Scent *of the* Missing

Scent *of* *the* Missing

LOVE AND PARTNERSHIP WITH A
SEARCH-AND-RESCUE DOG

Susannah Charleson

Houghton Mifflin Harcourt   BOSTON   NEW YORK   2010

For information about permission to reproduce
selections from this book, write to Permissions,
Houghton Mifflin Harcourt Publishing Company,
215 Park Avenue South, New York, New York 10003.

www.hmhbooks.com

Library of Congress Cataloging-in-Publication Data
Charleson, Susannah.
  Scent of the missing : love and partnership with a
search-and-rescue dog / Susannah Charleson.
    p. cm.
  ISBN 978-0-547-15244-8
  1. Rescue dogs — Texas—Dallas — Anecdotes. 2. Search
dogs — Texas — Dallas — Anecdotes. 3. Search-and-rescue
operations — Texas — Dallas — Anecdotes. 4. Golden retriever
— Texas — Dallas — Anecdotes. I. Title.
  SF428.55.C43 2010
  636.7'0886 — dc22   2009033783

Book design by Melissa Lotfy

Printed in the United States of America

DOC 10 9 8 7 6 5 4 3 2

PHOTO CREDITS: All photographs by Susannah Charleson except as fol-
lows: *Skip Fernandez and Aspen: Dallas Morning News*/Louis DeLuca.
Fleta and Saber: Mark-9 Search and Rescue. *Max and Hunter:* Mark-9
Search and Rescue. *Jerry and Shadow:* Mark-9 Search and Rescue. *Max
and Mercy:* Kurt Seevers/Mark-9 Search and Rescue. *Fo'c'sle Jack:* Devon
Thomas Treadwell. *Confidence on a rappel line:* Sara Maryfield/Mark-9
Search and Rescue. *Certified Puzzle:* Daniel Daugherty.

*For Ellen Sanchez, who always believed, and
brought a thousand cups of tea to prove it.*

For Puzzle. Good dog. Find more.

CONTENTS

Scent of the Missing is a memoir of my experiences as a field assistant and young search-and-rescue canine handler. Unless otherwise attributed, the perspectives and opinions expressed here are my own and do not necessarily reflect those of teammates and colleagues in the field.

Though this book is a nonfiction account of working search-and-rescue, compassion for the affected families and respect for their privacy have directed me to change names, locations, and identifying circumstances surrounding the searches related here. Who, where, and when are frankly altered; what, why, and how are as straightforward as one person's perspective can make them.

The dogs are all real. You can hold up a biscuit and call them by name.

Scent *of the* Missing

1

GONE

I N THE LONG LIGHT of early morning, Hunter circles what remains of a burned house, his nose low and brow furrowed. The night's thick air has begun to lift, and the German Shepherd's movement catches the emerging sun. He is a shining thing against the black of scorched brick, burned timber, and a nearby tree charred leafless. Hunter inspects the tree: half-fallen, tilting south away from where the fire was, its birds long gone. Quiet here. I can hear his footpads in the wizened grass, the occasional scrape of his nails across debris. The dog moves along the rubble in his characteristic half-crouch, intense and communicative, while his handler, Max, watches.

Hunter rounds the house twice, crosses cautiously through a clear space in the burned pile, and returns to Max with a huff of finality. *Nothing,* he seems to say. Hunter is not young. There are little flecks of gray about his dark eyes and muzzle, and his body has begun to fail his willing heart, but he knows his job, and he is a proud boy doing it. He leans into his handler and huffs again. Max rubs his ears and turns away.

"She's not in the house," I murmur into the radio, where a colleague and a sheriff's deputy wait for word from us.

"Let's go," says Max to Hunter.

We move on, our tracks dark across the ash, Hunter leading us forward into a field that lies behind the house. Here we have to work a little harder across the uneven terrain. Max, a career firefighter used to unstable spaces, manages the unseen critter holes and slick grass better than I do. Hunter cleaves an easy path. Our passage disturbs the field mice, which move in such a body the ground itself appears to shiver.

Wide sweeps across the field, back and forth across the wind, Hunter and Max and I (the assistant in trail) continuing to search for some sign of the missing girl. Hunter is an experienced search dog with years of disaster work and many single-victim searches behind him. He moves confidently but not heedlessly, and at the base of a low ridge crowned by a stand of trees, he pauses, head up a long moment, mouth open. His panting stops.

Max stops, watches. I stand where I last stepped.

And then Hunter is off, scrambling up the ridge with us behind him, crashing through the trees. We hear a surprised shout, and scuffling, and when we get to where he is, we see two men stumble away from the dog. One is yelping a little, has barked his shin on a battered dinette chair he's tripped over. The other hauls him forward by the elbow, and they disappear into the surrounding brush.

A third man has more difficulty. He is elderly and not as fast. He has been lying on a bare set of box springs set flat beneath the canopy of trees, and when he rises the worn cloth of his trousers catches on the coils. We hear rending fabric as he jerks free. He runs in a different direction from the other two — *not their companion*, I think — and a few yards away he stops and turns to peek through the scrub at us, as though aware the dog is not fierce and we aren't in pursuit.

Our search has disturbed a small tent city, and as we work our way through the reclaimed box springs and three-legged coffee tables and mouse-eaten recliners that have become a sort of home for its inhabitants, the third man watches our progress from the edge of the brush. This is a well-lived space, but there is nothing of the missing girl here. Charged on this search to find any human scent in the area, living or dead, Hunter has done what he is supposed to do. But he watches our response. From where I stand, it is clear Hunter knows what we've found is not what we seek, and that what we seek isn't here. He gazes at Max, reading him, his eyebrows working, stands poised for the "Find more" command.

"Sector clear," I say into the radio after a signal from Max. I mention the tent city and its inhabitants and learn it is not a surprise.

"Good boy," says Max. Hunter's stance relaxes.

As we move away, the third man gains confidence. He steps a little forward, watching Hunter go. He is barefoot and shirtless. "Dog, dog, dog," he says voicelessly, as though he shapes the word but cannot make the sound of it. "Dog," he rasps again, and smiles wide, and claps his hands.

Saturday night in a strange town five hundred miles from home. I am sitting in a bar clearly tacked on to our motel as an afterthought. The clientele here are jammed against one another in the gloom, all elbows and ball caps bent down to their drinks — more tired than social. At the nearby pool table, a man makes his shot, trash talks his opponent, and turns to order another beer without having to take more than four steps to get it. This looks like standard procedure. The empty bottles stack up on a nearby shelf that droops from screws half pulled out of the wall. Two men dominate the table while others watch. The shots get a little wild, the trash talk sloppier.

A half-hour ago, when I walked in with a handful of teammates, every head in the bar briefly turned to regard us, then turned away in perfect synchronization, their eyes meeting and their heads bobbing a nod. We are strangers and out of uniform, but they know who we are and why we are here, and besides, they've seen a lot of strangers lately. Now, at the end of the second week of search for a missing local girl, they leave us alone. We find a table, plop down without discussion, and a waitress comes out to take our orders.

She calls several of us "honey" and presses a hand to the shoulder of one of us as she turns away.

Either the town hasn't passed a smoking ordinance, or here at the city limits this place has conveniently ignored the law. We sit beneath a stratus layer of cigarette smoke that curls above us like an atmosphere of drowsy snakes, tinged blue and red and green by the neon signs over the bar. Beside the door, I see a flyer for the missing girl. Her face hovers beneath the smoke. She appears uneasy even in this photograph taken years ago, her smile tentative and her blond, feathered bangs sprayed close as a helmet, her dark eyes tight at the edges, like this picture was something to be survived.

I have looked at her face all day. On telephone poles, in the hands of local volunteers, over the shoulder of a big-city newscaster at noon, six, and ten o'clock. She is the ongoing local headline. She's the girl no one really knew before her disappearance, and now she's the girl eager eyewitnesses claim to have known all their lives. It's hard to tell what's real and what isn't, but for the most part that's not our job. We go where law enforcement directs us. We run behind search dogs who will tell us their own truths in any given area: *never here, was here, hers, not hers, blood, hair, bone, here, here, here.*

We humans aren't talking about the search, our first day at work in this town. Inappropriate discussion in a public place, and we are exhausted with it anyway. Though today's bystanders seemed to think we could take our dogs to Main Street and race them outward across all points of the compass — first dog to the victim wins — canine search-and-rescue doesn't work that way. Assigned to locations chosen by law enforcement, we work methodically, dividing a region into sectors to be searched by individual dog-and-handler teams. It's a meticulous process, but trained dogs can quickly clear a large area it would take humans days to definitively search.

Even so, we could be here for weeks. We already feel the trackless absence of this girl. Her hometown is small, but its outlying population is widespread, and there are places to hide a living woman or the remains of a dead one that cross lines into other states. Today we were sent to clear more "hot spots" — places where bodies have been dumped before. Shrouded, ugly areas they were too, scarred from previous events, but not this girl, this time. All day the dogs have been telling us: *Not here. Not here. Not here.*

I look at her photograph again. A big guy shifting on his stool blocks the ambient light from the bar, causing the girl's face to purple beneath the neon and the whites of her eyes to swallow the irises. Her gaze no longer connects. It's a condition that was true of her in life, some say. She has a history of scuttling head down, of sitting at the back of the class, never speaking unless spoken to, and even then as briefly as possible. She sounds uncertain on her voicemail greeting, enunciating her name with a rising inflection that suggests she isn't quite sure of it.

We hear fragments. The cumulative description adds up to a girl who began inching away from this town six years earlier, who saved her allowance and bought a junky car simply to have her first job at a truck stop in another town fifteen miles up the road, who saved her paychecks to buy a used laptop, and who had begun re-creating herself in variations all across the Web. *No judgment,* says a neighbor. *An accident waiting to happen,* says one interviewee. Authorities suggest she might be a runaway if it weren't for the methodical, calculated nature of her young choices. She might be a runaway if it weren't for her purse, cell phone, keys, car, and laptop left behind at her grandmother's house, the last place she was seen alive.

We're told she has a tattoo, inked by a trucker where she worked: a butterfly with the letter *K* on her left wrist. The tattoo is in honor of an online friend, Katie, who had slashed her own wrists in a successful suicide — or so it was rumored, until Katie returned to a chat room a month later with a new location, new name, new boyfriend, holding up her woundless wrists for photographs, laughing at the duped online friends who thought they knew her, who had responded to her loss with depression, Paxil, and new tattoos in her honor. April Fools, all.

Did our girl admire her, forgive her? I wonder. *Is this a copycat drama?*

I turn away from her photograph. She's not my daughter, but I feel a mother's impulse to push the bangs from her eyes, the rescuer's urge to put two fingertips to her carotid to check for a pulse.

We're a quiet group, tight and preoccupied. Still wired from the day's search, we lean forward over our food, weight on the balls of our feet with our heels lifted, as though we'll push up at any moment to go back to work. Unlikely. We're stood down for the night and have an early call in the morning. It always takes a while to let go enough to sleep, especially as a search presses forward over days and investigators' verbs begin to change from *she is* to *she was*. That little shift in tense is enough to keep us awake all night, revisiting the day's barns, ravines, burned houses, tent cities, and trailer parks, triple-checking ourselves against the signals from the dogs. To say this girl haunts us is to overdramatize. But we all mull choices made in the field long after we should be sleeping. I stab at my coleslaw and wonder when one of us will finally relax into the back of a chair.

In time, Terry, a canine handler, leans over to say to me, "Hey. I hear you're going to work a dog."

The others look up.

"Yes," I say. The word feels huge as a wedding vow.

I've been on the search-and-rescue (SAR) team for a while now, running beside certified dogs and their handlers, working as a field assistant responsible for navigation, radio communication, medical assessment, and other pragmatics of a working canine search team. After three years, I'm senior enough to have earned the next open slot to train and run beside a search dog. I am excited about this, but a little nervous too. Having run with more than a dozen breeds and their handlers, having searched night into day for the living, and having knelt over the dead, I'm aware how serious a proposition bringing a new dog to the team is. Working search is not a hobby or a Sunday pastime.

"What breed you thinking of running?" he asks. He handles a

Border Collie, a high-drive, obsessive-compulsive boy who is good all around, but particularly good searching on water.

"I'm not sure. Maybe a Border Collie. Maybe an Aussie. Or maybe a Gol ..."

"You give any thought to a Golden Retriever?"

I nod, and he tells me about his former Golden, Casey, a good dog with a lot of smarts and a lot of soul and a nose that never stopped. A good dog that died, too soon, of cancer. Though my colleague is not one who generally talks at length, his description is detailed. I see the shape of his Golden boy emerge. A sturdy fellow with a nice face and a wide grin — funny, perceptive, and compassionate. My teammate speaks, and his voice constricts. This dog has been dead for more than five years. Terry's love for the animal had been too raw at the time he began training his own search canine, and he couldn't go with a Golden. Listening to him now, I'm aware it's an open wound. Toughened by years as a homicide detective, he is still not in shape to have another Golden, he says, but he's safe enough recommending one to me.

And the breed has much to recommend it for search work: drive, stability, commitment to working with a human, congeniality, and nose. I already have other dogs and cats, and for reasons of amicability at home, as well, I'm also drawn to the idea of a Golden.

We speak of other search-and-rescue Golden Retrievers: iconic, much-photographed Riley traveling aloft in the Stokes basket across the debris of the World Trade Center and diligent Aspen supporting her exhausted handler as he presses his face to her back following a search of the collapsed Murrah Federal Building in Oklahoma City. This fine breed figures in virtually every aspect of search. Snow dogs, bomb dogs, drug dogs, arson dogs too.

"Got to love a retriever," says Johnny, a Lab man himself, and then he chuckles. "But, girl, no matter what kind of puppy, there's gonna be some housebreaking and chewed shoes in your future."

"And sleepless nights," says Ellen.

"And *poop*," adds Terry wryly, a cautionary finger up. "These high-drive dogs. All that adrenaline. When a puppy starts working, you just wouldn't *believe* the poo . . ."

I push away my coleslaw.

Leaning back in their chairs at last, the whole group seems pleased about my coming duress. They exchange young SAR dog stories, not one of them featuring angelic puppies poised for greatness. There's disaster in every punch line — "the neighbor's TV made him howl" . . . "ate right through the drywall" . . . and "then her *parrot* learned to bark." I look at the team trainer dubiously.

"This is good," says Fleta, rubbing her forehead. "A new pup-in-training always gives the whole team a boost." Her eyes are tired, but she grins as she lifts her glass in salute.

On any given day in America, there are as many as one hundred thousand active missing persons cases. A large percentage of these cases go unresolved. At the same time, the recovered and unidentified remains of some forty thousand people are held by medical examiners across the country. As a search-and-rescue worker in the field, I am caught by those numbers — they equal the population of a small city. I'm aware that we run dogs in the thin air between possibility of life and probability of death, and that while we search for a single girl whose weathered flyers have already begun to fade, there are thousands of others actively being searched. Or not. Knowing how many people are involved on the search for this young woman, I cannot imagine the number of investigators, grid walkers, pilots, ATVs, equestrian units, dog teams, and forensic experts of every kind needed to resolve all the others. I suspect geography, marginalization, and limited resources mean quite a few of the missing are short-term questions that go unanswered — or are never raised at all.

Our small-town girl disappeared in a slow news period. I wonder how much time she's got before funds run out, new local troubles arise, and she is crowded from the docket to take her place in local lore. The margin between SEARCH CONTINUES FOR

MISSING TEEN and UNIDENTIFIED REMAINS UNCOVERED IN
STATE PARK ten years from now seems narrow.

Time and numbers make me urgent. I cannot train my new dog
too soon.

Next morning's light is hard as a slap. The community has rallied
beneath a red, white, and blue striped tent donated by a used car
dealership half the state away. The structure is shabby; its attached
bunting is worn. The top line sags. A good wind could be a problem here, but the morning is windless.

At this early hour, the sun shines in at a slant, but it is already
too warm inside the tent. Two hundred or so volunteers jockey
for position behind the darker canvas of the wide blue stripes. We
suck down donated orange juice or strong coffee or both — an un-
wise choice. The port-a-potties have not yet arrived, and today's
search has staged in the middle of nowhere, from a plain so flat
that any thought of a quick whip around a bush to pee should assume an audience, both local and televised. A caravan of mobile
units from TV stations miles away has also arrived. Their antennae and cranes have already begun to extend.

We hear more cars exit the road and crunch across the gravel
and brush. Doors slam, and a voice from near the tent flap says
that the sheriff's here with the parents, and we should be starting soon. I don't think so. I read a similar doubt on the faces of my
teammates. *Hurry up and wait* is the case more often than not on
large searches, and this one, with its ambiguous geography and its
swelling ranks of volunteers, has become a large search. We were
told to be on-scene at 7:00 A.M., and we've been here ninety minutes. I think if we deploy by 9:30, we'll be lucky.

"I'm going to check on the dogs," says Terry, four bottles of water in the crook of his elbow. The dogs are crated behind the shade
of our cars with Ellen, a field assistant, in attendance. I can see
them through the tent flap. They look a whole lot more comfortable than we do.

Aware they are on-scene to work, the dogs are alert. Collie Saber, German Shepherd Hunter, Border Collie Hoss, and Buster, a Lab. They scrutinize all newcomers, nostrils knitting and ears perked forward, their expressions speculative. I wonder how they sort passersby: *old guy with a kidney problem . . . nice lady who ate bacon for breakfast, come* here, *nice lady . . . this guy's got two dogs — one of them, oh, one of them's in heat! . . . hey, that kid dropped McMuffin on his pants.* Terry's approach makes them turn and grin. Their wagging tails *bang-bang-bang* against the bars of their crates.

Here in the tent, a community group has made T-shirts for its members, purple T-shirts bearing several photos of the missing girl. WE'LL FIND YOU promise the shirts on the front. WE LOVE YOU they say on the back. Several participants have their video cameras out to record today's events. The sheriff walks in with two deputies and the missing girl's parents, and the group falls silent. A man whips his Tilley hat off. His friend with a digital camera continues to shoot: sheriff, mom and dad, TV reporter, crowd. A deputy's leaden gaze stops her. I hear the little *scree* of it winding down. She puts the camera in her purse.

The sheriff's briefing tells us little that gossip hasn't already introduced. Yesterday's search found nothing relevant to the missing girl. But, we are reminded, every area cleared contributes something to a final answer. The sheriff's baritone is edged with weariness, ragged on its ending syllables, yet he speaks well. His words are clear and urgent. The community group will be divided into four units who will work, geographically, across today's new areas. We should expect hardship, he says. These places are ugly and brushy and filled with debris from illegal dumping. High boots are recommended. There will be broken glass. There could be snakes. A woman in front of me, wearing shorts, sandals, and a baby in a papoose on her back, looks at her husband. He looks pointedly at her feet, and she sets her jaw and turns away.

The sheriff pulls the girl's parents forward. Though the woman appears shattered with fatigue while her husband's face is tight and reserved, it is his voice that gives way as he thanks the crowd. "Find our girl," says his wife in his wordlessness. She guides him away from the television camera, but he turns and gives the lens a long look in passing.

"All right," says the sheriff. "We've got no better reason to be here." The crowd stirs beneath the tent, convicted again. As two deputies step forward to divide the ground-search volunteers, I feel a tug on my arm. "We're going," mouths Johnny. He jerks his head in the direction of another officer discreetly leading us out of the tent and away from the crowd.

As we gather around the deputy and the dogs press their noses to the crate bars to smell him, he opens a map on the hood of a truck and shows us where we're headed. "The word is this may be it," he says. "We think she's here." He points to a spot and then makes a wide circle with a forefinger.

"Why here?" asks Terry. The retired detective in him is never far away.

The deputy shrugs. "Anonymous tip." He stares at the map a long moment. "That's all we've got."

The dogs quiver and circle and pee as we release them from their crates. A few bark excitedly as we load them into the trucks, engines and air conditioners on. Safe now in transport crates, they are ready to go. I can hear them winding themselves up behind the glass, scuffling and muttering, that signature dog sound that's more grumble than growl.

Three dogs work separate sections of the area we've deployed to, fifty acres of patchy terrain, dried creek bed, and dumped appliances. A variable wind has risen, strong enough to make a little thunder in our ears, but born of ground radiation, it offers no relief from heat. The dogs will use the wind, though. Turning east, north, then west, through binoculars I watch them sweep their individual sectors, heads up and tails visible above the bending grass, handlers following yards behind.

Collie Saber moves across the scrub at a steady trot, despite his heavy coat and the day's temperature. I hardly need binoculars. He is easy to see from a distance, a tricolored boy flashing against the dun terrain. Fleta follows, watching him thoughtfully, with Ellen in trail behind them both, taking notes. The scruffy field is flat. Saber's wide sweeps are clean and unbroken. At the end of the sector, they pause. The Collie looks back to Fleta and turns with a movement very like a shrug of his great ruff — an *all clear* that's readable even from where I stand. I see Fleta turn and shake her head to Ellen. A moment later, Ellen's voice crackles across the radio that they're coming in.

Max and Hunter are winding their way through a clutch of small trees that cling to the edge of a rainwater runoff gully. I watch the German Shepherd's great dark ears working independently as he penetrates the sector, as though there is much to hear skittering in the grass. A nervous prairie bird flushes yards away from where they walk, and both Hunter's ears come forward so rapidly that the light spots within them seem to blink like eyes. He doesn't turn for the bird, however, continuing on his course, nose thrust forward. He leads Max through the trees and they disappear behind them, visible only as an occasional twitch and flash of Max's red shirt as they work the rest of the sector.

Trained to alert differently on the living and the dead, the dogs' demeanor across the area is consistent. No pause, no head pop, no sudden, energized movement, no bark. Their passage stirs rabbits and shivers a few snakes from the brush, but the dogs communicate their disinterest. They all seem to agree that nothing's here.

The deputy watches quietly. "I hunt with a Lab," he says, looking out to Johnny and Buster. "Great dogs. Can't stop them."

Fleta has already returned with Saber. Max comes in with Hunter, shaking his head. Hunter takes a drink of water as fast as Max pours it and flops down with a sigh. A few minutes later Johnny returns with Buster. "Nothing," he says. "Except a bunch of baby rabbits in a washing machine out there."

"Aw," says Ellen. "Bunnies. How many?"

"Dunno," Johnny replies. "Enough to be breakfast, lunch, and dinner for the snakes."

"God." Ellen folds her arms across her chest and shakes her head. Ellen's worked ranches, but she's ready for any kind of good word here.

The deputy says, "Thing is . . ."

We look at him. His cell phone buzzes, and he walks away, muttering into it, one hand pressed to the opposite ear to block the wind.

A new search area, and we are moving fast. Ground searchers have found a location where the scent of death is strong, and third-hand word to the deputy by cell phone suggests the presence of possible evidence too. Now a potential crime scene, the area has been cleared, and the sheriff waits for the dogs. We'll use a different approach: one way in, one way out — a cautious trail rather than a wide sweep — to confirm or deny what's been found.

We park at the base of a shallow rise crisscrossed with bike trails and more dumped appliances, a whole host of abandoned cars. Our deputy gives a little jerk of his head as we look upward, waiting for clearance to deploy.

"Kids park here," he says.

I think of sex in this tangled, airless scrub and feel old. "Really?" I ask, doubtfully.

"The stars are nice," he replies. A little twist of his mouth suggests he knows this from experience, and I wonder if he's busted kids here or was once one of them himself.

His cell phone buzzes again. After a few moments he turns to us. "Thing is," he says, "there's a smell in a locked car, and an object not far away that may have been a weapon, and fresh clothes in the mud. Because this might be a crime scene — if not this one, then another one — we don't want you to track the whole area, but we'd like you to bring the dogs and see what they think about the car."

Fleta and Saber, Max and Hunter, Ellen and I follow the deputy up the thin trail to the top of the rise. A distance away, perhaps two football fields long, I can see a group of volunteer searchers watching us, their purple shirts dark as a bruise against the buff-colored ground. I hear the huddle of voices when the breeze shifts and I am downwind. At the top of the rise, the sheriff and two deputies are still and expectant. They turn to lead us carefully to the car in question, a battered blue '72 Impala. Just beyond it, a stainless butcher knife lies in the dirt. The knife is clean and bright. Next to the Impala, a pair of crumpled blue jeans rest in such a way that it appears someone dropped his pants right there and stepped out of them. The jeans remain in that position, the legs stacked, the fly open, the waist upward and wide. A thread of dust marks a few denim folds that I can see, but it doesn't appear to me that the jeans have been here long.

Ellen and I are taking notes as first Saber, then Hunter slowly circle the car. Both are experienced cadaver dogs, and though they sniff every crevice, neither gives a flicker of interest. Fleta shakes her head, and minutes later, Max does too.

"No," says Max. "The dogs say no."

The sheriff gestures us all closer forward, and the fug of decomposition is palpable. "Have any of you ever smelled a dead body?" he asks. Fleta, Max, and I nod and step nearer, and without thinking about it, we simultaneously put our noses just above the trunk. The air is thick and foul.

"This doesn't smell right," I murmur just as Fleta also shakes her head. I always have difficulty explaining it, but to me dead human smells different from squirrel, rat, or possum on the side of the road. Not just more scent — human death seems specific and particular. I don't know the why behind the chemistry. All that shampoo, maybe, or trans fat or antiperspirant, or maybe we're all pickled in Coca-Cola, like the urban legend says.

"Something's dead in here," says Fleta, "but I don't think it's human."

Max guides Hunter forward again, watching. "Where's the dead thing, Hunter?" he says. Off-command to find human scent, Hunter circles the car in the way of any curious dog, stopping warily and putting his nose to the back left wheel well. Max kneels into the area, then drops his head. "Got it," he says, his voice sad. "It's a dog."

We all bend down, and there, caught above the back axle, we can see a dog's paws and its limp head dangling. A medium-size mixed breed, brown fur ticked with black. The flesh of its mouth is pulled back from the teeth; the eyes are muddy and glazed. The pads are intact but slightly shriveled, and I can see a small white stone between two of them. This dog was either hit by the car or crawled up there to die. An uncomforted end. I hear the lazy drone of flies.

"Dead for a while," says Max.

"Well, okay," says the sheriff. He gets up stiffly. Though he is sunburned, the flesh beneath his eyes is gray.

"Got anywhere else for the dogs to search?" asks the deputy.

The sheriff shakes his head. "Don't have anywhere else for anybody." Then he adds, "This search is going to be a long one. Guess you folks can go home. We'll call you back if we get something for the dogs."

We stand a moment. He gazes along the rise to the motionless group of volunteers. Below us, another vehicle has pulled up and parked. The car doors slam, *thunk,* and — slower — *thunk.* The sheriff turns.

"Right," he says. "I'll go tell the parents."

He walks down the path, and they walk up toward him. As they near, I watch the sheriff stand a little straighter. The father, too, lifts his head and squares his shoulders and pulls his wife to his hip as they climb. And in that moment before they connect, on day thirteen of a search for a missing local girl, I wonder how they can bear the unknowing, what these parents most wish for — words that leave the door open or words that press the door closed.

Our cars are loaded for the long drive home, and the dogs are having a last romp in a small park along a stream. Two of the local volunteers on today's search stand with us beneath the shade of a pecan tree. One is about to drive back to her college for summer classes. The other has had a quick shower and will head another direction to her restaurant shift miles away.

One asks what we think the dogs know about this search. Do they feel what we feel? Does the search continue to trouble them, as we humans are troubled?

Fleta shakes her head, pointing out that from the dogs' perspectives, this search was successful. They were asked to do a job: *find the missing girl or indicate definitively she's not here*, and they did. Apart from three vagrants in a tent city, no one living or dead was there to be found. And after the day's sectors were done, volunteers hid so the dogs could find them, a quick and upbeat conclusion to a hard workday, a game that fools no one but keeps motivation high. These dogs are all praise-hounds. They played along, finding and grinning and capering.

No, Fleta suggests. There are exceptions, but usually the dogs let go of a day's search better than we do. We trust them to do their jobs, and they trust us to tell them they have done it well. And when we tell them, they believe us.

I watch them play. Common goals aside, these dogs are complete individuals in the field. I have searched beside Hunter's intensity, Saber's calm authority, and Buster's bounding accuracy. Even this evening's pleasure they pursue in different ways. The German Shepherd noses for critters in the brush, while the Lab snaps at minnows in shallow water, trying to catch them. We tease him, and Buster raises his head with muzzle dripping, looking fusty and bemused, but he grins at the sound of his name and tries for fish again. The beautiful Collie, Saber — much-admired and he knows it — rolls ungracefully in the grass, groaning *unnh-unnnh-unnhhhhh-mmmmmmm*. His white ruff is streaked with green when he gets up, and his coat splays every which way. He is thoroughly happy to be such a mess. "Brickhead," says Fleta, hugging him as he nuzzles her ear. "Doofus."

The Border Collie brings every one of us his ball. Hoss is a dog of great charm and is completely tone-deaf to rejection. It's time to leave, but he is persuasive. We throw and throw and throw again. "Fetch therapy" we call it, and it works. The local volunteers leave laughing, Hoss still petitioning them with his ball in his mouth all the way to their cars.

As we head out, I wonder what my own dog will bring to the work, to the team, and to me. I like the thought of a long drive home with a Golden snoring belly-up in the back of the car: a good dog who has worked well. A partner. A friend. After a search like this one, that companionship must take away a little of the ache.

2

DOG FOR THE JOB

I T's 102 DEGREES when I step out of the airport in
Midland, Texas, but my hands are cold. I've got a dog
carrier, a collar and leash, and a canine SAR training
vest. I'm wearing my team ID and a stunned expression I can describe only now as *deer in the headlights.*

After almost a year of research, breeder queries, and preemp-
tive puppy-proofing at the house, I am a half-hour away from the
Golden Retriever that will be my partner. Today there's little evidence of all the meticulous preparation: I look down and realize
I'm wearing different-colored socks and that in my blind scramble
to get from home to the airport at dawn, I also brought a new dog
toy, size-appropriate for a Great Dane, a stuffed red lobster with
"Cape Cod" embroidered on the claw. I don't remember picking it
up at the house. I don't remember pushing it through security. I
think the lobster is probably bigger than the puppy is.

"Where's the pet?" asks a cabdriver who sees me standing alone,
cradling the empty carrier and the toy.

"I'm going to be having some puppy!" I babble, waving the lobster as if to clarify. The driver shakes his head and backs away from
me, clearly figuring I'm not all there.

• • •

For so visible a presence in the public consciousness, the Golden Retriever is not an ancient breed. Though its early history is sometimes debated and there are folk stories of Russian dogs being the sire and dam of the first pups that would be Goldens, the Golden Retriever Club of America credits the Golden's origins to Sir Dudley Majoribanks, Lord Tweedmouth, who acquired the single yellow pup in a litter of black wavy-coated retrievers in Brighton, England, in the early 1870s. Lord Tweedmouth named the yellow dog "Nous" and added him to his pack of sporting retrievers at Guisachan House in the Highlands of Scotland, later breeding him with a liver-colored female Tweed Water Spaniel named "Belle." That mating yielded several yellow pups that would become foundation dogs for the Golden Retriever breed. "Crocus," a Nous and Belle pup, appears in photographs to bear a striking resemblance to the contemporary Golden. Golden Retrievers began appearing in British dog shows in the Retriever-Wavy or Flat-Coated category in the early 1900s, but the American Kennel Club did not recognize the breed until 1932. Goldens were a rare breed at the time.

Like their forebears, modern Goldens are intelligent dogs that are eager to partner humans in a variety of ways. Though bred to retrieve, they can also be talented, disciplined athletes in the agility ring and obedience trials. Many excel in tracking and at other scent-associated tasks. The AKC literature confirms they are loyal, loving companions. The breed's natural inclinations are all potential positives in the search field. I'd heard the general buzz for years, but during months of research prior to locating my puppy, it was good to see a solid reputation surface.

Now the Golden Retriever consistently places in the top ten most popular dogs in America — in part due to the word-of-mouth PR, perhaps in great part due to all the media exposure — a popularity that may contribute to the breed's serious problems. And there are some. In the open market, where supply meets demand, some smell the money to be made in Goldens, and commercial breeding can be haphazard. In the long months prior to finding my partner, I researched genealogies and read up on the breed's vulnerabilities, among them possible hip issues, heart issues, eye problems — and cancer, a common killer of Goldens, young and old. Hemangiosarcoma and lymphosarcoma: twin specters that shadow thousands of heartbroken posts on the Internet, lowering the Golden's average lifespan to ten and a half years. Deaths at age four or five are not uncommon. As a member of several online Golden Retriever forums, I read hard news from online friends and went to sleep some nights saddened by vicarious loss.

There were other caveats. For all their cuddly, genial good looks, Goldens are extremely social dogs who want to work beside their humans. The cute puppies that become grown dogs are ill-suited to haphazard training, intermittent contact, and banishment to the backyard. Hundreds of high-energy, anxious Goldens end up in rescues and city pounds every year, the result of poor choice-making on the part of owners who want a good dog at their leisure but don't want a Golden that jumps on them in the backyard, the ten-minute-a-day family pet now desperate for affection after long hours of abandonment. The collective research unanimously asserts that Goldens cannot be treated as accessories. This is true of all dogs, of course, but with a big dog like a Golden, the behavioral result of social neglect can be catastrophic for family and dog.

I was a newcomer to Goldens, but at least, I thought, I could promise attention, companionship, love. And work. The breed's drives and my own seemed right in sync.

I inquired with several Golden rescue organizations that promised to keep their eyes open for just the right young Golden that might work, but no solid leads emerged there. From pages of notes, I made ten breeder queries, nationwide. Four breeders indicated they had no new litters proposed for the year. Two had pups, but they were already sold. One seemed unwilling to believe I'd travel to get the right dog, no matter how much hypertext I used in my e-mails: *Plane! Car trip! Off for the summer!* Three others never responded. Nine months of close calls and almost-dogs that never came to pass — a whole series of Goldens that nearly came home to me. I had begun to wonder if a wiser universe was telling me something.

"No," said a neighbor, when I whined my frustration. "You said yourself this is more than a dog to be had and a thing to be done. You're being *prepared*." Gerand is a feng shui practitioner whom I've known to find a reasonable meaning in food poisoning and the bad chicken salad behind it, so I listened — and chafed — and waited.

In a moment of serendipity, a breeder who'd been recommended to me by five separate sources responded to tell me that she had a female named Spirit whose pregnancy was established, whose background was what I'd been looking for, and who might be very likely to bear a puppy with an aptitude for SAR. She sent me a link to information and images of her Spirit and the litter's sire, Ozzie, from another breeder on the East Coast. There was obedience, agility, and hunt in the merged background — good health and longevity too.

I already had notes on this breeder's line, but I took a day or so more to review them, imposing some kind of rationality while inside my heart leaped. Everything seemed right about this litter. I sent my application and puppy deposit and began a second wait for a Golden that wasn't yet born, charged with the idea that somewhere out there in the miracle of cell division and good dog DNA, my partner was becoming real.

"Look at that head," said Terry, weeks later. He was looking at a picture of Ozzie, my puppy's sire, a big boy with a genial, teddy-bear expression. "You've gotta smile at a face like that." I agreed. Another in the long list of reasons I wanted a Golden was the attraction factor. We search for children and Alzheimer's patients with some frequency, and I didn't want these victims more scared when they were found than when they were lost. I knew I wanted a light-faced dog with an open, kindly expression.

Terry looked at pictures of pretty mama Spirit, posed calmly in a "watch me" command, and he looked at my first pictures of her puppies, sent two days after the litter was born. Ten pups: nine girls and a boy. They looked like fuzzy tater tots, all butts and tiny ear flaps, their faces obscured as they huddled together. Each wore a little "collar" of colored rickrack for identification.

"I'm taking guesses," I said, pointing to the little tabs of rickrack. "Tell me which one you think will be my puppy, and if you guess correctly, I'll donate one hundred dollars to the Golden rescue of your choice." Terry pointed and picked. I'd played this game for a few days. Everyone had a reason for picking the puppy they did. "This one looks like she's protecting the others," one said. "This one has a big nose," said another. I made my choice last, picking a little blond pup curled on her side like a comma. In the picture, she was independent and apart from the others, wearing a yellow rickrack collar — and she was fat as a piglet, which suggested she could find something when she wanted it, and she didn't mind crawling over nine other puppies to get it.

As it happened, I guessed correctly, more fluke than intuition. "Yellow" and all the other pups were pretested for evidence of drive, confidence, and willingness to work for a human at six and again at ten weeks, and their breeder conferred with our SAR team head trainer. It was a close call indeed between this female and the little male. Breeder and trainer talked at length long-distance, and they made a decision for me — like an arranged marriage with four paws and a tail. I found out the day before I flew to Midland. "It's a girl," I was told. And she wore yellow rickrack.

Now it was just a matter of meeting her and bringing her home to join my family of three elderly cats and six adult dogs. I'd been raising dogs for years. I thought: *How hard could it be?*

Most of the animals in my house are rescues themselves. Coming from a family that always rescued cats from the pound, some part of me still draws energy from a rowdy, highly interactive little pack of animals, and I have one — a household of distinct personalities, none of them shy about expressing his point of view. A few dogs are fosters, living here on a temporary basis until they stabilize enough to be adoptable — plucked from animal shelters a day before their scheduled euthanasia. Excepting Pomeranians Fo'c'sle Jack and Mr. Sprits'l, the population here swells or decreases as this dog comes in to foster or that dog adopts a new family.

In the weeks preceding the new puppy, they were all aware of my changed motions, but only Sprits'l appeared deeply suspicious as I puppy-proofed the house, mutter-grumbling his way behind me, giving occasional "augh" barks of disapproval. He is a bright, fox-faced little guy, the color of a cigarette filter stubbed out into ash, which sounds ugly — but he is a good-looking dog. Sprits has small, dark eyebrows, and for a couple of weeks they were raised speculatively at the excessive housecleaning, the throwing away of once-loved-but-now-much-ignored small dog toys. The other dogs appeared curious but unconcerned.

Fo'c'sle Jack, the first Pomeranian in the pack, is much attached to me and has always been an easy dog. Jack came into the world mellow. Even though he was attacked by two large off-leash dogs as a pup, a violent event that shook both of us up for months, Jack recovered his equable nature. He doesn't rattle easily; he rarely barks. A soft and genial orange sable Pomeranian, his chief concern is food: *when's it coming, how much is coming, and by the way, you could give a guy a treat now and then*. With confident graciousness, Jack's seen foster dogs come and go. He was the least likely to be affected by this change, I thought, especially if I brought in a puppy of a breed known for its dog-friendliness.

By contrast, rescued Miss Whisky is all nerves, stretched tight as a violin string about to snap. When Whisky's previous owner, an elderly woman with advancing Alzheimer's, put a kitchen towel over a gas burner a few years ago, her whole house went up. The woman was pulled from the bedroom alive, and on his way out another firefighter found Whisky crouched in the kitchen between the refrigerator and a cabinet, semiconscious, the long fur of her tail already burning. He pulled the dog free, but in the aftermath of the fire, the woman's son placed his mother in a care facility and turned Whisky over to the pound. A poorly bred, cowering, traumatized black Pom with few social skills, she was given little time. A rescue organization got her out of the shelter, and I took her a few days later, the fur of her tail still crimped and scorched from heat. She is calmer now, but reactive: new neighbors throw her, the scrape and clunk of the mailman throws her. In truth, a strong breeze can still throw Whisky some days. She's in a state of almost permanent exclamation. Though she wags and smiles, her eyes are wary, and she barks about everything like an old record on the skip, shrieking a high note: *Wow! Wow! Wow! Wow! Wow!*

Whisky's staccato bark makes Salty Sophie blink, as though she winks away kickboxing butterflies. Sophie is the smallest of the Poms and perhaps the pluckiest. Another rescue, Sophie had been found duct-taped in a cardboard box and tossed in a Dumpster in Florida. A passerby heard her whimper, extracted the little dog, and then took her for veterinary care — despite the fact she could not keep Sophie herself. She came to us shaved free of mats and ticks, but with serious medical conditions: a collapsing trachea and congestive heart failure, both of which impair her breathing, particularly on hot, humid days. Despite her rough history and medical problems, Sophie is a cheerful, upbeat little dog, a round and waddling creature eager to keep up with household events. Dinnertime inspires Sophie to dance a doggy mambo, and occasionally she gets too excited about her coming food and falls over, dazed and blue about the mouth. But after a moment's pause, she is up again, does a little box step, and makes a honking sound through her nose, the closest she gets to a bark. Sophie is unruffled by the fosters who pass through on a layover to their new homes, and I think she'll get along with a new dog — even a larger dog — just fine, as long as the puppy has a little sense and equilibrium, thereby not sitting on small Sophie or spinning her silly on a race through the house.

The senior statesman of the household is Scuppy, aged twenty-one, another rescue who has already taught me much about how a smart dog works the wind.

A friend first e-mailed me about Scuppy after seeing a Petfinder ad pleading his case. A very senior dog who had been the pet of an elderly couple, he was abandoned when the couple died. Neighbors later said that the couple's adult children simply opened the front door and let the old Pomeranian out. Blind and deaf, he had wandered along the street, crossing traffic and colliding into unfamiliar fences for days until someone took him to the pound. There, the shelter's attending vet recognized Scuppy as one of his own former patients. A phone call confirmed the old dog's abandonment. No, the family denied, their mother's dog had died years ago. They knew nothing about a dog, about this dog, about any dog. Nothing, even when the vet's digital photograph exactly matched the stray Pomeranian sitting in a cage at the pound.

The shelter staff had made something of a pet of him as long as possible, but his age and disabilities made him unattractive for adoption. When I called eighteen hours before his scheduled euthanasia, the attendant on the phone wept. The Petfinder ad had been removed, she said. Scuppy couldn't be adopted because he was unneutered, and the law prohibited the adoption of an unaltered pet. But the shelter vet believed he would not survive surgical anesthesia due to his great age, and thus neutering was out of the question. One way or another, it looked like Scuppy would be put to sleep.

I asked about his health apart from the listed disabilities, and she said his condition was good for a dog both elderly and lately neglected. He was an active, mobile dog interested in exploring; he was gentle and responsive to touch. He was just very, very old. The shelter staff had been looking for someone to give him a soft place to live out his last months. But the decision had finalized today — he couldn't be adopted. The woman's voice was weary with the finality of it.

"What about foster?" I suggested. "Could I . . . sort of permanently . . . foster this dog?"

She put me on hold.

"What time can you get here?" she asked when she returned to the phone.

"What time do you close?"

"Five-thirty," she said.

"I can be there by five-thirty."

There was a pause. "Come at six," she said, and hung up the phone.

We met behind the shelter later that evening in the dark, where I signed paperwork I couldn't read. The young woman advised that the normal pet insurance that came with adoption was not available for fosters. Another attendant in the shadows, with bright-red hair lit only by the occasional flare of his cigarette on inhale, said I wouldn't be needing insurance, anyway: an old dog like Scuppy didn't have a whole lot of time. There was a little bundling movement, backlit in fluorescent from the shelter's half-cracked door. The two hustled something into my pet carrier, then scuttled back into the shelter. The whole thing was as quick and dark as an exchange of state secrets, and I would not have been able to recognize either one of them on the street in daylight. It would have been creepy if I'd not sensed how much these two wanted to avoid putting down yet another dog. Especially this one.

In the car, I unzipped the top of the carrier and saw him for the first time, a "clear orange" Pomeranian, his face sunken and white with age. His ears did not flick the way a hearing dog's would, and when I gently lifted his chin, I saw his clouded eyes. He was the oldest dog I'd ever seen. Toothless too. Accepting change with equanimity, he yawned, showing a wedge of bare, pink gums. I kept one hand down beside the old boy as I drove, feeling the soft, exploratory huff of his breath against my palm.

Once home, Scuppy accepted the other dogs calmly, submitting to their sniffs and prodding and circling without fuss or complaint. He clearly bewildered them, but something in his demeanor kept them respectful. At suppertime, he stood beside them in the kitchen, barked when he smelled dog food, and put his nose to his bowl as though he'd had this houseful of siblings his entire life. When he finished, he bobbed his nose and scented incoming air as I opened the back door for the other dogs, and he too headed outside, feeling his way along the porch to the ramp leading to the yard. There he revealed unexpected abilities. As he walked the backyard to become familiar with it, Scuppy marked the fence perimeter every few feet, demonstrating a bottomless bladder and a genius ability to meter his pee. He marked an entire fence line in that first single outing. The other dogs stood together and watched him, not one of the little males attempting to best the old boy by peeing over his mark.

He would mark further across the following days: trees, shrubs, the birdbath, a coil of garden hose, a clutch of flowerpots at a fork in the flagstone path leading to the garage. The outside water bowl too, which deeply offended the other Poms until I washed and raised it a little, allowing Scuppy's mark to land on the bricks beneath.

Scuppy clearly loved to be outdoors, and once he'd marked his territory, he never collided with objects again. He would walk the backyard for hours, then sit in the soft grass and lift his nose at the passage of squirrels on the fence or a fluster of pigeons beneath the feeder. When he was ready to come in, he would give a polite, solitary bark from where he sat — a little upward inflection like a query — *errrrr, now?* There he'd wait to be picked up, cuddled, and brought into the house. I learned that I could stand upwind of him many feet away and, waving my hands at knee level, would see him give the signature head pop of recognition I'd learned from the on-scent search dogs. When Scuppy caught the scent of me, he would rise, turn, and follow it to the source, his small tail wagging. And so it was that I learned how to call blind, deaf Scuppy and realized he could come when called just by the scent of me — even across the entire yard.

Having hidden electrical cords, replaced loose mattress batting, and installed some puppy gates, I took up all the cat toys and the small-breed toys, and I told the Pomeranians they'd just have to understand we couldn't have a puppy chew-and-choke hazard around for a while. The Poms tilted their heads when I spoke to them and looked even more speculative. *Something's changing,* their expressions said, *and it don't smell like bacon.* All this commotion began four weeks before Spirit's litter was due on the other side of Texas and fourteen weeks before I could bring the puppy home. I knew it was early, but I lay on the floor and tried to imagine this world through a Golden puppy's eyes. I wondered, in turn, what she would teach me and when.

When she sees me for the first time, Puzzle's expression is skeptical. I am another in a series of strangers bending over the x-pen. She considers and quickly rejects me, immediately gives me up for better things. A tug toy is more interesting. The open-bottomed bucket on its side, more interesting still. Our meeting is not a Hallmark moment between us. Mama Spirit welcomes me with soft generosity, but her blond, dark-eyed daughter with the fuzzy bottom turns away.

I sneak glances at her as Kim and I go through her puppy book and discuss her diet, vaccinations, and pending training. Puzzle isn't the biggest pup of the litter, nor the smallest. She moves through the x-pen with a bit of swagger, boxing toys, taunting her siblings until they wrestle. I see her swipe a stuffed duck from her sister and shoot a glance my direction. Puzzle drops the toy her sister wants and sits on it.

Somewhere in all of that, I think, *is my partner.*

Kim lifts her from the x-pen and puts her on the floor. "She knows 'Sit,' 'Stand,' and 'Come,'" Kim says. "And she should be pretty much housebroken."

"Sit," I say to Puzzle, who waits a molasses half-beat and then sits. And yawns.

"Good girl," I praise her.

Yada yada, her expression suggests.

I have never seen so intractable a puppy. My previous pups had cuddled at first meeting, but this one looks like she could spit at me like a llama. And might.

You have other dogs, I reassure myself. *This isn't all that new.* I want this ten-week-old Golden to be impressed with me, somehow—because I find her beautiful and full of possibility, and my heart is tight with months of waiting for her.

"Come," I say to Puzzle. She glances at Kim, then stands with elaborate slowness and saunters over. When she reaches me and I pick her up to praise and cuddle her, Puzzle doesn't yield. She leans back with stiff paws against my chest and gives me a long, level gaze.

I love her immediately. She hasn't learned to love me. But in her willingness to come I sense an ethic, and in her scrutiny I see intelligence. I think of the hard places we will go that need both: the disaster sites and gang-riddled neighborhoods, the lakes, the crime scenes and small town with a single missing girl whose case is ongoing, whose fate remains unknown.

I return the puppy's gaze. What began as a late-night conversation in a bar has emerged as a Golden Retriever braced in the bend of my arms. She feels solid and capable. She feels right.

"Hi, sweetheart," I say to Puzzle. "Are you ready to go to work?"

3

INTO THE WIND

I CAME TO GROUND search-and-rescue from the air. The route was not direct. While I was working as a flight instructor in the early 1990s, an experienced student once asked me to fly with him to an area where he'd had a problem on a runway a few days before. A police officer and a talented pilot working on an advanced rating, he had been carrying other law enforcement personnel on a clear autumn day in his single-engine aircraft when, on landing, his plane shot off the end of the short, lakeside runway and down a small embankment before coming to a stop.

No one was hurt, the plane wasn't damaged, but he was an experienced pilot and the event concerned him. He wanted to discuss that landing with me and revisit the runway for touch-and-go practice. From his description of the plane's performance on final approach and the long, long streaks from his tires still visible on the asphalt when we got there, I suspected wind shear was responsible, and that his headwind had shifted to a tailwind at an unfortunate point in the landing sequence.

We had different conditions the day we revisited that airstrip, but we worked his touch-and-goes anyway. After a handful of successful, unassisted landings proved to him that the runway itself and his technique for landing on it were not an ongoing problem, he asked if I'd mind a flight around the lake before coming back to the runway to shoot more landings. The request surprised me a little — flight time is expensive — but I agreed.

A cold front had passed the day before. This afternoon was beautifully crisp and clear; low pressure had swept the air clean. From a plane flying low in this kind of weather, you can see the herringbone of wind on water, the definition of individual leaves, the colors on a bobber at the end of a fisherman's line. We made a circle of the lake's long shoreline, my student flying at the regulation altitude. I noticed, however, that his scan of instruments, sky, and ground included a lot of glances straight down, and having flown with him so long, I knew also it wasn't part of his standard procedure.

"What are we looking for, David?" I finally asked.

He didn't answer for a moment. Then he said, "We don't know what he did with her."

Without further comment, we circled the lake into evening, alternating who flew the airplane and who looked for the body of a woman along the lake's ragged shore.

That's how I began working search. In later months, through some grapevine I never completely understood, I gained a clientele who hired me to fly the press or personnel from other law enforcement agencies over variously troubled locations. For some clients, it was a matter of budget. My fixed-wing aircraft was less expensive than a helicopter. For others, it was an attempt to be nondescript: small planes in high-traffic areas attract less attention than rotorcraft. A few said they'd heard I was confident with the airplane; when asked to fly low and slow and stable, within regulations I could do it.

We flew over crime scenes and followed off-road trails suspected as body dumps. We traced the trajectory of downed aircraft in deep wood. As altitude restrictions expired, I flew with photographers over what remained of the Murrah Federal Building in Oklahoma City and the Koresh Compound in Waco, Texas. We plotted the paths of tornadoes. We circled livestock stranded on high ground by flood. From the vantage of a high-winged Cessna, my passengers — often press or insurance photographers — documented public and personal catastrophe. They unscrewed the window bracket for an unobstructed view and leaned outward as the slipstream held the window up. "Again," they'd gesture with a little twirl of the index finger, and around we'd go another time.

Not every client was clear about our objectives. Once, a man I took to be an insurance photographer (he came with multiple bags on shoulder straps), turned out to be the son of a rancher who had died. We unscrewed the window bracket so he could photograph the homestead in a long-shadowed sunset, and he did so, but when that was done he opened what I thought was a second camera case, drew out a large velvet bag, and prepared to drop his father's ashes over the family ranch. This kind of flight request is common, but problems are common too. It's a hire that recommends a good briefing. I saw what he was doing, was just about to give him — *hey!* — a quick word on ashes and slipstream when he, ahead of me, began to pour. Wind carried the ashes back through the window into the airplane, where they whistled around the tiny cabin and ended up all over us.

"Sorry," he said after an appalled moment. I tried to smile and felt the sheen of grit across my teeth, like I'd been testing pearls.

Not long afterward, another client had a similar request, but she was more straightforward on the hire and asked to sprinkle her father's ashes outside the small town along the interstate where he'd grown up. We had a good briefing on procedure, and I knew she understood, but when we got to the location she opened the window, took the soft case in her hands to hold it ready, then to extend it and pour — and dropped it entirely. The bag landed like a flour bomb in the middle of a Taco Bell parking lot just off the highway. We could see the astro-shaped burst of ash across the pavement.

We circled a little while in silence. I was thinking about the incident report I might need to file with the FAA. I don't know what she was thinking.

"Dad loved their Enchiritos," said my client at last, and she shut the window.

My own recent transitions were just as clunky. The flight career was still a fledgling; my twelve-year marriage, shot through with its own disasters, failed. And then I was alone. The family worried about my faltering income in "a man's profession," about their daughter newly divorced so young.

They worried about me in airplanes, but flight was perversely my good fortune. Then, as now, it was a mental and physical discipline, a blessed remove. I flew as often for hire as regulations allowed, grateful for the money of course, but I would have flown for free. During the period of divorce, I moved to a seedy, affordable apartment so near a runway that in the middle of the night I could identify individual planes by the grind of their starters, see the alternating flash of the airport beacon — green-white-green-white-green-white — like the *lub-dup* of a heart across the graceless walls of my bedroom.

It was a different time for general aviation before 9/11, when civilian pilots were not so readily framed as a threat. I would unlock the flight school on sleepless nights and check out a Cessna 152, file a flight plan, and go up to admire city skylines or make cross-country jaunts in the dark — flights I recall now for the occasional camaraderie over the radio with air traffic controllers and the night-flying freight dogs, but remember most for their exquisite aloneness. Moon and silver ground and the comfort of the Lycoming engine's cat-purr drone. I would set one radio receiver to the navigation facility closest to my home airport and the other receiver to the facility closest to the point of arrival, and I flew with the counterpoint of their Morse code identifiers beeping out of sync in my headset — literally the sound of where I was going and where I had been.

Though I think my family worried I might be suicidal (which I was not), and I know they would have been frightened to learn I flew in the middle of the night, flight gave me perspective. I think of those flights as private, invisible stitches across Texas in the dark, binding me to a world outside my own grief. Martha Graham once commented that she never thought of a dancer as alone on stage, that he or she was "always partnered by the surrounding space." It was a concept worth borrowing. And what space. On a clear night in still air, the stars were so close they shook up other senses, tempting me to open the window and put out my tongue to the spangle. I would have bet they had a taste, like pop rocks, maybe, or wasabi.

Other nights a blanket of stratiform cloud stretched wide above the little Cessna, and I flew small and secret, like a child with a flashlight under the blanket, flying beneath an eiderdown beautifully up-lit at its edges by the lights of cities on the horizon. The ground went dark for long passages over rural areas, defined by the deeper black of an occasional lake or edged by an interstate highway stippled with traffic. Small towns lay tidy as a tic-tac-toe grid beneath a handful of streetlights. But the peace and order were flecked occasionally with buildings afire, with the *uh-oh-uh-oh-uh-oh* twist of lights from emergency vehicles speeding down an unlit road. I could see them thirty miles away.

It wasn't in me to imagine my own catastrophe. Though there was one late night on an approach to the home airport's north runway that I felt a distinct unease at three hundred feet above the ground in the landing sequence, a sensation I couldn't validate with a crosscheck of the instruments, the sound of the plane, the feel of the air across the wings, or the sight of the windsock on the field. The unease was as profound as a waking shake on the shoulder, an imperative "go around." I followed instinct and aborted the landing, pressing the throttle forward, stabilizing the airplane, and retracting the flaps as airspeed allowed. The second approach was virtually identical to the first, the landing and rollout uneventful. I taxied to the ramp and shut down the airplane, then walked to the edge of the tarmac and gazed out at the runway in the dark, wondering about my little mystery, looking for anything that might have been a problem on the first landing.

Nothing. South end of the field was quiet. I could hear wind tunneling through the windsock across the runway — a keening little song like a pissed-off fairy in a bottle. The beacon's double flash pulsed across the hangars, the planes, the tarmac, and me. Nothing. Nothing. Then movement: a stray dog winding west through the shadows at the end of runway 34. He paused and turned to look my way, caught by the scent or the sound of me. Was the dog what I had sensed earlier? Where had he been the first time I was approaching to land? A gangly, spotted mixed-breed, he blazed red in the glow of the runway end lights, his head lifted in a carrying posture of intelligence. We looked at each other a long moment, in our separate ways making sense of threat and possibility. The dog seemed to make his mind up first. When he turned and loped into the black field beyond, I felt an unreasonable urge to drop my flight case and follow.

Restless. I'd been feeling restless. The encounter with Runway Dog both provoked an urge for change and informed the relationship with my own dogs at home. In the months after that late-night experience at the airport, I paid even closer attention to dog ways of negotiating the environment. Eyes, ears, tongue, nose, pads — and that magical word *vibrissae*, the whiskers of the muzzle and eyebrows that can even perceive changes of airflow — I watched my little housedogs and saw them respond intuitively to a concert of sensory perceptions. Many of their skills were similar to stick and rudder skills I'd learned to use as a pilot — moving air is a whole kaleidoscope of changing textures, palpable to the pilot's hands, feet, and seat of her pants — but even the most sheltered dogs of my crew were better at making whole-body sense of their surroundings than I was.

When a leaf fell into a burning citronella candle and ignited on the back porch, three of the littlest dogs in the house raised their noses simultaneously, nostrils working, before they brought eyes and ears to bear and turned their heads to look in the direction of the fire, separated by a screen door and six yards away. Scent first indicated change; sight and sound were used to make better sense of it. Though all three dogs grew excited, Mr. Sprits'l alone ran to find me one room away, quivering and barking furiously, every hair electric, leading me back to the trouble. (When Sprits'l is excited, he tends to spin rather than travel in a straight line; this made our trip back to the porch rather like following a dreidel.)

Not a little fire. I extinguished the bucket of flame that had been a candle, thinking all the while about the clarity of Sprits'l's message: *Not normal. Not right. Back here. No, back here. Fix this.* He had not simply barked at the flame; he'd not run to another dog to telegraph the news. He'd come to me without hesitation, and when I went out the door to take care of it, Sprits did not attempt to follow. I realized that to this dog there were certain givens in our relationship, and that I was not only a bringer of food and a scratcher of chest, but I was also a trusted protector. I knew that, but I didn't know *he* knew that.

What else would dogs tell me? What else did dogs know?

Curiosity led me to consider volunteer opportunities with working dogs — dogs whose job descriptions included making sense of a changing environment and communicating that change to a human. I wanted to try for that kind of connection. And our large urban area presented plenty of opportunities. Depending on level of interest and commitment, I learned I could be a puppy-raiser for guide dogs, a once-a-week socializer of assist dogs, and — most interesting to me — an assistant in the field on a canine search-and-rescue team. They were all time-intensive opportunities, especially SAR. Three to seven training hours a week, plus expected home study, plus emergency calls.

One friend asked, "Does it pay well?"

A relative sighed, "You are never going to marry again."

My oldest friend understood. "Of course," Marina said. "You've got a history of getting out there. It makes sense you'd want to learn to fly a dog."

• • •

I visited the K9 team I would eventually join after finding a 1995 photograph from the *Dallas Morning News* that I'd cut out during the aftermath of Oklahoma City's Murrah Federal Building bombing. Skip Fernandez, a canine handler with the Miami-Dade County Fire Rescue team, sits on the ground with his head bowed and eyes closed against the back of his Golden Retriever, Aspen. The caption states that they have worked all night, and they look it. They are dirty. The dog sits rolled over onto one hip, propped up by her front legs. She looks tired. Her expression is subdued.

I don't know why I originally clipped the photo, but when I found it six years later, I felt convinced. While some disasters needed air support, almost all of them needed dogs on the ground to locate the living and the dead — and partners beside them to translate. Though the process itself was a mystery to me, I was eager to understand dogs better on their own terms. And perhaps I had something to contribute: As a pilot I had begun to learn the workings of the wind. I could talk on the radio. I wasn't squeamish or afraid of the dark. Surely that was enough to make a start at this. Nothing about the work looked easy, but canine search-and-rescue looked like work I wanted to do.

4

PUZZLE HAS LANDED

THE BAGGAGE HANDLER at ticketing doesn't speak much English. He makes a gesture when I bring Puzzle up to the counter — a funny little shoving motion that I can't quite make out, until he does the push gesture and a twist of his fingers, and I realize he's telling me that Puzzle should be in a hard-sided carrier to go in the belly of the airplane.

"No," I say. "This is a search dog in training, and she's coming home in the cabin with me." I show him the soft-sided, under-the-seat carrier. Puzzle will fit inside it, but I've been told earlier by the airline that because she's a search dog, she will be able to ride in the cabin in my lap or at my feet, as long as she has the appropriate credentials. Our trip home together involves elaborate explanation with some backstory; uncertain, the baggage handler shakes his head and leaves to find the ticket agent, who comes out wiping her hands, a daub of mustard on her nose.

"So what is this puppy supposed to do for me?" she asks a little skeptically, but she grins because Puzzle has suddenly turned on the charm, wagging and smiling and pawing at the agent's extended fingers.

"Well," I say. "She's not going to do anything but love you at the moment and maybe mooch a French fry, but she's passed her first aptitude tests, and she's heading home to train to be a search dog." I show her my team ID and Puzzle's green in-training vest, the smallest size of which is still three times too big for her. She looks like a puppy in a barrel.

The woman glances at the ID and the vest. "Wow. You are my first search-and-rescue dog," says the agent. She rubs Puzzle's ears, causing a sensation so pleasurable that the puppy's eyes almost cross.

"She knows 'Sit,' 'Stand,' and 'Come,'" I respond proudly — thinking, *boy, I hope she still does* — and resting Puzzle on the counter.

"Sit," says the agent, and Puzzle plops down on the counter with such gusto that she knocks my driver's license to the floor, grinning with her tongue out sideways. She clearly adores the woman, who leans closer. Puzzle licks the mustard from her nose.

"I couldn't do it," says the agent.

"Do what?"

"Train a puppy and then give it up to someone else."

I lean forward to help her untangle Puzzle's forepaws from her hair. "The good news," I say, "is that I won't have to make that choice. I'll be her working partner. She'll be a search dog, *my* search dog, but she'll also live with me."

"Ohhhhh — so she's going home, then," says the agent, handing me a boarding pass.

"Yes," I answer, reaching for the pass awkwardly, realizing Puzzle has somehow flipped in my arms and is butt-upward, her tail waving gently beneath my chin. "She's going home."

In the airline terminal, Puzzle is extremely social with two passing pilots, a child pushing her own stroller, and the three TSA agents who pass her among them after her collar, harness, and vest set off the security sensors. She tilts her head so winningly at a cowboy-booted man on a cell phone that he hangs up and crosses the gate area to pet her.

"Now this looks like a dog that could get away with anything," says the gentleman.

I tip her up to look into her face. "This sure looks like a dog who will try."

"She's got a good head, good big black nose. Gun dog?" he asks.

I shake my head. "Search-and-rescue."

"Bless you, Ma'am," he says, then, "You'd better give this one something to do *fast*."

He pets Puzzle, engulfing her head in his large hand. Then he walks away with a chuckle, with a better-you-than-me shake of his head.

By contrast, our flight attendant, who later catches sight of Puzzle out of the corner of her eye during a trip down the aisle during the flight, gives a nervous little shriek. I feel sure the young woman saw the puppy come aboard, but now Puzzle sleeps upside down in my arms, her round belly upward, feet akimbo, head limp and lolling backward toward the aisle. Gravity has pulled down the puppy's ears and lips and bared her fangs. Her eyes are open but unseeing, rolled up in her head with the whites exposed. It's not a good look. It's not even canine — more Hell-Spawn Bunny of the Undead.

"It's a *puppy*," says my seatmate, helpfully pointing to the paws, the nose, and the tail.

"I'm sorry," stammers the attendant. "F-for a second, I thought I was seeing some kind of a . . . a . . . mutant."

"She's going to be a search dog," I add. I exhibit the little green vest.

"Oh. I'm sure she'll be very good," says the flight attendant. But her expression is shifty. She hurries away.

The exchange has roused Puzzle a little. A couple of *huh? what?* snorts, and she stretches all four paws upward, trembling with the extension. She is briefly stiff as roadkill, then relaxes. In less than a minute she begins to snore: a treble *skkkiiiiinnnnnnnnnk* from just behind her nostrils, then a deeper *skkunnnnnnnnnnnk* farther back in her muzzle. Her eyes roll slowly upward again, the whites staring dully across the aisle toward two other passengers.

One grins. The other flinches and turns back to his in-flight magazine.

I look down at Puzzle and consider that I've never seen a Golden puppy photographed from this unflattering angle. There are probably reasons for that.

"She doesn't have to be pretty," says the grinning man across the aisle, his voice kind. "She just has to be smart."

The Poms look like they've been to a horror show.

Puzzle's nap aboard the airplane has refreshed her, and she has entered the house all bounding energy and curiosity. It takes her only moments to put her nose to the butt of every Pom that rushes forward to inspect her, to flush a cat from the laundry basket, and to knock over a row of plastic bottles I have set aside for recycling. Now she has suddenly discovered the stuffed lobster that's made the trip with us, and she takes the over-large toy in her mouth, rushing up to little Sophie with it, shaking it meaningfully: *booga-booga-booga, lobster-booga!* Sophie honks and skitters, her dark eyes wide.

Undeterred, Puzzle drops the toy and prances up to Maddy, one of my oldest cats. Maddy has seen dogs come and has seen dogs go, and, totally fearless, has found a *laissez chien* attitude serves her well. She flops down on the floor as Puzzle approaches, squinching her eyes shut as though the puppy is something to be temporarily endured, like an enema. Puzzle moves very slowly, giving Maddy a thoughtful nose-over. The introduction seems to be going well until the puppy gets to Maddy's bottom. Some curiosity there gives Puzzle pause, and she huffs a snort straight up Maddy's backside, which causes the cat to loft with an insulted squawk and leap for the back of the couch. Maddy misses, overshoots, lands hard behind the couch, scrambling two other cats hiding back there — and they jointly riot, heading for the closest high thing any of them can find: a large potted ficus in a ceramic pot by the window. It is a big tree, in a big pot, but they are three senior cats with weight issues and motivation. As they struggle to climb frail branches, their weight overcomes the ficus, and it tips over before I can dodge the couch and get across the room.

Four things happen almost simultaneously. The tree falls, the pot shatters, the cats shoot apart like pieces of exploded TIE Fighter, and Puzzle leaps into the debris with the first bark I have heard from her: a bright, happy *hark!* of satisfaction. When I pull her from what's left of the tree, she has already snuffled into its root ball, emerging with a triumphant expression and a dirty nose flecked with Perlite. I get the sense that if a puppy could waggle her eyebrows at the lot of us, she would.

Wow! Wow! Wow! Whisky shrieks about the new dog in her house.

Augh! replies Sprits'l, apropos of it all.

5

ALL THE WRONG THINGS

PISSED AT HIS GIRLFRIEND, says the brother of the boy who is missing, or at least that's the version we get from the officer who interviewed family members an hour ago. *Pissed at his girlfriend and hitching a ride with a friend to Austin for the weekend.* He left the house before supper and slammed the door and headed right, said the brother, who watched him walk down the hill and out of sight. He was still wearing the khaki pants he'd worn earlier while waiting tables, stained with grease and ketchup. He was so mad he didn't stop to change. Just threw his things down and pulled on another shirt as he walked out the door, before their parents got home.

Two search dogs, however, disagree. Charged by their handlers to determine direction of travel, both dogs show little interest in the route suggested by the missing boy's brother. The dogs have been sent out to trail the boy separately, the second handler unaware of the conclusions drawn by the first team. Neither dog confirmed the brother's gestured route. Two officers clearly believe the dogs, while one is torn. The brother's story is brief and consistent. I've heard it twice myself, and it's not difficult to imagine the boy slamming out the door and hooking a right toward his friend's house, hitching a ride to Austin, and leaving the girl behind.

The friend in Austin, however, says by cell phone that he last saw the boy in question earlier that day at school. If he'd gone to Austin, says the friend, he didn't get there with him. And he adds, "Like his parents would even *let* him go."

The missing boy is a good-looking kid, two school pictures tell us. Last year's photo has a little baby fat that's missing from this year's shot. His hair is longer too. He appears confident and capable — he looks into the camera easily — and he was either cavalier about his sophomore picture or ill-prepared for it. He's wearing a faded, wrinkled T-shirt in this most recent photo, and his hair is mussed. There's a little tuft of it sticking upward from the back of his head, like a cowlick that aspires to a miniature peacock fan. His grin is crooked, and there's a pink scar from the corner of his mouth that points to his jaw. He appears uncertain in the freshman photo, but in the sophomore shot there's a little "dare me" expression in his eyes.

We get a lot of school photos in the pre-brief of searches for missing children, but sometimes a family will bring out their own candid shots too. It would be good to see a picture of this whole boy in the context of his house, his neighborhood. The way he dresses. The things he carries, values. But not this time. His parents, who made the 911 call after searching awhile themselves, offer a school picture and little else.

They stand silent on the porch of their house. His two younger brothers straddle bicycles a few feet away in the driveway. The bicycles are sized for smaller riders. Both boys have their feet on the ground and their knees rocked outward, their forearms resting on the handlebars. Though they stand apart, the family resemblance is apparent between parents and sons. Even at midnight in the shadows, I can see their faces settle into the same lines, pale and remote in the thin light of a waning moon and the streetlight one house over. They do not talk to one another or touch. They stand together but not together, the tension between them palpable.

The parents do not come forward to speak to us or to meet the dogs that will search for their son. It can go either way on a search; some families want that connection. Others do not. Neither has the community rallied to this search, which is also unusual. Though we see the occasional flick of light when a curtain is drawn back, no neighbors come out to support the family or speak with the police.

But before we arrived, the boy's mother located the jacket her son had tossed over the chair in his bedroom. A meticulous woman: she paid attention to the concept of a "scent article," bringing the jacket out caught between salad tongs so as not to touch and contaminate the fabric with her own scent. The officer that briefed us leads Jerry and Shadow again to the jacket now lying on the sidewalk of the house. Jerry directs Shadow to smell it, and she takes a brief, thoughtful scent. She knows the scent, has smelled it before an hour ago when sent out to confirm or deny the brother's statement. When Jerry commands her to "Find *that*," she ignores the eastward path the boy's brother says was the last way he went, choosing instead to wind her way north in the darkness. I am assigned to field assist the pair in this sector, and I follow a few steps behind, taking notes and watching Shadow. She avoids the street and the sidewalk of her chosen direction, sidestepping instead to an alley bounded by a mangled, uneasy fence that separates the neighborhood from open field beyond.

The wood and wire fence sags with the remembered weight of all the people who have climbed it. The field beyond is dark, broad, and scruffy—and for sale, weathered twin signs at either end seem to suggest—land waiting for development, only minimally kept neat. A line of trees bounds the far eastern edge of it. From this distance, the trees seem to hunch forward toward the field, like a line of vultures waiting for something to fall. The police say this field is a common thoroughfare for the dog-walkers and teenagers of the area. The dog-walkers let their dogs "run loose and shit free," as one officer puts it, while the teenagers use the field as a shortcut to a pizza joint and a convenience store. Sometimes the kids simply walk into the trees, for drugs or sex or both. The field and that stand of trees is a concern, a likely venue for poor choices or drug deals gone bad. Two busy streets intersect at the far edge of the wood, creating an area that is both quickly accessible and relatively obscured. There have been other kids in trouble there; other crimes across the four years the land has been for sale. Earlier this evening, police already searched into the tree line. They've found nothing.

Shadow walks along the alley, slipping through the infrequent light. Her liquid movement before us is beautiful: now a silver dog, now black, now silver, now black as she crosses in and out of the dark. About seven houses from where we began our sector, she slows, pauses, and mutters to Jerry. She puts her nose to a fence, then moves around the side of it, pawing at a warped gate buckling outside its frame, a gate that no longer aligns with its catch. Shadow is interested here. Very interested. She sticks fast with her nose to the gate.

Jerry moves to the front of the house to see its address, then calls the location to the officers in charge. They confirm this house is the home of another friend of the missing boy. But the officers have already visited it. Having spoken to the friend and his parents, they determined the boy is not there — though he'd visited there frequently, always coming in from the back gate through the kitchen. They say Shadow must be interested in old scent. The scenario is logical enough, and Jerry directs Shadow to move on. She does so with reluctance and some grumbling, a low, musical singularly Husky note. Her lope away seems unwilling.

Jerry wonders if anyone has checked with the boy's girlfriend. I call the question in by radio as we move northward down the alley to a dark area where a street lamp has gone out. We move with flashlights only now, Shadow glowing in the distance ahead of us. She pads steadily forward, but without the excitement of a dog on the scent she's been asked to find. Occasionally she pauses and turns her head to look back at us. Her pale blue eyes snap as they pass through the flashlights' beams. She turns away and lopes on.

The radio crackles; we have turned the volume down to prevent disturbing the neighborhood asleep. I murmur against the mike and hold the radio to my ear. Incident Command confirms that the girlfriend has been reached. She had no information about her missing boyfriend and (this said in low parenthesis) seemed surprised by any question that the two of them had fought. Jerry shakes his head and we walk on, coming to the end of the alley and turning eastward toward another street and a reverse sweep to the south.

Shadow grows less interested the farther we move east. She sparks again only once as we are southbound the next street over, crossing purposefully between two dark houses with us tiptoeing behind, then across the street. She mutters a little, working quickly, and as we watch the direction of her interest, Jerry recognizes we've returned to the front of the same house that she had originally engaged before. We call in second interest and head back to finish the sweep we'd briefly abandoned.

I can hear handlers calling Incident Command from their sectors southwest, southeast, and northwest of us. Routine calls noting time and location, none of the dogs showing any interest at all in their assigned areas.

Tonight we use an additional resource. One member of our team is a professional man tracker out of a police department in California. He and another FAS team member have begun "cutting sign," looking for footprints or other indicators that might confirm or deny the brother's story, anything that might suggest the boy's direction of travel. They know his shoe size and his height, have a fair approximation of his stride. By flashlight they will look for evidence of transfer: crushed grass in the road, alley dust in the grass, fresh mud on the depressed wire where someone has newly climbed over the fence. Man tracking is a painstaking process that requires good vision and an ability to note the signs of disturbance left by any creature that crosses ground. Terry's long experience makes him fast and efficient. Webb, his assistant, has caught on to the job quickly.

Jerry, Shadow, and I are at the farthest bound of our sector when Terry calls to Incident Command. He and Webb have found what appears to be likely prints in the grit of the alley we had first walked along. Not our boot prints; these belong to someone else. No sign that someone had gone over the wire and into the field today, but three prints in dust and tamped grass a few steps away suggest track—they lead to the area where Shadow had put her nose to the worn gate and held fast.

Jerry and I look at each other a moment. Shadow has worked ahead about a house-length, loping quietly southward now on the fourth street of our sector, but her demeanor suggests we are nowhere near the scent she has been told to seek. The other dogs are coming in. *Nothing*, their behavior tells their handlers. We conclude a final sweep and head back to the command area ourselves. As we walk, I can see flickers of light in my periphery from all quadrants: the other teams returning. Their flashlights punctuate every step, occasionally silvering the eyes of the dogs now trotting quietly beside them.

At Incident Command, two officers have agreed that fresh track and a dog's intense interest is enough to justify a second inquiry at the house seven doors to the north. They will return to that house and wake the family. Team by team, we head back to command and begin drafting our sector reports, chewing our pens and sketching sector maps, writing the narrative that explains who searched the sector, how it was searched, any problems in the sector, any area where the dogs might have shown significant response. We write, but we are all turned a little toward the command post radio. Our own radio is silent. I can occasionally hear the murmur of the police communication from the line of parked police vehicles near us, somehow sounding matter-of-fact and urgent at the same time, but nothing across ours.

Almost simultaneously, the dogs look north: noses up, ears wheeled forward. Their postures mark the boy's return before we see or hear it. He walks slowly back to his house with a police officer on either side. His head is down, and he walks with his arms folded across his chest. His right hand, beneath the fold of his left, is clenched into a fist. His parents meet him at the center of the yard, and the three stand rigid there, the boy and mother silent, the father speaking in short, emphatic tones with the officers who brought him back. The two younger boys retreat into the house. We never see them again.

After an exchange we cannot hear, one officer invites the dogs to meet the boy they have searched for. Perhaps the officer has seen them straining and wagging where their handlers stood. At the invitation, the handlers gesture and the dogs come together, and it's like a little ballet as they converge on the spot where the boy stands. Collie, German Shepherd, Husky, two Labs. From dropped shoulders and long arms, the boy turns his palms backward to allow the dogs to sniff, but he does not connect with them. He does not look up. Not at us. Not at the police. Not at his father who, after we begin to pack up for the night, lifts his hand as if to strike his son, then gives him an angry push into the house.

"Sometimes," says an officer, "it's tough to know if you've done a good thing or not."

6

FIRST LESSONS

THERE'S A STORY told about an experienced handler working a training scenario with a young dog who'd just begun to learn to search. The three-story warehouse where they sought a single volunteer victim was an ideal training environment: full of stacked crates, landscaping tools, out-of-season holiday decorations, window-cleaning equipment, discarded office furniture, and the occasional makeshift bed for a homeless person who'd snuck in. The lighting was poor. There were dark stairwells and disused elevator shafts, strange air currents and dead corners where scent hung motionless. The building challenged even experienced teams. But this dog was keen, and this handler wanted to give the building a try.

Working from the almost-empty ground floor up, the two swept the entire warehouse, and the Australian Cattle Dog pup hesitated in only one spot — a patch of cement strewn with the moldy remains of Halloween hay. He worried at the hay a little before the handler directed him away and upward to the second floor. From there they worked slowly through the still air, threading their way between the corridors of outcast computer desks and finding nothing. Up to the third floor, even more congested and dusty, peppered with pigeon feathers and owl droppings. They worked the room edges, the corners, and made back-and-forth sweeps across the middle of it through debris. The dog showed no interest at all. Knowing they had one planted victim, the handler reversed the search and again swept the third floor. Nothing. Second floor. Nothing still. Losing faith in the dog due to its youth and relative inexperience, the handler began opening crates and tilting boxes over, hoping to either find the victim himself or stir the air enough to shake loose significant scent. The dog did not respond. In frustration, the handler took the dog back to the first floor and moved through it again, quickly. The pup moved back to the flat scatter of hay, and the handler called him away from it twice, directing the dog to the edges of the elevator door.

The story goes that the dog had now had enough, ignored the handler and marched past him, oblivious to further commands, trotting out of the building straight to the head trainer and plopping down in her lap. The trainer says that when the handler came out, his face flushed with anger, the dog turned away. She says the dog too looked disgusted, like "ain't *he* a piece of work?"

After a few moments' debrief, the trainer asked if the dog had shown any interest in anything in the building at all. The handler dismissively mentioned the hay. The trainer stood up and led the pair back into the building, where she ran her foot across the hay and revealed a grate in the floor, and beneath the grate, a ten-year-old child sat patiently in the space of an air duct, looking upward at the three of them.

I've never heard how the story concluded — if the handler made nice to his dog at that moment, if the dog shrugged off the incident in the way of good-natured canines, how the pair of them fared on later searches. But the tale in all its versions is always cautionary, its warning perpetual: trust the dog.

It's not as easy as it sounds, because the handler developing trust is also raising a puppy still prone to scatterbrained antics. Many SAR dogs begin training as soon as their inoculations for rabies, distemper, and parvo allow it, between ten and twelve weeks old. Energetic, playful, sometimes highly distractible, they are introduced to search through "runaways," a game where a friendly assistant holds the new puppy and the handler runs a short distance away to hide. The assistant cries "Find!" and releases the dog, which ideally runs immediately for the handler and is praised and rewarded for the glorious find. Handler runaways are repeated enough times so consistent behavior is seen from the puppy, and then roles are reversed: the handler holds the dog and the assistant runs to hide. If the pup seeks the assistant as readily as she had sought the handler in previous exercises, learning has taken place — both for dog and handler. The dog has learned that "Find!" has an objective and a reward, and the handler has taken a first step toward trust. It's an encouraging moment when a handler sees his new dog willingly look for another person just as readily as he'd naturally run for the handler whom he has begun to love. When we see the dog successfully find a wide variety of people hiding in different places during "runaways," the dog demonstrates consistency and the handler's confidence rises.

From there, simple searches continue — one victim in a "sector" — but the victim's within a close, limited range of location. Now the handler cannot see the volunteer victim in hiding. And small as it may be, the sector is a mystery to the team. This is the moment when a basic understanding of wind direction and air currents makes all the difference to dog-and-handler strategy. It's also the moment where distractions for a young dog may tell — a blowing leaf kicks off a puppy's prey drive and off she goes to chase it; passersby fifty yards away tempt a friendly dog to break off the search and trot over to petition for petting. Another dog crosses into the puppy's field of vision, and the opportunity for play is irresistible.

It's a tough time for a handler, who can make several wrong choices at this crucial moment for a young SAR dog. Overdiscipline, and the dog can associate working search with punishment and become less willing. Overindulge, and the puppy learns that search is a casual, when-you-get-around-to-it affair. Perhaps the worst temptation is to deny that the young dog lacks focus at this point in training, to use your own eyes to find the victim and credit the dog with the find. Most training teams have an experienced handler or trainer supervising the search, but the opportunity to overcompensate for the dog's young nature still exists. More than false pride is implicated. Crediting a pup with more success than he has earned may push him into harder training scenarios that he is ill-equipped for; a frustrated dog (who may also intuit the handler's frustration) can quickly lose the sense of adventure and fun that fosters a consistent will to work. And the handler's confidence has taken a serious blow. Hide the puppy's immaturity at your peril. Eventually there will be search scenarios where your eyes can't do it and the dog, moved ahead in her training too fast, isn't willing to.

At eleven weeks old, Puzzle is all paws, fat belly, and big head. Her nose is large and very black, and she seems willing to use it to achieve a goal. There is a lot to smell in this house: food on the stove and leather shoes in closets, the other dogs and cats, and because the house is pier-and-beam, every mouse and squirrel running under the house too. She is not yet ready to begin search training. While we wait for her final Parvo vaccinations and the vet's all-clear to put her paws on new ground, we begin scent games in the house, designed to teach her to find things on command and to associate successful finds with praise. One game involves passing a treat from hand to hand behind my back, then extending both closed fists to the puppy, asking her to identify the hand with the treat and to bump that hand with her nose. Puzzle catches on quickly, and after a few attempts she recognizes the difference between faint scent (was there) and stronger scent (is there now), and she happily bumps my hand with her nose, sometimes chattering at me with yaps and moans to underscore her choice.

The Poms, too, enjoy the game. Blind Scuppy is invariably accurate. Fo'c'sle Jack, who loves food above all things, learns that the quickest path to a reward is to get the correct hand and be quick about it. Mr. Sprits'l is wary of the game. Inclined to sniff both hands critically, he tilts his head and considers in the way a gourmand might judge a mouthful of foie gras: *I smell the treat, but is it up to my personal standard?* When he chooses the correct hand and gets both treat and praise, Sprits takes the treat with great care, trotting off to private spaces, where he will work it with his paws and deliberate.

We play the "Which Hand?" game for a few days, then progress to a hidden treat beneath one of three clean, upended flowerpots. This advanced game requires that Puzzle not only identify the correct pot but also begin to maneuver to get to what she seeks. I watch these early efforts at problem-solving with some amusement. Puzzle lacks small motor skills and any sense of physics. She's inclined to identify the correct pot and then scoot it across the porch by bumping it with her head, the treat dragging along with it as she goes. After one such effort, she flops down on her bottom and barks angrily at the pot, then turns and barks indignantly at me. The message seems clear: *This won't cooperate, and it's All Your Fault.* Metatext aside, she has made a good choice. When she barks for my attention, I pick up the flowerpot and she gets her treat.

I am happy to see her accuracy and her perseverance. In the days that follow, I notice she pushes less and instead stands over the chosen flowerpot, barking for my attention much more quickly. I hope that this is the beginning of what will be direct, communicative alerts on Puzzle's search finds — a sort of *I've done my job, now you do yours.*

The games get more difficult, and I begin to hide the treats in the house and yard: under objects, on top of fence posts, wedged in the *V*-shaped branches of young trees. Puzzle is eager to play, and for a distractible puppy likely to abandon a butterfly she's chasing to flush a bird instead, falling over her own feet as she goes, Puzzle is all focus when the treats come out and I put on her little "search" collar that signals the work is about to begin.

The Poms watch us. Though they too get to play scent games

at least once in our daily training, I recognize they are aware that Puzzle gets more training and more treats. Feeling the pressure of hard gazes, I look up once in the backyard and see a row of three little fox faces staring out a bedroom window at us. Mr. Sprits'l gives a mutter, then an outraged *Augh!* of protest when the puppy scores her third treat in a row. I realize then that as soon as Puz can safely work outside the yard, we need to begin our training elsewhere. I am ill-versed in dog dynamics, but it seems to me that at least some of the Poms recognize the puppy's unfair share of my attention. Later that afternoon, we play again in the house, each dog taking turns at this scent game or that one. Sprits'l successfully finds a treat beneath my right foot, and when I raise my shoe he takes it after a long, guarded sniff. "Good boy!" I praise him as he stomps off — the treat in his mouth, his ears cocked back and his posture stiff with scorn.

Puzzle, in turn, watches the Poms. She is especially fascinated by Scuppy. The old dog navigates our yard quite easily, missing objects he has previously marked, sidestepping other dogs in his path as he orients to their scent and movement. Every once in a while I see a hint of what must have been his younger sense of mischief. He will pad slowly and quietly toward a huddle of pigeons, then make a little burst of speed and a bark like a toy trumpet with a mute. With only his nose to go by, Scuppy clearly demonstrates how scent moves, where it sticks, and how it pools. Watching him, I am aware of subtleties that he translates easily, though I cannot smell them at all.

Puzzle treats the old dog with kindly deference. She's inclined to rush and tumble the younger Poms, but she carefully sidesteps Scuppy and does not interfere with his flushed pigeons or his path through the yard. Sometimes she follows him as a sort of wingman. Other times she simply observes.

I leave the back door open and watch them lie together in the yard and ferret the scent of bird versus squirrel versus man-with-a-baby-jogger and girl-with-a-dog. Sometimes their noses bob together. Other times it's in a little sequence, like they're doing the Wave. One night I slip out the back door and stand half the backyard away, upwind of them and silent. It's a warm, humid, windless evening. I lean over and wave my hands, wondering how long it will take both dogs to catch scent enough to notice. It takes only moments. Their noses bob with recognition, and Scuppy stiffly rises, wagging, ready to come to me. Puzzle turns her head in the easy pivot of a young dog and smiles from where she lies across the slate. When she sees Scuppy heading my way, she too gets up and follows at a careful distance. Scuppy finds me without a misstep, puts his nose into my hands, and groans as I rub his soft ears, and Puzzle, sometimes competitive and pushy for attention, does not push him away.

Though I am eager for the day when Puzzle's safe to train with the team, I recognize how much she's learned from all the dogs here at home, quite apart from human instruction. She's a whole-sense dog who will perk her ears at a baby's cry two doors down or pause at the sight of a squirrel through a window, spinning with excitement as Sprits'l yaps through the glass, but it's Scuppy's unwitting instruction that engages her most. A friend asks, "Are you sure it's safe to leave the old guy alone with her?" — a question I have never asked myself. Puzzle's twice his weight now and probably ten times his strength, but in the backyard beside him she moves gently, as though crossing a stream stone by stone. She models his thoughtful inspection of the yard, corner to corner, scent by scent. She mimics his position when they jointly lie across the cool slate sidewalk in the evening. Best of all, she learns from Scuppy that human scent has value.

Imagine you are walking through a small-town neighborhood at midnight, the houses dark, televisions gone silent, the cars and lawn mowers stilled. Though the cumulative daytime noise level is down a few notches, you move, nonetheless, in a world of sound. This is a time when you can hear small, specific noises and perhaps identify them — the drone of separate air conditioners from three houses in a row or the jingle of collar tags hitting cement when a sleeping cat on a patio rolls onto its side. The ting of one pipe of a wind chime stirred by a moment's air. The strike of a match as someone sits smoking alone in the dark. The chirp of two crickets in conversation. They think better of it and stop their love song as you pass. Eighteen-wheelers on a highway half a mile away. Your own footsteps, of course, and the quality of them, down to the squidgy press of rubber soles on asphalt or the crunch and squeak of gravel you disturb.

Then imagine that it's your job to locate a single radio playing softly in the alley behind an unknown house in a five-square-block area. You could just run around randomly — hopeful of catching the sound by chance — or organize the process, sweeping back and forth down streets and alleys, attempting to quickly locate anything that sounds like it might be a radio. And though the old AM transistor you search for has a tinny, signature sound, when you move too quickly, that sound can be overcome or disguised by other noises. So you methodically work the area, and at some point in the process you believe you hear it. You move left or right, forward or back, turning in an attempt to narrow down the location, getting warmer or colder, as we say in children's games.

Warmer now and closer still, and the sound is undeniable, refining and separating itself from all others — you're hearing Sinatra or 50 Cent and then a PSA on sleep disorders. That definition makes things easier, and in a matter of moments you locate the house, the fence behind the house, the transistor radio sitting on a lawn chair just inside the fence.

Though you've engaged a different sense, in this scenario you've worked something like a search dog, moving through an area in a systematic fashion, acquiring, then filtering out environmental norms to hone in on a specific element. When we watch a SAR dog work, the process seems magical, but when we translate it to human sensory capabilities, we better understand what we ask the search dog to do with her nose: let every other smell go and find only *this*.

SAR dogs can demonstrate any number of nose-driven skills.

Air-scent dogs are frequently used in relatively unpopulated areas to find living victims. Trained to locate and follow the cloud of human scent made by the microscopic skin rafts we shed and odors we create just in the process of living and moving — think of Pig Pen, from the Peanuts cartoon, and you've got a fair visual on the evidence we leave — the air-scent dog is invaluable on disaster sites and in the wilderness lost-person scenario. Working quickly, a good air-scent dog can determine if a search area has no living person in it or, alternatively, hone to the scents of an injured family or a single person within a large search sector. Children, young people, or athletes with their higher metabolisms shed more rafts and create a greater cloud of scent. Those who are relatively motionless, like babies, or have a slowed metabolism, like the elderly, release fewer rafts. Even so, air-scent dogs are often successful at locating Alzheimer's patients who have wandered away and ended up stuck in brush or debris, unable to extricate themselves. An air-scent dog works very fast and largely nose up until near the source of the scent.

Trailing and tracking are terms often (incorrectly) used interchangeably. There are many approaches to both activities. The purist may note substantial differences in the two techniques: trailing uses a scent article; tracking may not, for example, or tracking is more likely performed "head down" on a harness, while the dog's head position moves up and down for trailing, and the lead is longer. There are those who might argue both claims.

Generally stated, trailing dogs may follow both scent in the air and scent that has fallen onto foliage, objects, cement, or dirt in trail. Using a scent article from a specific person, the handler exposes the dog to the scent and then instructs him to find more of it and follow. These dogs may work head up or head down and, once on the scent, trace the movements of the person they seek as closely as possible. Trailing dogs move quickly and randomly, their path transcribing the wide swath of scent left by a specific moving person. As noted in Jen Bidner's book, *Dog Heroes,* mid-twentieth-century experiments with suspension devices demonstrated that trailing dogs are able to follow a person who has never touched the ground.

Tracking dogs, on the other hand, may follow a combination of elements: disturbed vegetation and scent left by footsteps on the ground. An excellent tracking dog — sometimes called a "cold-scent dog" — can follow a path that is days or weeks old, even if the track has been blurred by the passage of numerous other people. This technique is often attributed to the Bloodhounds we associate tracking runaway criminals in novels and film noir, their nose-down posture as famous as their throaty bays. Bloodhounds are, however, excellent trailers on a cold scent too. The Bloodhound is famous for its number of scent receptors: 230 million as compared to other scent-working dogs, whose estimates range between 200 to 220 million. And both, of course, outstrip our human gift of scent. With forty times fewer scent receptors, we are significantly unversed about the spectrum and prevalence of human rafts.

Human Remains Detection (HRD) and cadaver dogs are trained to alert on the remnants of human death. The two terms are not necessarily synonymous. Cadaver dogs specifically recover deceased humans and locate skin, hair, bones, blood, and the indeterminate mix of scents made of semen, urine, sweat, and the process of decomposition, which has an evolving scent of its own. HRD dogs are also often able to discriminate between human and animal ash. These dogs may alert over graves from a century before. One of the most remarkable possibilities with the HRD dog occurs when human remains are buried near the root structures of trees. HRD dogs may put up their paws and stretch to alert on the relevant tree, which exudes human scent as part of its photosynthesis and related processes.

Search dogs can also effectively work from boats on water to recover the drowned. Though theories vary as to what, exactly, the dogs catch scent of from the water — some say the creation of gases an intact body creates, others suggest the more straightforward scent of natural oils, skin remnants, and decomposition — the SAR dog can be extremely useful to recovery dive teams and drag crews who need to narrow the range of an underwater search.

Skeptics abound. A SAR team's quickest allies come from the public who run hunt dogs, or those who work seizure-alert or cancer-detection dogs, from law enforcement officers with search, bomb-, or drug-sniffing canines of their own, and from those who are willing to suspend disbelief for the moment to learn. And the dogs don't necessarily make it easy to believe. To the uninitiated, a dog in a sector that doesn't have a workable scent can look suspiciously like a dog having a good time in the bushes. And a dog actually on a scent that's wavering in conflicted air can look downright confused — checking empty corners, turning circles on a sidewalk, or snaking sideways for a moment to pick it up again. It took me six months of running with experienced handlers before I could begin decoding the subtler signals of a searching dog in progress. And the dogs too finesse their skills with experience. Every time we train, I learn some new pause or movement from dogs I've worked with for years.

Where skepticism becomes a problem is at the point of deployment. A team can be called to a search because someone in charge has brought in all available resources, only to arrive and find that search management isn't sure how to assign the dog teams and is pretty much convinced that dogs are useless anyway. Persuasion and explanation on-site take time, time that some situations can't afford. And so the condition perpetuates itself: Bloodhounds are sent out to run a city park days after an abducted child has been taken to another area, or air-scent dogs are asked to track a single scent only after two hundred volunteers have grid-walked through the field the day before. Dogs are not "the magic bullet," as one trainer I know often says. Search dogs are a resource like any other, and their work must be understood if they are to search effectively.

"We hate to see the dogs come in," one detective said to me a few years ago. "It's a sign of defeat — means we've turned a corner and that the victim is probably dead."

I said, "Hey, we have dogs that do live finds too. With our dogs, it's such a priority that they certify in live finds first."

Perhaps he sensed I was about to go into an unwanted rafts and metabolism lecture or worse, into some fanciful realm he usually reserved for neighborhood psychics on a crime scene. "We only use dogs for human remains," he said definitively, shaking his head. "Live people just don't smell bad enough."

Head trainer Fleta holds Puzzle in the soft grass of a local fire training facility. Ahead of us is a railway tanker, to the left a double row of demolished cars, to the distant right a simulated disaster site, the "debris pile," where Puzzle will eventually learn to find victims buried in rubble. Today's training includes Puzzle's first "runaway" searches with the team. The objective is simple: find the woman who is now unseen and get the treat she took with her.

Puzzle may not yet have shown any deep affinity for me at home, but on command from Fleta she scrambles across the grass to find me where I've hidden behind a car. She gallops ungracefully, rounding the corner of a smashed vehicle too quickly. The physics of puppy fat and wayward legs aren't with her, and she falls over with a little skid, righting herself with a shake and continuing on to where I crouch. She wags wildly as we praise her. We do a second find-your-handler runaway, and the second time she measures her pace a little better. We see her briefly hitch at the place where she'd found me previously, but when I'm not there this time, she lifts her nose, snags a thread of scent, and pivots at that nose point, changing direction, heading for me in the new spot. This is a moment of revelation for both of us. Puzzle learns that sight has its own limitations and that in this game, scent prevails. I have the opportunity to watch her blink-quick decision to trust her nose.

We repeat the game with a reverse of position. I hold Puzzle while Fleta shows her a treat, then cover her eyes as Fleta runs and hides thirty yards away. At the command "Find!" Puzzle trots forward a few steps, then dashes wildly in the direction Fleta traveled. Following behind, I notice with some amusement that the puppy is wagging so hard her tail's propeller action almost seems to make her fat bottom loft. "Good girl!" I hear from Fleta. "Good girl!" I also praise. Puzzle takes her treats and trots back to what she must think is the starting point. She flops down in the green grass, snitzes once, and tosses her head with a grin so wide it eclipses the rest of her face. She looks like a little blond Halloween pumpkin laughing there, full of merry confidence and more than a bit of mischief.

The squirrels at home are less enthusiastic. Puzzle's nose has become a problem for them, and I see three lined up on the roof of the garage, leaning forward on their paws and cussing the puppy in long-winded bursts of angry chittering. I watch one deliberately push a broken stick until it falls and hits her over the head. It's a small stick that she ignores, because at the moment Puzzle is head down in her fourth newly dug hole. Quick and intent, she paws at the soft earth rapidly, her bottom high and little plumes of rich black dirt shooting out from between her legs. The more she digs, the more the squirrels scold, and as I watch I soon realize why: Puzzle is digging up their buried pecans. She doesn't eat them, preferring instead to drop them on the slate sidewalk, mission accomplished, then turn to nose across the ground to a new spot with a likely nut beneath.

It's eight in the morning, and as I look around the yard four holes are in plain sight. There could be more around the corners at the edges of the yard. In the half-hour since her breakfast, Puzzle has undone a single squirrel's long workday, unearthing a week of winter food. There is no doubt the squirrels are watching and disapproving. I guess that these three are probably residents and that it's their hard labor she's made short work of.

She turns her attention to a flowerpot whose plants have long since died dramatically. The coleus lies in a limp Sarah Bernhardt pose over one edge of the pot, but Puzzle is far more interested in the other side of it. The squirrels and I watch as she raises up on hind legs and balances her forefeet in the dirt, then begins scratching a hole in that uneasy position. It's slower work, involving balance and great care. I watch her occasionally pause to consider the hole, and at one point she puts her nose down into it and huffs. I hear the echo of her snort against the sides of the terra cotta, and I see a little blizzard of dirt fly immediately upward into her eyes. She lifts up, blinking a little, her nose black with dirt to her forehead, the tips of her paws also black to the wrists. She hops down from the pot, sauntering toward me in a posture of quiet triumph. The squirrels riot across the shingles as she drops a sheathed, very black pecan at my feet.

But before Puzzle and I can interact about the digging and the pecans, she stiffens, lifts her nose, and then trots to the edge of the backyard. She stands there a long moment, nostrils working, though there's nothing I can see through the thin spaces of the privacy fence. She huffs and moves forward, her tail slowly beginning to wag. I still see nothing.

"What have you got, Puz?" I ask her, just as I hear the rapid *tip-tip-tip* of paws and the harder, ungainly slap of feet as Gerand and his new dog, Token, approach the house. I can hear Gerand gasping, *Slow . . . down . . . dog . . . slow . . . down . . . dog,* but Puzzle wuffs happily and races Token on the other side of the fence, and neutered though he may be, it's the female dog Token pays attention to. He sparks to her unseen energy, showing off, perhaps, connects through the fence, then makes a little revving sound and pulls Gerand harder northward. Puzzle presses her nose to the place where he was, savoring the delicious last scent of them as they leave us. She heaves a little sigh, sits down with a plop.

"Good girl to let me know they were coming, Puz," I say, though I know she doesn't understand.

I haven't talked to Gerand in weeks. And it sure doesn't seem

7

TRUST FALL

WHEN YOU STAND at the edge of a building with your heels hanging free over the side, kinetics create a delicious little tension that travels right up the nervous system to your brain and to your heart — a hot, silvery sensation like breathing mercury or swallowing sparks. Standing there now, at the top of the "high-rise," a tall building used at the fire academy, I feel wind strum my rappel line, and I consider mortality. Or simply humiliation: a misstep that sends me flailing over the side to smack against a wall on the way down and my own late correction on the line that forces a teammate at the bottom, working safety, to pull taut and suspend me there like a spider caught in her own long thread.

There are a dozen ways to get stupid on a rappel line and just a few ways to be cool. I don't fear heights, which is in my favor. I'm still working on cool. I've already kissed brick a few times today, blowing out the left knee of my fatigues. Both my elbows are bloody and bruised.

Today marks Puzzle's third weekend to train with the team, and it's also the day that human teammates are scheduled to rappel and work on high-angle rescue. We are at a fire department training facility, and rookie firefighters are half a football field away from us, working a large engine, fighting a simulated tanker blaze. We have watched them climb a long ladder and sway there, and now they release water from that high angle of attack. This is the maneuver, backlit by flame, which we see so often in movies.

Autumn plays tricks with us. It's warm this morning, and a light wind carries mist as far as Puzzle's crate, which I have placed in the shade of the ladder tower a distance from where we work. Some dogs are prone to separation anxiety, a concern we don't want Puzzle or any young search dog to share, and so she is crated at a distance with her stuffed lobster and a treat and something to watch — in this case about twenty young firefighters working the tanker. She lies comfortably there, lifting her nose and squinching her eyes shut, happy about water in any form and particularly happy about this mist on a warm day in the shade.

When I walked away a half-hour ago, she didn't whimper. *A good sign*, said a colleague to me, but I remind myself that Puzzle hasn't yet seemed concerned when I've left her in any venue. I can see her from where I stand seven stories up, a blond bit of pocket fluff against the dark floor of her crate.

Earlier we rappelled from the ladder tower, much closer to where Puzzle lies, a three-story structure open on all sides planted in the middle of a parking lot. It's no great height, but the backward launch from the top of it can still be scary. I envied the double-handful of us that launched confidently backward with an arc of a jump and a landing soft as an astronaut on the moon. Three little swings and two little touches to the building and they were down on both feet, looking up and grinning to the rest of us. My own descents lacked that easy grace, characterized by an awkward spurt of trajectory that resembled a hippopotamus giving birth on the run. I had some trouble rappelling from the ladder tower, which has no walls but does have an open metal framework along the sides. The experts among us managed to *gaboing-boing-boing* down with their feet precisely contacting the framework. Not me. I either missed the framework entirely, swinging completely through and then banging it hurtfully on the way out again, or contacted the metal braces in a sort of straddle, a right smart rap on the backside, on the *ischiopubic ramus,* said one of our paramedics, which somehow made it hurt more.

Now, at the top of the high-rise, the wind is blowing warm and fitful from the south. We are rappelling down the protected side of the building out of the wind, but up here on the roof in queue for our turn to drop, the wind puts hair in my eyes and whips the sleeves of my T-shirt, making me feel a little shaky, a little scattered. I'm about tenth in line, with plenty of time to watch and learn. Or not. I peer over the side to Deryl, holding the line on the ground. He is an imposing man, but from the roof he seems small. When I go over the side, it'll be Deryl providing safety if I forget how to rappel. From here, it's not the size of the guy that makes me feel safer, it's the intensity of his focus. A good man. He would be quick on the line to stop my falling self two beats before I might know I'd lost it.

I move away from the edge of the tower. I look at the teammates ahead in line and realize that ten years ago, probably none of us would have forecast we'd be on the roof of a building together, preparing to step off the edge of it. Backward.

"You couldn't pay me to do that," said a visitor to a booth the team had hosted during a neighborhood safety fair. She was speaking collectively, gesturing to the brochures and photographs we had at the booth depicting the working life of a canine SAR team. They are candid shots without airbrush, and in them we are rappelling with dogs on line with us, pushing through mesquite thorns in the wilderness, sweating in 105-degree heat on the debris pile while we traverse it behind our dogs, watching for signs of human scent. When I told her that we are an all-volunteer group, she gave me a little laugh and a doubtful twist of her head, and said, "You do this for *fun*?"

It's a common question, and one I'm often at some loss to answer. *We do it for service* would be the summary response, and accurate too, but sounds a bit lofty, and canine SAR folk are not generally a lofty group. We trudge through Dumpsters too often, carry our dogs' warm poop bags too frequently to claim much glory. Though certainly some of the training is fun, the work itself is challenging in every respect.

Behind every experienced handler with a dog or assistant in the field is an implied rigor: years of training scenarios and practice searches — three to seven hours weekly in all types of weather, campouts involving ten to fifteen hours of wilderness training, classes in everything from scent theory to medical assessment to meteorology to report writing to building construction and situation size-up and, following that, required exams. And for many, daily training on some aspect of SAR, whether decoding dot-dashes from a Morse code CD or tying figure-eight knots on a bight with a sample bit of rope. And work with the canines at home too — a reliable dog on a disaster site may have hundreds of hours of "Heel" and "Down" and "Stay" from his handler, training that proves he can control himself amid chaos and respond appropriately on command. Early in my experience with the team, a colleague said, "To work volunteer SAR, your idea of what makes a good weekend has to be flexible."

A news reporter once mentioned off-camera that our volunteer status surprised her. She had figured "canine SAR teams were made up of elite, paid professionals." I'm not sure how she typified elite, but paid wouldn't apply to most canine SAR teams I know. The reverse is true: most of us pay to be able to do this. Canine SAR units are often not-for-profit organizations, but contributions rarely equal the yearly expense of running even one dog. Unpaid we may be, but *professional* we strive for. Canine SAR is part of America's long, worthy tradition of volunteer emergency response, going back to the earliest days of colonial firefighting.

Among our team members are a few common denominators. About half of us are former military. A good few are former or current first-responders — police, paramedics, firefighters. We have professional dog trainers among us. A handful of pilots. A few scuba divers and a couple of rock climbers. But we are also students, entrepreneurs, bookkeepers, schoolteachers, engineers, tech support personnel, and one of us aspires to be a pastry chef. Though our working backgrounds are disparate, we're generally outdoorsy and unafraid of getting dirty. And we all love dogs. It's also safe to say we share a deep sense of responsibility toward our fellow human beings, driven by an impulse to serve that training intensifies and the search field completes.

Canine search-and-rescue attracts a lot of interest — an interest that increases in periods following catastrophe or after a particularly riveting news story illustrates the poignant connection between a dog and the human he has found. Many teams have no lack of short-term volunteers, some who are simply interested in the work as a hobby, others who believe it's a simple matter of putting a family pet in a vest and walking around until he finds something, still others who are attracted to the media attention and vicarious glory. And some, of course, who have both an urge to contribute and a willingness to give up, in our case, weekend mornings and some weeknights to training. Work with our team also means risk: even in training we may crawl over unstable rubble, hike through wilderness and emerge from it bloody, or lie in crushed vehicles on a hot summer day while waiting to be found by a young search dog that is still learning.

Our team requires that new members train first to assist dog units in the field. These field assistants learn and are tested on map, compass, and GPS navigation, first aid, situation size-up, crime scene preservation, interviewing, interagency response protocols, and radio navigation before ever taking to the field to assist on a first search. Advanced training follows, with written and practical tests administered by NASAR (the National Association of Search and Rescue), FEMA, and the U.S. Fire Administration. Field assistants, or the FAS team, perform invaluable services during searches, freeing the handlers to concentrate on their dogs as they jointly work a sector.

Training and testing thoroughly is a long process, and many volunteers are surprised by all that the commitment involves.

Pushing through thorns in the sleet isn't fun. Wading through a floodwater debris field poxed with illegal dumping is nasty. If the poison ivy doesn't get you, the blisters will. And then there are the insidious, sulphur-resistant, omnipresent chiggers. A month or so into training, newcomer attrition is high.

It would be easy to think about quitting now. A colleague just ahead of me balks at the edge of the building. She did well rappelling off the ladder tower, but the distance down from this greater height seems a long, mortal drop onto brick and cement. Some loose-lipped sadist ahead of us in line talked about a recent rookie SWAT cop who'd come to grief by being careless during a shorter rappel (two broken ankles and four front teeth gone!), and the story has made a few of us pensive, a few of us a little manic — *ha,ha,ha* — as we cover our shaking knees.

My teammate feels the pressure of her indecision. No one rushes her, but we all want her to make the rappel. *I* want her to make the rappel, perhaps a little selfishly. Every success encourages the rest of us, gets us a little further from the image of the limping, gap-toothed former cop who can now hoover peas off a spoon. When I point out to her that she's a flight instructor who routinely teaches students how to recover spins and that this, by comparison, is no big deal, she seems encouraged, and in a swift, decisive moment calls out to Deryl on safety, checks her equipment, and steps over the edge. Her descent is quick and smooth, and we cheer when she lands squarely on both feet. *She made that look easy,* I think, as I hook onto the line, call down to Deryl, and stand poised at the edge of the roof.

Patience is as much a part of working search as commitment. When you consider the volunteer SAR team made up of adults from widely differing backgrounds, there's strong likelihood that they won't all be good at the same things. A great dog handler may struggle with compass navigation; a hard-charging brush buster who can search in the wilderness for days may get a little claustrophobic training in tight spaces; the compassionate field assistant who can imagine how a lost child might think may struggle with theory involving building construction and collapse. At our best, we are a collaborative team of teachers and simultaneously a team of learners. At our best, we remember what it was like not to know something.

I was fortunate as a field assistant — many of the required duties were similar to those needed to fly an airplane. Navigation, radio communication, and emergency protocols were already a part of my thinking. Translating those procedures to ground SAR wasn't difficult. The dog work was new, however, and I struggled for some time behind handlers in the field, all of whom seemed to want something different — *stay right beside me, stay fifty feet back, clear the area ahead for hazards before we get there, let the dog go in first* — an inconsistency that frustrated me until the training day when I ran after four dogs in the same sector, one after another in quick succession, and I saw, at last, that each one of them worked a given sector differently, taking to the terrain according to their individual gifts. The quick-scented and somewhat heedless dog needed more help avoiding hazards than the slower, more cautious dog who worked an area with efficient, deliberate care. Some dogs enjoyed moving quickly and, pack-oriented, wanted the presence of their human counterparts just behind them. Other dogs preferred to blaze ahead and communicate back across a half-acre of brush. I must have tried many a handler's nerve with my early one-size-fits-all approach to assisting them in the training field, but not one of them yelled at me for it, a compassion I admire, a patience I have an uneasy feeling I'm going to have to learn.

The young woman who rigged today's rappel system comes forward to me. She is patient, silent for a moment while I stand there, intuiting perhaps that I'm reviewing procedure and making sense of the physics behind the rappel. Or she may think I'm nerving myself up. All of which is true.

"I would like," I say, "not to slam into the wall this time. I understand what's got to happen from the point I step off the edge to the moment I connect against the wall, but somehow I'm just not moving quickly enough to do it."

She says, "If you can get past the idea of the fall, you'll step off and get your feet right. Right now, I think you're stepping off and going into a kind of fetal position, so it's your knees that hit the wall."

Fetal position. Though I don't think I feel scared, I'm amused that when I step over the edge, some part of me still curls up and cries Mommy. I'm not sure what I feel beyond a desire to get down neatly and with no new wounds.

She adds, "Try to think of it the way you would if you were stepping from one building to another over a gap that's seven stories down. Don't fixate on the hole. You want to visualize stepping off with one foot and connecting to the building across the gap. The fall is not the big deal. It's not the empty space that matters. It's the arrival."

That's a philosophy I'll have to remember to pass along to Gerand. "I'm sorry I'm taking so long," I say to the young woman.

She gives a little okay-by-me shrug, then says, "If you feel anxious about the force of the fall on the line — even though we've shown it's safe — you know you can *crawl* off the side of the building. That might help. Just lie down along the edge, pivot your legs off, bend at the waist, and find the wall with your feet, then establish tension on the line and start rappelling down."

Crawling off the building sounds almost as bad as fetal position. Her suggestion sounds easy and bloodless, but definitely uncool. *I can't be too bad off,* I think, *if my ego's still capable of wincing.* No, I have to trust this young woman, and I have to step over the side. I remember the scores of fourth-lesson flight students who took a deep breath and gave me a thumbs-up before I demonstrated their first stalls, their faith in me overcoming every instinct for self-preservation that screamed, "You're going to make the airplane *stop flying*?" Their actions shame me now. I look at the young woman and say, "I trust you." I give her a thumbs-up.

"On belay," I shout down to Deryl, who confirms the belay, and then I step backward. This time, there's a funny little *whoosh* of wind across the flat of my ears, a double buffet, as though the winds at the top edge of the building decided to smack me on each side of the head.

Three seconds of freefall aren't much in the grand sum of life's uncomfortable experiences, but they are memorable. It's a little like touching a fork to a filling while stunt-doubling a crash-test dummy just before the bang. My descent from the high-rise is safe enough — a little jump, an arc of a swing, and then several controlled collisions down and down and down to the ground. I walk away from the rappel with all my teeth intact and no new holes in the knees of my fatigues, but the knuckles of my left hand are scraped, as though I took a swing at the wall somewhere along the way.

The teammates above and below me cheer. Later I may be in for much teasing (was I upside down at one point? I have an uneasy recollection of the ground rushing up), but right now they're all about my success.

I've got to get better at this, I think. After I learn to make my own descents with confidence, there will be a point where I'll be put online with Puzzle, and we'll be raised and lowered together. Dog-and-handler rappelling works differently; it lacks the graceful *gaboing-boing* of the solo descent, but Puz will do better if the handler holding her on the way up or down is assured.

Puzzle squeaks happily when I open her crate, emerging from it wiggly and more overjoyed to see me than ever before. She squirms and mutters as I hold her in my lap, kissing my face and then sniffing carefully every bruised and bloody spot on my arms and knees. Teammate Michele says, "See! She's glad to see you." Birgit adds, "Looks like she knows she's your puppy now." I hope so. What's changed in the past ninety minutes? Perhaps she scents the slightly shaken cocktail of me, post-rappel: the adrenaline, sweat, torn skin, and blood. Perhaps her joy is a matter of timing.

She wants out of the crate, and I'm the one to free her. This sudden sure-do-love-you change is another of her dog mysteries.

I take her to socialize with the rest of the team. Some cuddle her, others bend down to rub her belly when she rolls over to expose it. Petting her is not an easy process. Our teammates are dog lovers, but they also know this socialization lays a strong foundation for the puppy who must learn not only to be a partner, but also a member of the larger pack that is our team. These are her instructors, her mentors, and the people who will hide for her hundreds of times, in all conditions and all weathers, as she trains toward certification. But for now the lessons are simpler: this is a fun place to be; trust and affection are the standard; humans are here to be partners and here to be found.

My colleagues try to hold conversations while Puzzle ping-pongs between them. She moves quickly among dogs and humans alike, and while I'm prepared for her puppy bounding and freakish attention span (*Is that a treat? What is a cigarette? Did you see that bird? Hey, this dog's got balls!*), my height, my center of gravity — and my steady stream of apologies — slow me down. Puzzle trips a teammate, runs completely under the belly of one dog, and steals the last part of a chew treat from another. I arrive just in time to see Collie Misty shoot yellow Lab Buster a thoughtful look. It's a brief communication — *discipline this youngster or let her slide?* Both dogs turn their heads away from Puzzle, allowing her the thievery. For now.

"That puppy license won't last long," says Fleta with a laugh.

"I'm surprised she's so dominant," I hear over my shoulder. "I expected a Golden to be softer."

She's not soft when it's her turn to search. At the command "Find!" Puzzle catapults from my arms, trips over her own feet while trying to lift her nose and run at the same time, spins angrily at her tail, and then ricochets across the rubble to locate the volunteer victim shrouded by debris and tall grass. We hear a little *oof!* as Puzzle lands on the young woman's chest. It's a successful find, but not a graceful one. The praise afterward goes straight to her head, and as we leave the search area, she saunters up to one of the senior dogs and starts to shadowbox. I see the wrinkle of his dark muzzle, just a little rickrack showing of bared white teeth. A warning. The four adult dogs standing there simultaneously lift their heads and turn away from her, a doggy snub executed like synchronized swimming. I'm not sure how much of it registers with Puzzle, who bounces off a couple of their backsides before she pogos across the grass to get the toy in her crate.

I look at my dog, now tugging at the embroidered left eye of Lobster. She has him gripped in fat paws, and she's working him over with a will. I hear little *pup-pup-pup* sounds of black thread pulling free. Every once in a while, she lifts her head to make eye contact with the nearby dogs or humans, her expression a little like a challenge, a little like a brag — a *wouldja get a load of me.*

A colleague puts his arm around my shoulder. "Good rappel there at the end," he says. "You landed on your feet. And you don't look like you lost too much blood." He grins toward Puzzle. "Fourteen weeks," he says in the same way one would say "tax audit," as though he remembers his own dog, as though Puzzle's age is a statement of condition.

"She's a natural disaster," I say and smile at her.

"A force to be reckoned with," my teammate amends. "But count all the plusses. You're doing good," he adds.

We both look at Puzzle, who has now beheaded her toy and makes *ack-ack-ptui* sounds, spitting out soggy bits of red plush. She smiles up at us with a wreath of Lobster's former innards around her muzzle. She appears to be having a very good day.

But I must look dazed. I can't imagine ever being able to step over a ledge and descend placidly with this dog. At this point, I can't imagine taking her off lead and expecting to ever see her again. After a moment, my teammate shakes his head and pats my arm. "Don't worry," he says. "It all works out. Remember she's got you. And you've got us."

8

SIX DAYS DOWN

A STEADY RAIN is falling when the pager goes off this morning, a rain that continues as we make our way out of town twenty minutes later, a rain that silvers the highway in the light of traffic inbound for the city. It is early and still very dark, and the rainfall — slow and insistent — is the kind guaranteed to make us sleepy, even though we've got coffee in a Thermos, oldies rock on the radio, and a cryptic note on the pager that indicates we will be looking for a drowned man likely six days down.

Which is unnatural, this failure to surface — a big man, we've learned, believed drowned in a small body of water in warm weather. According to our refloat tables, his body should have appeared days ago. A teammate and I discuss this as we drive. The situation suggests many things the team has seen before, among them the possibility that he's tangled in something beneath the surface, that heavy clothing has affected his buoyancy, or that his body did refloat days ago unseen and is now caught in shoreline debris, that local wildlife may have claimed and dragged him, and — apart from all of this — the chance that he may not be there at all.

The calling law enforcement agency believes he is.

I consider the effect of water on a victim submerged six days. If we do find the body of this man, the distortion will considerable. Horrific. I feel little internal latches begin to flip as the analytic part of my thinking steps forward and my other, more vulnerable responses head for cover. I have never seen a tidy death, and this one is unlikely to be the first.

A body under water still produces scent available to a dog.

"What are they smelling?" a reporter once asked me. "Perfume? Garlic? Laundry detergent?"

Yes, perhaps, but more so the distinctly human tissue byproducts that rise naturally to the surface and are released into air passing over water. Blood may be part of the scent artifact too. Unless in motion due to current or caught and suspended by something underwater, drowning victims always lie face down in the water, heads hanging, which causes blood pooling and any postdeath injuries to seep. Some theorists suggest that the friction of water against skin and the friction of human body against underwater objects actually cause more scent production from a water victim than would naturally be produced by a victim on land.

The scent of underwater victims is also subject, like a sailing ship, to multiple forces. The scent of a victim in rivers or moving floodwaters is carried by current before it is released into the air, where it moves according to wind direction and terrain friction. The scent of a lake victim may be fragmented and distorted by the chop of passing boat and ski traffic. Additional factors like water temperature and composition, depth of water, and depth of victim sometime complicate the relationship between the victim and the rising point of the victim's scent.

Dogs working water are rarely able to hover directly over the location of a body in the water. Rather, from boats or shoreline they indicate the location where scent is first available to them above the surface. Our team uses multiple dogs for this effort, ruling out certain areas as "null" — or no indicated scent — and defining areas by GPS where more than one dog has indicated scent source, dogs and handlers ideally refining that information to determine areas of faint, stronger, and strongest scent. The teams work "blind," meaning that they do not know the nature or location of information passed on from the previous canine unit, the better to ensure that similar indications are not influenced for one handler by the handler who has gone before.

Not yet a handler with a certified dog, for this search I will be working along the shore or on the water with another dog unit. Buster, Belle, Shadow, Hunter, or Saber: all are experienced water and shoreline recovery dogs, partnered by handlers long with the team.

While my colleague drives, I inspect my worn gaiters by flashlight. Warm weather has encouraged the snake population, and though I have a live-and-let-live philosophy about them, I know our blundering press through the brush along a shoreline can provoke a snake to strike in self-defense, if not aggression. On scene, an officer confirms this. "Lotta snakes out there," he says, with a gesture of disgust across the lake.

The rain has stopped, but the air is heavy and close. The area we will search is small by our standards — a wattle-shaped inlet off a thick neck of the lake, a good fishing spot that doesn't take much effort to get to, bordered by a sheltered boat dock. The shoreline is ugly and unkempt, a tumble of yellowish brush and trees fighting dumped garbage for space. The winning trees extend awkward branches over brown water. Thick bramble competes below. The shoreline appears impassable from where I stand.

During a momentary wind shift, I can smell rotting debris and the stench of something dead from the opposite bank. The dogs lift their noses but do not react. One of the officers tells us this is a prime crappie fishing spot; locals have been dumping old furniture and Christmas trees, dead cars and small boats here for years to give the fish a place to shelter and breed. Plenty of folks dump along the shore too, not to improve the fishing, but just because they can. "One-stop dumping," he calls it: do a little fishing, drop a lot of trash.

We look at one another. The boat work on this search should be relatively straightforward. The shoreline work will probably be more difficult. There's no scramble among us for the easier search, and I'm proud of that. Most of us stand with gaiters in one hand and a PFD in the other, ready to go whichever way the Incident Commander directs.

Meanwhile, the dogs are schooling among us. Two yellow Labs, a Husky, a Collie, and a German Shepherd. Their heads bob slightly as they ferret the thousands of scents drifting around us from the water, the shore, and the Dumpster behind the convenience store nearby. I watch their noses work and their ears prick to passing sounds, and I wish, as I always do, that I could experience the sensory world they interpret with calm curiosity.

We do not have a picture of our missing man, but his half-brother in another state has sent a photo. Apparently the two men are so similar they were mistaken for each other as children, and they are still much alike. We look at the image of this virtual twin. It is a birthday shot over a small cake ablaze with black candles. The twin's eyes squint shut with laughter. His moving hand is fuzzy where he tries to shield himself from the camera. From him we get an idea of size, muscle mass, and hair color. The first two are relevant to the victim's refloat projections; the third may be significant when we begin to work along the shore, where birds and other creatures sometimes furnish their nests with hair.

We're told the man we're looking for had come out here several days earlier to fish off the side of his boat. He was last seen arguing with a stranger outside a local fast-food restaurant, where he clutched a fresh six-pack to his chest, pointing first to himself and then toward the lake in an exchange no eyewitness can clarify. This account provokes ongoing speculation, raising the question of possible foul play—if not on his boat, then on another one, or somewhere else in the immediate area.

A couple of conflicting stories suggest the missing man may have been seen later on his boat, still docked, a little while before a late-evening thunderstorm hit. One version describes a man in the shadows sitting on the side of a boat that may have been his. Whoever he was, he ignored a friendly warning about the approaching storm; without reply, he stared across the inlet to a midpoint on the water where nothing moved.

Though officers shrug over the latter account, saying everyone wants to get in on the story and small towns make new ghosts fast, one of the search dogs shows interest around the victim's boat. Hunter paces restlessly along the dock, straining to cross onto the boat, but aboard it, he appears frustrated, as though the space has convoluted the scent. His handler remarks that this is interest, strong interest from his dog, but he is cautious. Hunter may be indicating human scent from what remained of the owner's personal belongings still aboard. His early interest is noted, and we all head to our separate sectors to confirm or deny the presence of the missing man there.

An hour later as Johnny, yellow Lab Buster, and I press forward through unforgiving brush, Buster works as quickly as the thick scrub and debris will allow. Thorny vines snag our clothing and our bootlaces. One particularly stubborn branch catches both my boots and penetrates my leather gloves, then flips the radio out of its holster when I cut myself free. Johnny says, "They'll all be on their second sectors by the time we get halfway through the first." I don't know whether to pity or envy naked Buster, who is scratched liberally but able to move much faster than we are.

And he is moving fast.

There is any amount of human scent here, but it is old, old scent that Buster wisely disregards. Decaying car seats, beer cans and Styrofoam cups, disposable diapers a decade old, shredded by a thousand field mice in nesting season. The promised snakes are here too. Most of them whip quickly away from our approach, but in the deepest part of the shoreline thatch, one young fellow, perhaps two feet long, slips over a low branch toward us, then pauses and coils with a neat little snap, his head flattish and his mouth gaping wide. Steady Buster gives him a peripheral glance and changes direction. Johnny and I do not stay long enough to differentiate the snake from his nonpoisonous imitators, though Johnny knows I am interested in snakes. Sidestepping, he grins and asks if I happened to notice whether there was a single or double row of scales on the underside of that tail. I did not, and I don't go back to look. It is enough that the snake was there, brilliantly patterned and smiling widely upward, the tip of his tail a shivering yellowish-green.

The dead thing I could smell across the water turns out to be the remains of a cow, in so strange and awkward a position that she appears to have been dumped there a while ago. The local wildlife has worked her over, and at this point she is mostly hair and hooves and curves of whitish bone already braided with vine. Buster acknowledges the cow but is not fooled by her scent. He continues forward through our sector, a strong and sensible dog who communicates clearly that while there are many interesting things where we are, not one of them is the reason we are here.

The dogs on the water have something else to say. I can see the last dog unit returning to the dock. In a series of blind searches where handlers did not know the response of previous dog units, three dogs have confirmed one another, indicating strong human scent from the water in a chain of points leading back to the docked boat. Two dogs have returned to the spot where Hunter strained to get at the water to chew it, his best method for discerning submerged human scent. One dog shows intense interest; one of them fully alerts a few feet over.

Two officers look down to the murky water surrounding the dock. A crappie hole encouraged by debris is not the safest place to send down divers, but that will be the next step in the search and recovery of the missing man, whose untouched six-pack still sits on the boat.

Having completed the search, Johnny, Buster, and I return. The team stands down. We write our sector reports — this is what we searched and how we searched it; this is how the dog responded. We notate wind, terrain, direction of travel, and percent of coverage. We debrief in the parking lot, reviewing the environment, the weather, the known, and the unknown about the victim. The dogs could not have been more unanimous in their signals to us. They are relaxed now, praised and satisfied, lying in confident postures. I make a map for my own notes, drawing Buster moving with long speed streaks behind him, with wheels instead of paws. I add little sketches for both the snake and the cow.

The divers say they'll let us know what they find after their own difficult searches, but they expect to find the missing man there, caught in debris or fishing line. Crime or misadventure? Those are the conclusions, long coming, that we rarely get. But I stroke Saber's cheek and think of a local family needing some kind of word, of the half-brother waving away his birthday photograph, and of the man caught beneath his boat waiting to be found. "Good dog," I say to Hunter, as Saber leans into my scratching hand and groans. We drive home beneath a sky that cannot commit to sun.

9

HOUSEBREAKING

GOOGLE "GOLDEN RETRIEVER" and "tempera-
ment," and you'll likely come up with happy para-
graphs describing the Golden's sweet nature,
companionability, and eager desire to please. These are famous
qualities, and it's no wonder that the Golden is one of the world's
most popular dogs, the figural presence in TV commercials and
greeting cards. Oh, those cute puppies, knocking over a houseplant, tumbling down a hallway with a roll of toilet paper! Theirs
is a moment's mischief. Puzzle's shenanigans work overtime.

The Pomeranians are a little stunned at puppy behaviors from
a dog that rapidly triples their weight. When she dances and boxes
and bows in petition for play, they scatter for the first few weeks.
Puzzle gets more action out of Maddy the cat, who after the first
startled introduction seems to quite enjoy the puppy. In fact, the
cat is the first four-footed member of the household who keeps
Puzzle in line. Maddy stalks Puzzle when she is sleeping, creeping
up behind her, circling, staring at her with a calculated, misleading benevolence, then popping her nose with a paw, causing the
puppy to wake from her deep sleep dazed and scrambling for a cat
that has long since skittered across the room and out the door.

Puzzle's not the only one who wakes stupid. Insomnia leaves me fuzzy-minded in the early morning, and I'm not yet used to the new dog rhythms. Puzzle, however, is housebroken. One early morning when she grumbles and I don't take the hint that she needs to go out, Puzzle pops me in the face with my house shoe. I open my eyes and watch her eyebrows knit and her expression change. She looks dubious and vaguely disappointed. Clearly she hopes I'm a little smarter after the slap.

Unfortunately, she has to do this the next day also. She wants to go out. I don't wake up. She wants to go out a little harder. I can be slow. And in time Puzzle figures out that if she slaps me, runs away with the house shoe, *and* drops it at the door, I've not only made the connection, but the one-shoe-on/one-shoe-off stumping to the door has thumped me awake enough to be able to unlock it.

Certainly there are softer ways to wake, but Puzzle's insistence interests me. Eventually she'll need to tell me other things, and there will be complicated, difficult moments when she has to fig-ure out how to communicate what she knows. I imagine a few dog trainers would have something to say about this whole process with the shoe, about the metamessage of the slap to the head, about my slow responsiveness, about who's really in charge in these early days. But I can't argue with her success. I learn to wake at the first mutter of her grumble, and once I've demonstrated this for a week or so, she never slaps me with the house shoe again.

The other dogs have not reached a similar accord. Though I make allowances for the clumsiness of a developing puppy and her universal interest in provoking play, Puzzle's sideswipes of gen-tle eight-pound Jack seem to cross another line. She is testing her place in the pack and challenging any dog she considers a rival. She carefully steps around little Sophie, with her labored breath-ing and congestive heart failure, and treats five-pound Scuppy kindly, but for reasons I don't understand, Puzzle targets Jack with dedication.

It is an unfortunate choice. While on a leashed walk with me in 2002, puppy Jack was attacked by two large dogs running free, an attack that nearly killed him before I could kick the big dogs off and fall over him to block them. In the presence of Puzzle's swaggering dominance, her sideswipes and bared teeth, he — at four and a half years old — first stands his ground, then cries out and gives in to the five-month-old pup when she pins him down, his tail in her teeth. The line between play and bullying blurs here. I am inexperienced with it, and I'm never far from that 2002 attack. Apart from whatever it means in dog logic, Puzzle's new behavior worries me.

She is a dog who's got some lessons coming, I think. *She's a dog who needs to learn to respect me and to get some comeuppance from larger playmates, from a pack.* My little crew hasn't found their ground with her yet. But on neighborhood walks, we meet other dog owners with mature, puppy-friendly big dogs, and play-date interactions seem to ease some of the tension at home. *A tired puppy is a good puppy,* says the truism. In our case, a tired puppy seems less interested in collaring a Pomeranian just for the hell of it.

Weeks pass. At SAR, the team continues to let Puzzle mingle with the grown dogs. We watch carefully and hope they might check her pushiness. Only one of the males has so far given her a growl that means business.

"Can you hear them counting to ten?" one handler says to another about the dogs, as I rather desperately redirect Puzzle elsewhere, a wiggly and manic process, like juggling six baby sharks and a tuna.

The universal expectation was that she'd be pliable, friendly, and willing to work. The work part is true enough, but at home she retains a stubborn streak and the occasional tendency to bully. Puzzle on a playful scramble sends three Poms rolling like fuzzy croquet balls, yelping in surprise, but worse, she again corners Jack in the hallway minutes after they all have eaten, and when he backs against the wall and squeaks in fear, she jumps him, taking a mouthful of his ruff as though she were about to shake prey. She already outweighs Jack several times over, and in the tumble of them I cannot tell if this is extreme play or aggression. But it doesn't look good. I am between them and have the dogs apart in only seconds, Puzzle bemused and Jack trembling. This was unexpected and far too close a call, and I realize there are all kinds of problems with my inexperience here. I hire a dog trainer right away.

There is the old, old joke about the airline pilot so accustomed to a jet's roar that when its engines suddenly go silent, he screams, "What was *that*?"

I understand.

Silence in the household with a new dog can indicate a puppy sleeping or, more insidiously, a puppy occupied somewhere in the nether regions, ripping up carpet, chewing electrical cords, backing Pomeranians into corners and staring, staring, staring. Unless Puzzle's crated, unless I can see Puzzle sleeping, silence usually signals trouble. All those qualities that were a good sign on her aptitude tests — intelligent, curious, assured, resourceful, strategic — can translate differently at home. Intelligence directs her to prize open the latch to her crate, pad silently out, then wiggle through folding closet doors. Curiosity leads her to sample the cats' litter box (robust! salty! with just a hint of salmon back!) to taste-test my shoes (patent leather shares the same bouquet of dead cow but is more delightfully resilient than suede). At one point I walk down a hallway and find a Hansel and Gretel trail of buttons leading out of my bedroom. Resourceful, strategic: Puzzle had woken from a nap at my feet, tiptoed away on soft paws, jimmied into my closet, and de-buttoned five shirts back from the cleaners. Fortunately, she wasn't interested in eating them. The number of buttons dropped equals the number of buttons missing. She just likes the feel of them in her teeth, the little snap of release. Self-confident: when I catch her in misdeeds and scold her, she does not look ashamed.

I am, however. I thought I was prepared for the realignment of priorities any puppy brings, but either she is sly or my distraction level has made me oblivious, or a little bit of both.

The obedience trainer is frank. "You aren't being enough of a leader, here. She's a smart dog, and she's got time to think too much," Susan says. "Smart dogs are tougher than dumb dogs. For a while, you want her thinking what you need her to be thinking. You want her doing what you tell her to. It should be: sit for petting, sit for treats, sit for no reason at all other than I told you to. She should think her middle name is 'Sit.'" Susan's direction: watch her carefully, keep her directed, reward her for good behavior, set some standards, and make her stick by them. In fact, my leadership over all the crew is lacking. Make *all* the dogs stick to the rules.

I say "Sit" so much that even one of the cats drops his bottom at the sound of the word. I say "Sit" so much that when a salesperson hovers over my shoulder and interrupts me for the fourth time in a complicated transaction, I hold up my hand and reflexively say "Sit," as I lean over the contract. He blinks. I blink. "New dog," I say in apology. "Ah," he replies and points at the picture of his black Lab, all muscular intensity with a shining head. "How old?" I ask. "Ten months," he says. "Yours?" "Six months," I answer. We have a moment of empathy. He does not, however, interrupt me again.

Walks are also a challenge. The world is fresh and new to Puzzle, and my neighborhood is in a state of upheaval. Old houses are demolished for new-builds, and the sound of destruction and the smell of overturned earth is everywhere. Puzzle strains at her lead, occasionally porpoising to leap for some provoking scent. Downwind of a dog friend in a backyard two blocks away, Puzzle goes theatrical. *It's Roxie! Roxie! Roxie! and she's way up there and I'll DIE if I don't go VISIT.* She has a Roxie moan, a Jack-and-Lady grumble, an Annie mutter. The sounds are so separate and singular that at one point a friend on a walk with us recognizes the difference. "Oh," he says when Puzzle lifts her nose and mutters, "Annie must be out." She is.

I am not opposed to dog friends or playdates, but I'd like a better walk from Puzzle, a loose lead, a heel. "Keep her busy on her walks," says Susan. "Make her go on *your* walk. Be consistent with your words. Don't give her time to think about what she'd rather do."

In a few months, I get a casual, acceptable trot ahead from her, punctuated by only a few spasms of pull. The lead is frequently slack. I feel less like I'm walking a chain saw. But "Heel" Puzzle seems to find insulting. She veers away on her lead like a reluctant teenager in the company of a parent. We are irrevocably bound, but terribly uncool. She seems to be sure I'm unnecessary. She prefers to think I'm invisible too.

Even the sight of the lead is enough to set her spinning. Puzzle is young and winds up easily. Quick movement from me or a high, bright word, and she starts to ricochet across the house. I begin to approach walks as though I were headed for meditation, winding things down half an hour before we're likely to go out. I try speaking more quietly, moving more calmly and with greater purpose. I turn off the TV and the radio, and I avoid giving all the dogs high-energy treats. I am just one notch away from lighting incense and beating a few low-key brass gongs with cloth mallets before I suggest "walk" in a whisper.

Like the Poms, Puzzle is also keenly aware of body language, and though I try to disguise my intention to take her out for a walk until the moment I head for the leash, the puppy seems to anticipate me by minutes. I don't know what she senses in me; there is no noticeable routine of timing, clothing, or movement that I can see, but when I have a walk in mind, I notice her sudden omnipresence, and then her escalated breathing, and then a certain oingy-boingy quality that knocks over chairs and thumps pictures a-tilt on the walls. It is as though she can hear the bat's-squeak of the idea across the synapses of my brain. Sprits'l takes a cue from Puzzle and begins to bark, racing in circles in front of the door. Puzzle may be the one going out, but five-pound Sprits'l is just the man to scold her for what she's about to do, what she may do in the future, what she has certainly done in the past. To her credit, Puzzle accepts his noisy chiding with goodwill. She sidesteps Sprits'l and heads for the leash rack. She is all about the walk. I wonder if she can smell me mentally gearing up for the adventure with her that often feels like a cross between street fighting and deep-sea fishing.

Friends try to help. One night a teammate and I are both going to take Puzzle for her evening walk. Ellen has witnessed this spectacle in the past, and tonight we decide that we'll use the long SAR lead, which has a sense of weight and gravitas, and that we'll wear the puppy out with backyard games, wind down for an hour or so, and then take her out when she is mellow. Mellow. *As if,* Puzzle's expression seems to say when we bring her in from forty minutes of fetch and chase in the backyard.

"Maybe," Ellen says, "we should just up and go in the middle of a TV show. You know . . . sit and watch the show and then, all of a sudden, just get up and go." It is a good plan, meant to teach the puppy spontaneity and adaptability, but the truth is we hope to sneak the walk up on Puzzle and to teach her there's no need to make a fuss about something she does twice every day, anyway. No need to dismantle the dining room. The Poms do not have to be woofed, nor the cats flushed upstairs in happy anticipation.

Our plan fails on several levels. Puzzle is lying on the floor, tenderly beheading a stuffed octopus when I get up. She immediately drops the toy and rolls onto her chest to watch what I'll do next. I head for her long lead, and she's at my ankles, happy and wiggling as I snap it on. She's delighted with it. Gathering a knot of black webbing in her teeth, she trots toward the door with her head up and her fuzzy tail waving. As I move for my house keys and Ellen bends to re-tie her shoe, Maddy flashes through the room and right under Puzzle's nose, then skitters away. It is a direct provocation and one that Puzzle cannot resist. She scrambles after the cat, her long lead trailing, and before I can grab it, the end of the lead catches under the leg of the china cabinet. The cabinet shudders but does not fall. Before we can shriek "Puzzle, stop!" the lead snaps taut. Puzzle scrambles after Maddy, the uneasy cabinet makes a little hop, then pivots somehow on two feet that are free, turning ninety degrees clockwise on squat legs like a glass sumo wrestler, before its weight stops the puppy. Through some miracle of physics, the cabinet rests upright and perpendicular to the wall after the dance step, its curved glass intact. The china and crystal inside have shifted but have not shattered. Ellen and I gawp, wordless. I'm reminded of those magicians who can pull a tablecloth out from under a laden table and leave dinner, wine, and candles intact. Puzzle has felt the check on her lead and sits like a good dog, her expression a little wistful as Maddy rounds a corner out of sight.

Ellen finds her voice before I do. "Did you see that?" she shouts, waving her arms at the china cabinet. "Did you — DID YOU SEE THAT?" Her pitch rises to dog whistle altitudes and Puzzle gives a little woof. High octaves out of humans are very exciting. I extract the dog's lead and tell Puzzle to hold her sit, which she does, but I can feel the happy vibration of her down the long length of webbing. The puppy flashes me a loopy, tongue-sideways smile. A cat, a scramble, a spin, and a shriek: this is the way all walks ought to begin.

10

SOMEONE ELSE'S STORM

A SPONGY EVENING on the verge of spring, and I am driving up I-35 in a caravan of eight other cars. A teammate sits beside me. Frances has her knees propped on the glove box and her peanut butter sandwich on the dashboard. She's clearing waypoints from her GPS and humming along to Santana. I've got a Thermos of coffee wedged next to me in the seat. We've got a long drive ahead. The team has been preemptively deployed against bad weather in another state, and we're packed for several days of possible searches, heading out to serve as field assistants to the handlers with certified dogs.

We've driven north out of city lights and into the enveloping black of rural night sky, but we lose stars, too, by the minute as we head into the storm system moving toward central Oklahoma. On radar, the system's greatest violence and repeating hook echoes suggest that tornadoes are likely again in an area barely recovered from multiple disasters across the past decade. So we've been deployed to a staging area just outside the storm's projected path, the local police and fire departments now aware how long it can take specialty search-and-rescue teams to get to a disaster site after the fact. We'll move three hours closer to coming trouble, but not too close to become victims ourselves. With any luck there will be no trouble at all.

But the longer we drive, the more the angry sky defines itself. We watch the roil of cloud to cloud lightning and see, from one splendid chain reaction across the horizon, a dozen flashes and three separate cumulonimbus anvils backlit in perfect formation, firing on one another like ships of the line in the age of fighting sail.

To stay alert on the road, Frances and I trade storm stories. Frances grew up in New York and had never witnessed a tornado before she got here, but the first year she was in Texas as the young bride of an ex-military man, a storm out of nowhere hit when she was alone at the farm. The sky of that storm, she says, was unlike anything she'd ever seen: purple, silver, and green, pimpled with mammatus clouds — beautiful and surreal.

When the storm released, she heard all the windows of the house pop, as though the pressure in the house had suddenly changed. Hail the size of softballs killed some cattle, spooked horses in their stalls, and took out all the baby trees in the front yard. Hail fell so loud and so long, it was enough to make you crazy, she says. When her in-laws called afterward to make sure she was all right, Frances shouted into the receiver, unable to hear the caller and hardly able to hear herself.

This was her introduction to extreme Texas weather. It was enough to make her wish she'd married a guy from Rhode Island.

Frances says worse than the storm was her husband coming home to find out she'd forgotten to put his candy apple red '67 Mustang GT in the garage. She was too young to have gotten married, and things had gone south just afterward. They had been in all kinds of standoffs for months after the wedding. Thinking back, she says she might have forgotten the Mustang on purpose to shake things up, bring the storm inside a little, at least to know where she was with him, which it turned out was nowhere, but at least she knew.

Donny screamed at her for days after the storm, every time he caught sight of the GT's smashed windshield, the cratered hood peeling paint. When he threw a skillet and threatened to kill her dog, she packed while he was at work. She loaded his old army duffle full of clothes and that was it. Frances was eighteen at the time. She took her poodle and left, stepping over split baby trees, walking past the smoldering livestock that had died in the storm, piled into a mound to be written off as a loss, doused with gasoline, and torched.

"What about you?" Frances asks. "Do Texas kids just get used to this?"

I tell her that of all the things I could have been afraid of as a child, it was storms that scared me most. Which came first, storm phobia or *The Wizard of Oz*, already showing on television when I was small? While some of my playmates feared the flying monkeys or the talking trees, and others were spooked by the Wicked Witch of the West, for weeks after a rerun of *The Wizard of Oz*, I dreamed only of storms — nightmares I still remember — all lowering sky and wind rising, a whirl of flightless chickens, a tornado on the horizon, and the storm cellar bolted shut.

I had tangled reasons to be afraid, living with my parents near an air force base in an era of nuclear tension, housed on the leading edge of the Midwest's Tornado Alley. If The Bomb didn't get you there, said the sixth-graders (who knew it all), the tornadoes would. I was pretty much terrified of both. A few of the big boys talked about missiles in Cuba ("just a hundred miles away!"), little missiles with lasers and big ones with The Bomb, all of them most definitely aimed at us. But tornadoes were the stuff of better stories. Some of the sixth-graders had seen the Wichita Falls tornado of '64. Others pretended to have seen it. Those big kids fascinated and frightened us with their catalogue of bizarre outcomes: a toothpick stuck in the side of a car; a Cocker Spaniel found — still alive! — thirty miles from home *with its ears pulled right off its head;* a picture of a solemn, suit-wearing farmer holding a bald chicken, its exploded feathers plucked clean by the passing storm. Sometimes two boys would fight over whose uncle had the chicken and whose daddy had the earless dog. I had given up on Santa Claus by this time, but for some reason I believed every story from the sixth-graders about the tornado of '64.

Their tales were indirectly validated by our teachers. We were thoroughly prepared for disaster. On first-grade field trips, we memorized which buildings had the yellow and black FALLOUT SHELTER sign (post office, hospital, big school) and which did not (movie theater, grocery store, church). We learned which buildings were the safe places in storm or nuclear attack. The rules were simple: hear the siren, run for the sign.

We watched a lot of *Duck and Cover!* in those days. I still remember animated Bert the Turtle retracting into his shell at the first sign of trouble, the goofy kid in the jacket with the fur collar dropping his bicycle and flinging himself headfirst against a curb, the smiling teacher pointing out two types of nuclear attack on the chalkboard, the neat rows of schoolchildren hiding beneath their desks when something bright flashed white outside. When we ducked beneath our desks during drills, the rows were not so perfect, and our teacher didn't smile. Some kids giggled while the sirens wailed. A five-year-old first-grader, I always cried.

Tornado warnings caused sirens spring, summer, and autumn; civil defense drills brought sirens at least monthly year-round. The sound of that horn, just blocks from my house, the way it wound up and down its wail, went right through me. A latchkey kid after school while my parents searched in vain for childcare, on stormy afternoons I would hide in the closet beneath the stairs when the sky went black and the sirens went off, turtling like Burt, apart from my family like Dorothy Gale, ducking and covering and waiting for the house to fly.

I spent a lot of time in that closet. I can laugh a little about it now. "Duck!" I sing to Frances, ". . . and cover!"

She says, "You were one spooky kid."

• • •

The southbound side of the highway is ablaze with headlights, people running from the storm; northbound traffic is sparse. "Looks like we're heading the right direction," says Frances. She has eaten her sandwich and pulled on her boots. We've finished the coffee.

The storm stretches wide, west to east in front of us. Lightning, now cloud to cloud, now cloud to ground, reveals five intact super-cells. One cell northwest of us surges powerfully upward, and its churning base has begun to droop toward the horizon.

We drive north in still air past all-night fast-food restaurants. It's business as usual for them, with lines of cars wrapped around the drive-through. (*Not a safe place,* I mutter.) Burger by burger, they seem impervious to storm. But we are twitchy with expecta-tion. We've turned off the music and turned up our team radios, the squelch crackling with storm discharge. I take off the cruise control so I can feel the car beneath my feet. I expect a blast of wind at any time.

A couple of years in Tornado Alley had its effects. When I was di-agnosed with an ulcer at six years old, my parents made arrange-ments for me to stay awhile with my grandmother. She was my fa-vorite relative, living in a small town with calmer weather — on the surface, this was a very good plan.

None of us remembered that my grandmother lived only a few blocks from the firehouse. One day just after our arrival, I was out-side playing barefoot in the grass when the fire siren went off — an all-purpose, small-town horn used to alert volunteer firefighters or warn of a coming storm. It was a higher-pitched, long-winded cousin of the civil defense sirens of Tornado Alley. When it wailed on that sunny afternoon, I didn't have a lot of logic going. *Hear the siren, run for the sign.* The closest one was the post office three blocks away. I ran across the yard for the house, to save my family, but ran straight into a patch of stickers, fell, ran again, fell again, and lay screaming with my arms over my head, curled into duck and cover.

The siren had to stop before my parents found me, doubled up, being sick in the grass. I remember my mother's stricken face and the single look she exchanged with my father. "There's not a storm," she said, bewildered. "There's not a storm." I wasn't able to tell her the sirens were terrifying enough. I feel compassion now for my parents, out of money and possibility, whose sick child had fears she couldn't explain. They had no other options. When they left a few days later, I knew why I stayed behind.

We watched them go, and my grandmother had her own ideas about storms and Susannah. She was in no mood for a summer of wailing. The next time the firehouse horn sounded, she held up a hand. "Ehh," she said, with a shushing motion. "Not every siren has to do with us. Not every storm is ours." She said what we needed was a little "equanimity." I had no idea what the word meant, but I used it every chance I could.

Now three state troopers and two trucks full of storm chasers pass us. Plastered with logos, their vehicles are whiskered with equipment, and they are driving fast.

"Would you do that?" Frances points to the storm chasers. "I'd do that."

I nod. *Me too.* Somewhere along the way, fear of storms had turned to fascination.

"DPS says stop at the Holiday Inn," crackles Johnny over the radio. We have come far enough.

We exit the highway in tandem, right blinkers flashing. They are a shocking red against the storm's white and black. We meet in the parking lot and climb out of our cars to move around while we can, stiff from sitting and sore from straining forward to see the weather ahead. The wind is strong, the air electric. Released from their crates, the search dogs pee and race and quibble with one another, stretch in the bending grass of a neighboring field.

"They feel it," says Deryl. We all do.

A state trooper pulls up. His car is muddy and already dinged with hail pocks. He has a rain cover on his hat. "You folks good to go?" he asks. He looks tired already, and this storm is young. "Probably won't be long now." In the radio calls of his colleagues, we hear a distant siren wail.

"We're ready," says Max.

One hour. Two. Three.

Hunter's head rests on his paws, but his eyes are open and his sensitive ears flick left and right as the pitch of the moving storm changes and one distant siren gives up as another begins to wail. Saber lies on his chest, his graceful head turned to the northeast. Though they lie almost immobile, I watch their nostrils twitch, and I imagine all that they must process between the local, familiar scent of teammates, the nearby restaurants, and the millions of shattered, disorganized town and country scents stirred by winds miles away.

Saber looks thoughtful, a paw extended to the side of his crate and resting upward against it, the pads touching the wire frame lightly. It's an attentive posture, the way an adult would hold up a hand and say *Hush!* to catch the second sound of something. The movement of Saber's nose is slight but precise. A change of scent: I see his head lift almost imperceptibly and turn an inch or so to the left, his nostrils working more rapidly. I look in the direction of his change. Moments later a restaurant employee appears from behind a brick wall surrounding a kitchen door. He carries a white paper bag in his hand. It looks like take-out: late supper, perhaps, early breakfast. In the dim light, I have an impression of short dark hair, dark pants, a white T-shirt, and running shoes. What does Saber know of him? A baseline scent of individual young man, plus soap and fry-cook grease, and the onions he ate on liver earlier in the day, a hint of vanilla and jasmine on his jacket, left by the embrace of a girlfriend, plus the white bag contents: the hamburger, the cold, greasy fries, and the wedge of pickle with a half-inch smear of mustard along its edge? One thing is certain: the dogs get more of him than I do in the shadows. When the young man gets in his car to drive away, Saber releases him of interest, turning his head slightly back in the direction of the storm.

We've parked close together; we talk car to car. Frances and I were not the only one trading storm stories, we learn as the team waits for word to deploy or stand down. Many among us have been caught out by violent Texas weather — survived flash floods, tornadoes, hurricanes. Several members of the team have worked Oklahoma tornadoes before, most notably the 1999 F5 tornado that began in Chickasha and tore through Bridge Creek and Moore before dissipating. We speak now of that past history and what these storms can produce: mass casualties and injuries, entire neighborhoods leveled, landmarks obliterated. In Moore, Fleta says, even firefighters born there could no longer always be certain where they were amid the rubble. She describes established neighborhoods where nothing left was more than waist high, the dogs threading their search through twists of raw metal, jagged wood, and shattered glass. A hard search on the humans, tough on the dogs — in some cases, human scent from survivors, the injured, and the deceased torn to fragments and strewn wide.

Moore had its oddities too. Max speaks of trees stripped of leaves and of bark, and of one tall tree blown completely bare, a desperate squirrel still alive and clinging to the slick of its topmost branches. The Toughest Squirrel in the World, Max calls that guy, a bright memory in Moore amid much darker ones. And just down the street from what might be the Toughest Dog too. On one neighborhood search, Max saw rubble shiver from a collapsed house across the street, and as he ran to assist whoever was moving beneath it, a battered Rottweiler emerged. Buried in rubble for two and a half days, injured and frightened, the dog had nonetheless dug his way out. Rescue responders led him to a local group that was there to provide veterinary care and help families recover their lost pets.

Sometimes, Fleta says, the loss gets even closer than you'd expect. In one sector, as she and Saber searched for victims down a

street of flattened houses, the firefighter working beside her gestured briefly to the rubble of the next house they approached.

"Empty," he said. "No need to search that one."

"How do you know?" Fleta asked.

He said, "Because it's mine."

I look at the dogs that have deployed with us on this search, lying quietly in their crates. Some of them are storm phobic at home
on their own time. But now in the environment of search, when
they can smell and feel as well as hear the storm, it's curious to me
how they seem to let their fear go. Several of these dogs are Oklahoma and Texas tornado veterans: they've spent plenty of long
days circling the rubble on command, expressions thoughtful as
they made their way to the center of this tumbled house or the
ragged edge of that one, finding dime-size fragments of the deceased in the remaining eggshell curve of a bathtub.

These are the searches that test the whole handler, the whole
dog — equanimity and stamina in good measure. After the search
for human casualties had been made in Moore, the same dog units
went out to assist dazed residents returning to what was left of
their homes. Some families needed help locating emergency
items — medication, insurance documentation, and the like. Others just needed hands to help remove mementoes left intact. Still
others wanted nothing more than the solace of the dogs. Many
residents turned to them, having lost their own. After disaster, the
Moore handlers say, a search team's job description expands. We
come to search, but we do *whatever*, Max says. You have to get a
little bigger, give up your fatigue and your ego and your own fears
to meet the need.

We sit all night.

"Damn lucky," says the officer who stands us down, eight hours
after we deployed. He's referring to the towns that lay along the
spent storm's path and were, apart from downed trees, hail damage, and lost power, spared disaster. The worst of the weather had
skipped across open fields, he says, and there were already storm

stories, reports of strange sights — a tractor overturned beside a truck left untouched, a windmill that had fallen and somehow trapped a cow in the mangle of it, the cow apparently uninjured *but really pissed off.*

No persons missing, no civilian casualties known. Damn lucky, he repeats. Damn close. The officer thanks us for being willing to sit the night on standby. He says, "Glad you were here, but really glad we didn't need you." We thank him, and we all exhale.

Here is equanimity. The dogs are always ready for whatever. They shrug off the night of standby and are running now, racing like puppies across the muddy field. We're also a little goofy with relief, and we play too, tugging toys, throwing balls. We set up practice searches. Dog by dog, they find those of us who've disappeared for them, leaving paw prints on the windows, the wet of their noses streaking the cars where we hide.

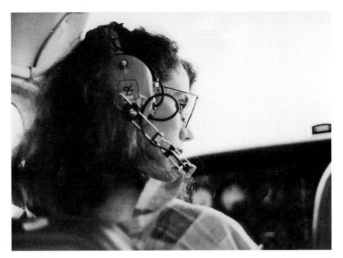

Piloting a Cessna 172 in 1995.

Dade County search-and-rescue handler Skip Fernandez and his partner, Aspen, rest together after working all night in the rubble of the Murrah Federal Building, Oklahoma City, April 1995.

Fleta and Saber search the rubble after the F5 tornado in Moore, Oklahoma.

Max and Hunter in a stream bed.

Jerry and Shadow rappelling, 2003.

Johnny and Buster in a wildlife preserve that requires on-lead searches.

Max and Mercy work in the chill air of an early morning.

Terry and Hoss search the wildlife preserve.

Fo'c'sle Jack is a certified therapy dog and enjoys interacting with children from the bow of his dread ship *Pork Chop* at charity events.

Ellen and Scuppy, age twenty-three, at a Christmas presentation for nursing home residents. Sociable and kindly, Scuppy became an unexpected role model for Puzzle.

Mr. Sprits'l on the couch he claimed — and Puzzle ate.

Puzzle, Fleta, and I observe Johnny and Buster finding a volunteer victim buried in debris. Moments later, Puzzle will duplicate the effort for her first formal search.

I found him! Puzzle and Matt, her first victim. She has swiped a piece of charred wood as a memento.

That's a lot of vest for a little dog. Puzzle relaxes off-lead at her second training session.

Left: Scent work in a fire academy "burn building"—Puzzle is twelve weeks old.

Below: Puzzle demonstrates "postural echo" in a gentle first greeting of Pomeranian Misty, subdued after the death of her owner just forty-eight hours before.

Search-dog training builds stamina and confidence. Puzzle works a fire escape in 2005.

Teaching the dogs confidence on a rappel line is a team effort.

Above: Vines, thorns, and the occasional snake: the Wilderness certification test in Texas.

Left: Puzzle posing after a morning on the debris pile—eleven months old.

Left: Mission ready: Team Puzzle after the challenging Urban/Disaster cert test.

Below: The backyard "playhouse": *La Folie des Chiots.*

Happy at her work: a certified Puzzle finds a photographer in a ravine on a training search.

11

RUNNING WITH THE BIG DOGS

WHATEVER OUR TROUBLES at home, a different dog hits the ground in the early days of our search lessons. Puzzle has learned all the signals that suggest she's about to leave the house and head out to work. It does not take her long to assimilate the clunk of ice in the mini-cooler, the zip of my steel-toed boots, and the jingle and snap of her treat bag on my belt to know what they mean. She rushes out the back door and into the yard ahead of me, wearing the special harness that is another signal we're about to get down to business. Puzzle is all retriever. She has the lifted head and switchy prance of a dog born to carry things for their partners, and she swaggers around the yard with her own lead in her soft mouth. She is small but extremely prideful, dragging much of the webbing behind her as she trots beside me toward the car, crooning *wrrooo-ooo-wroooo-oo-oo*, universal Golden for *dig me*. This is just the kind of reaction we want from a search dog — self-confidence, awareness, and joy in the work to come.

But at the door of the garage she pauses, and there I see her first hesitance. Puzzle is quick to make connections, and just as she knows that certain clothes and objects mean search training, she has also associated car trips with nausea. At the door of the garage, I see her pause, drop her lead, and back up a little. She is torn. When I encourage her toward the Jeep (*Hey Puz! Oh boy! Let's go to work!*), she is all mixed signals. She wags and simultaneously scoots backward, plopping her bottom down and whimpering, miserable with the conflict of wanting to go but really, really, really not wanting to throw up all over the back seat again, a condition I understand and share.

Car sickness is fairly common in dogs. I had a Sheltie that invariably vomited in the first five minutes of motion and then loved every minute of any car trip, even those to the vet. He would wholeheartedly retch up whatever he had in him, then flash a hey!-beg-pardon-for-the-puke grin, and wiggle and wag the rest of the way. Puzzle has thrown up only once in the car, but she's drooled a little and hung her head several other times, and it didn't take much to sense that she felt awful. At three months old, she doesn't seem to be particularly afraid of the vehicle itself or its smell, or its shape, or the rumbling of the engine, but within a few minutes of any drive, she is trembling, and in a couple of minutes more, I can see her head droop and her nauseated salivation begin. She is a long way from grinning about it.

Remembering the puppy that flew home belly-up and snored through moderate turbulence, I believe the car sickness is a problem we can outwit. Unsure if she feels sick because she's afraid or if she's afraid because she once felt sick, I first try modeling fearless canine car travel. While she sits in the doorway, I bring Sprits'l out to the garage, where he bounds into the car and puts his paws up on the back window, grinning and yapping an ecstatic *neener-neener* through the glass at her. Puzzle is unimpressed with the effort and oddly seems to feel no urge to one-up the Pom behind the window. They take a short car trip together. Sprits is joyful; within a couple of blocks, Puzzle's head and ears are down. *Love the car,* Sprits'l Morse-taps across the window with his paws. Puzzle's sullen expression suggests: *Hate the car. Hate the drive. Think I hate you too.*

Other tactics are marginally successful. I begin feeding her at least an hour and a half before a car trip, giving her food a chance to settle. We try puppy ginger snaps. A little Rescue Remedy on her tongue or paws. I bring out all the tricks that flight instructors use to help nauseated student pilots: I raise the seats so that Puzzle can get her bearings and see out, redirect vents so that she stays cool, fresh air blowing over her as she travels. Airbags are dangerous for dogs, so I cannot put her in the front seat, but in the back seat I move her closer to the center of the vehicle, securing her to the seatbelt with a special canine harness for a sense of security, hoping also to eliminate any swing or yaw she might feel farther back.

We make a party out of it with friends and much praising, we vary short trips with longer ones, and sometimes we just go hang out in the back of the Jeep without going anywhere. Once she jumps into the back seat of her own accord — a huge jump for a small pup — and I am very proud, but this is no new standard. Puzzle does not quickly learn to love a car. She tolerates the drive and, I believe, understands it's the necessary evil that gets her to search training. Some days, she heads into the garage with only slight reluctance. Other days, she sits on the sidewalk and sighs into the darkness, following only when I take up the lead and walk her into the garage. Once in the Jeep, she gazes stoically out the window while we back out and begin to roll, gulping a little as nausea seems to threaten, rise, and abate.

Where car travel may be a misery, search training itself is a quick and early joy for Puzzle. By the time we pull into the parking lot, her nausea is forgotten, her paws are up to the glass and her nose to the crack of the window. I hear her breathing change as she *huff-huff*s the delicious scent of human teammates and the dogs schooling among them at knee-level. She wiggles as I unfasten her seatbelt harness and secure her lead, and she scrambles across the asphalt to greet all comers, wagging so hard that she pops herself in the face with her own tail, and no matter how many times she's done it, still looks surprised and affronted by the smack. She whips her head in a startled *who did that?*— but it's an insult that quickly evaporates in the presence of greater joys: dog friends! people friends! and *Oh! Oh!* the men of the team.

Puzzle is something of a hussy, as one teammate calls her, a man's dog, and though she's fond of the team's women and shows a particular affinity for Fleta, our lead canine instructor, it is the men of the team who make her go weak in the knees. Puzzle is all about the boys: petitioning them shamelessly for attention and petting. Most of these guys love her too. They are longtime dog owners, well-versed in the perfect scratch and ear rub. A few of them pick her up and strum her belly like a banjo. Others cradle her and rub her ears until she completely relaxes and her head dangles upside down. Sometimes she shoots me a look from this exalted position, and the message is pretty clear: *They're big, and they're strong, and they are so much cooler than you.*

Now one of them has gone missing. Puzzle would really like to find the former Marine voluntarily buried in the woodpile. We stand fifty yards away, watching as Johnny and Buster work the mound of charred debris. Our head trainer watches us, I watch my dog, and Puzzle watches Johnny and Buster. She is quiet and intent at the end of her lead. When Buster makes the find, she strains a little toward the scene, as though she wants to see the moment of connection. Buster likes to fetch a ball as reward for his searching, and off he scrambles after it while we watch. Puzzle's ears briefly perk at the sight of the ball, but she turns back to the debris pile with a fixed expression.

I have seen hundreds of training searches, but now I look down at Puzzle and try to imagine how she frames all of this. In intermediate dogs, we sometimes get the sense of wry exasperation: *Look, I found this guy twice today already, not two hundred feet from his own car. I'm telling you, he is freakin' hopeless.* Advanced dogs often seem to grin in conspiracy: *Okay, I know you're going to hide her in the trickiest place you possibly can, and I'm still gonna show you it ain't no thing.* But for Puzzle this is all still new. I wonder if Matt's predicament bemuses her — *hey buddy, whatcha doing in there?* — and if she can already clearly distinguish between the scent of normal human energy and genuine fear. Perhaps she saw Buster search the pile, make the find, and get to chase a ball afterward, and in all of that she sees the search as the greater game. There's no way to know.

We turn our backs and Matt, the Marine, is reburied in the woodpile, covered again where Buster had made short work of finding him. Maneuvering downwind of the pile, I give Puzzle the "Find!" command and off she races to the debris, circling it without question and giving a little happy hop of excitement when she picks up Matt's scent. She takes a moment to negotiate the loose debris, but when she gets to Matt and he weaves out a hand to touch her nose, she's all happy grins and wiggles. "Good girl!" we praise, and from beneath the debris we can hear the mutter of Matt laughing, praising her too. I offer her a bit of beef jerky with the *good girl.* She takes the treat daintily, and then drops it absently, unchewed, preferring to caper while we lay on the petting and praise.

As we carefully extract Matt, Puzzle steals a piece of burned wood from the debris pile. Matt carries her to the team to show off her success, and she has her head up, her trophy in her mouth. "Good girl!" they all praise. *Rooo-wooo-wrroooo,* Puzzle rumbles, wagging around the circle, showing off her burned stick. *Woooroo-woo.* I know the sound, but it's the first time the team has heard it from her. It's the sound of a dog who thinks she's hot stuff.

A harder lesson is learning to take her turn. Dogs that are not actively searching are waiting to search or are in "rehab," resting quietly with a bowl of water in the shade, recovering from a previous search and physically preparing for the next one. Puzzle will come off a search quietly, but her eyes follow the other dogs, and she springs to her feet when she hears the distant shout of handlers giving their dogs the "Find!" command. She watches and quivers, and occasionally when she can get the scent of a victim from where she waits, she whips her head around to look at me with great urgency and moans. *Put me in, Coach,* we call the yearning expressed by a line of search dogs, watching a distant dog and handler work a new scenario, waiting their turn. They all would be happiest if they had every search. Though their frustration is apparent, I believe that all that watching instructs the dogs too.

Puzzle enjoys her early days of search work. Our trainers say the dogs often catch on far more quickly than the handlers do, and Puzzle is quick to demonstrate that she knows what "Find!" means and that she doesn't care who she's finding. She likes the challenge; she likes the hunt and the strategy to get to the victim; she loves the praise. What I cannot tell in these early months is how best to reward her. The Labs and Collies and some of the German Shepherds of our team love to fetch a ball, and I try this with Puzzle, who cheerfully fetches in the backyard. After one training search, I take out a beloved tennis ball from home and throw it for Puzzle, who looks at me skeptically and ignores it. She watches the arc of the ball and the bounce and roll that follow, then looks at me as if to say, "You want it, *you* go get it." Search training does not seem to be the time or place for fetch in her view. Treats are possibly the better reward.

What Puzzle responds to most is the celebration that follows a successful find. Praise goes straight to her head, and she trots from a search expansive — chin up, high-stepping with her tail waving a happy flag. She croons her signature rumble until she's acknowledged by bystanders. In these early months, the work itself is Puzzle's best fun, and I get the sense that if I really wanted to reward her for a good search, I would give her another one.

Puzzle in the wilderness can move much faster than I can. Chalk it up to youth. Chalk it up to four paws on the ground and a lower center of gravity. Chalk it up to motivation too. Puzzle is from a line of dogs who love fieldwork, and she immediately shows me that crashing through brush and fording creeks to find a victim is most excellent fun. While I consider myself somewhat outdoorsy, wilderness search in Texas is never just a tidy hike through friendly wood. A wilderness search invariably means deep brush laced with mesquite thorns, poison ivy, and rugosa rose branches. Puzzle presses through such brush with equanimity, disregarding the pops and scratches and thorns in her paws. I have more trouble, bundling through the brush like a wounded bug, tripping over vines, thorns tangling the straps of my pack, snagging my clothing and sometimes shredding it as I pass.

An early morning cold front has passed on our first long day of wilderness training. We are all a little stunned by the shift from an 85-degree afternoon yesterday to a 36-degree morning today. The humans have swapped T-shirts for parkas, and we stand in a knot together, our shoulders hunched against the climate we're not yet acclimated to. The dogs, however, are bristly and alive with the cool, electric air, and as every one of them has some form of field impulse in their makeup, they look toward the wood with anticipation. *This*, their waving tails seem to say, *is gonna be great.*

Today's training will rotate between three sectors. Some feature wide plains of tall, stiff grass. Other sectors are mostly brush and huddled stands of trees, so thick that inside the huddle it is difficult to see open field beyond. The air is dense and heavy, but it's moving a little too. This morning's twelve-knot wind will shift scent in interesting ways, and when the ground warms after a few hours of sun, the same terrain will offer all-new scent patterns.

The dogs go into this with few preconceptions. It's the handlers who must be on their toes, and the risk for all of us, and particularly for me, the new handler, is that we'll search the dogs too rigidly according to our expectations, rather than trusting them to tell us where the scent actually is. Puzzle's urban work at the fire academy has shown me that when she's clearly got the victim, she is not a subtle dog. Her huge, happy alerts are visible sometimes to bystanders in the parking lot from a hundred yards away. But wilderness work demands that I be able to decipher when she has begun to pick up scent (interest), when she has narrowed it to a general location (indication), and when she has found the source itself (alert). And the heavy brush may prevent her from alerting the way she typically would. I watch the big dogs and their handlers head out into sectors, and I remind myself that when it comes to decoding my dog, I am a kindergartner at best. We have two objectives: Puzzle needs to find the victim, and I need to know when she's on her way to finding him.

I also need to learn how to watch my dog and stay upright. Our first wilderness sector, though not large, is uneven — full of gullies and sinkholes and unsteady stones, all of which are hidden beneath tall grass. The wind is from the north, and we begin sweeping east and west from the southern, most downwind point of our sector. The idea is that a dog may catch first scent at the farthest downwind point of a search area and, if so, will indicate and head for the victim quickly and efficiently. Puzzle quivers when I ask her if she's ready to work, and on command she barrels away from me. She moves quickly, but not as quickly as she will after losing that puppy weight. She's tough to follow, even so. Puzzle's nose and tail are up, and watching her, I fail to see a dip in the ground ahead of me. I fall flat for the first time, a right smack. I pick myself up, take two steps, and fall again, this time tangling my compass in the small branches of a young tree. Puzzle pauses briefly at the sound of my *oomph* and *oomph* again, but when it's time to move deeper into the sector and sweep the other way, she races ahead without concern.

On the second sweep, I see the sharp, characteristic pop of her head and a little push in her gait, as though an elf has kicked her in the backside. *She has something,* I think. We continue the sweep, but on the reverse pass, when she pops her head again parallel to the first, I'm sure she's got the scent. I let her have her head. Puzzle takes off northward at full speed, and I stump along behind her, tripping once but staying upright as I watch the flick of her tail through the brush, then falling flat again in a clump of brambles just as she bounds into a stand of trees. As I pull myself up a fourth time, the two field assistants running with me exchange looks.

"Are you all right?" asks one. I'm not sure if he's asking about possible injuries or just my curious inability to run without falling. They aren't having any trouble with it, clearly. But then, they aren't learning how to run after a dog, and I haven't learned how to watch mine and where I'm going at the same time.

In the stand of trees, I hear a yip, then a little grunt and a laugh, and I find Puzzle wiggling over Max, who's buried beneath a camouflage tarp. Max is an old hand at this and somehow manages to pet her, praise her, and extricate himself from his hiding place simultaneously. She is aware of her success and turns to each of us for the praise due. When the two field assistants compare GPS readings, she bumps them for second acknowledgment. I give her a treat and again, she accepts it politely but with no great desire, gives a halfhearted chew, and drops it. *Wroo*, she croons lovingly to Max and the two field assistants. *I need better treats*, I think, *or maybe I just need to understand what really motivates my dog.*

I ran behind many other dogs before Puzzle joined me, and even as we train together, I continue to work as a field assistant behind certified dogs on actual searches. Though it's easy for a new handler-in-training to dismiss this opportunity, running behind other teams is some of the best handler training there is. Because field assistants operate at some distance from the canine unit, we are often able to see parts of the nonverbal communication between dog and handler that even handlers cannot see from their closer position. Our handlers all use similar commands, but from the moment of encouragement and release, the partnership is unique. There is much to learn.

Jerry and Shadow have a relationship framed by easy camaraderie, absolute authority on Jerry's part, and their mutual understanding that she knows her job, he knows his, and Shadow doesn't need to be micromanaged. She isn't. She's a dog of great presence. Even strangers who meet her will mention the aloof carriage, the regal bearing. We call her "The Queen," not because someone came up with a nickname we all adopted, but by default. No other descriptor fits.

Shadow works off-lead entirely. After Jerry's low command and a bob of her head in acknowledgment, she enters a sector with immediate purpose. She is not a nervous or an effusive dog; her assessments are cool, but the humans behind her can clearly see the process of her choice making. Left, not right, scent, no scent. She enters an area and meticulously clears it with wide, confident sweeps, Jerry following quietly behind. There is no mad dashing and great noise with a Shadow/Jerry search, but it is highly efficient. When Shadow enters an area of interest, she moves immediately to it, hones scent to the victim quickly, and sticks there. She's a talky girl who often discusses the find—in long strings of multiple syllables—with Jerry when he comes to reward her. Shadow likes her beef jerky. She will take it with great care, eat it thoughtfully, and then talk about it as a human might give several points of critique. If Shadow believes more treats are in order, she's not above putting a paw to your knee and telling you so explicitly.

In contrast, Belle, a yellow Lab, is a dog of high energy and great dash, who quivers before her release and races into a sector at a speed even the most athletic of us could not match. I was a victim on one of her early wilderness training searches. Buried deep in brush up a small hillside, I remember hearing the distant "Find!" command and seeing Belle flash by below me within seconds, with her handler and a field assistant struggling through the brush in full gear behind. When Belle caught my scent and altered course, she leapt over brush and had to belly-crawl in to get to me. She remained there and had begun her happy bark of success well before handler and field assistant were able to clear the brush to get to us.

"Good dog!" Cindi cried, waving Belle's beloved ball, her reward.

"Oh . . . good . . . God," panted the field assistant, "the only way to follow Belle is stark naked and greased like a swimmer."

Cindi learned early that working Belle was not so much a matter of keeping up as recognizing Belle's communication from a distance. Belle's signals are broad—fast and muscular, a lot of motion, a snapping at the air as she narrows to the find, and a bark of excitement to say she deserves her ball.

Max and Fleta's first dogs, Hunter and Saber, were two of the team's foundation dogs. They are the senior dogs of the team with a large number of searches behind them, and both now approach retirement. I regret that I came to the team too late to witness their early careers and the dialogue with their partners as it evolved, but I have seen the end result. Hunter has long been a hard-charger in the field, known for pushing through debris and digging out victims, if he must, to show Max where they lie. His finds will not go unnoticed. Saber, by contrast, moves like the senior statesmen of search dogs. He is calm, methodical, and precise, and true to his breed's background protecting sheep, Saber is known for an intense, protective victim loyalty at the point of find. A confident boy with a stubborn streak, Saber early taught Fleta how a search would progress and how she would pay attention to his signals in the field. With Saber, there is no room for sloppiness or inattention.

Max began training his second partner, Mercy, a white German Shepherd, in 2001. Fleta's second partner, another Roughcoat Collie named Misty, arrived in 2003. On the surface, it might seem that choosing the same breed for second partner would make training the new dogs easier, but though the dogs shared a handful of common physical traits in the field, they were each unique — Misty as gregarious as Saber was cautious, Mercy's subtler signals demanding a watchfulness not required by Hunter's broad, masculine alerts. *Every dog is a new conversation,* says Fleta.

I am learning to speak Puzzle, and maybe she is learning to speak me. We have a little time — hundreds of training searches to become fluent in each other, months of work before we will challenge our certification tests as a canine team. It is a rigorous curriculum for both of us in wilderness, urban, and disaster environments. Canine teams emerge from this prepared for all live-find work, whether a missing child in a neighborhood, five Boy Scouts lost in a state park, or an unknown number of survivors trapped beneath a building collapse. When I look at Puzzle, the prospect seems years distant, but sometimes she runs into her practice sectors with an intensity that suggests I'd better learn the grammar of her soon.

Puzzle's eagerness is clear, but she has more energy than finesse. Her wayward motor skills are funny. On the "Find!" command, she gallops away with great joy, then slows to a thoughtful lope as she first enters an area that seems to have live scent. I watch her work across the wind and begin to refine how she uses her nose. From that easy trot, the first strong scent that snags her attention literally seems to hook her by the nostrils. I watch her pivot while the suddenly lifted muzzle appears to stay in one place. When she's got scent, Puzzle's nose directs all her actions; she turns where it goes, and simultaneously there's a little kick-in-the-pants movement and a quickening of gait. Her tail, once idly swaying, begins to wag.

The closer she gets to the scent source, the quicker she moves. These early searches are easy finds. Though fully hidden, the victims are within Puzzle's access, if not her immediate sight. She pushes aggressively through brush to a scent source in the wilderness, but in closed building scenarios, where scent may slide along walls or hang in corners like ghosts, she must work harder to move from faint scent to stronger and strongest. I hang back while she mutters in frustration, clearly catching the scent but not able to see the source. It's the same kind of sound one occasionally hears from a person who's lost her car key in her purse: *I know it's here somewhere, but I just can't find it.* This is her problem to solve, and with a few words of encouragement (*Work it out, Puz*), I wait for her to find her own way in to the victim she cannot see.

When she does, the transition from indication to alert is obvious. I see a bounce of excitement just before her bottom drops, her tail wagging hard enough that her whole back end sways. Occasionally she makes a little whine of pleasure, particularly if the volunteer victim is someone she knows well. Her early alerts are puppyish, and I wonder what she will keep of these markers as she matures, and what she will lose. At this point, her final alerts have begun to evolve. They are clear to me and unaggressive toward victims: she no longer jumps on their chests, scratches them with a forepaw, or presses her face to theirs to lick. I hope her paws-off alerts will continue. I praise her hugely for them. Victim-passive alerts will be more appropriate in the field, where someone could be hurt or afraid of dogs, or if the find is located in the middle of a crime scene that would be better left unmauled by a happy, successful search canine.

On a Saturday morning in late spring, I lie wedged beneath two slabs of cement tilted sideways over chunks of concrete and mangled rebar. I've been here about an hour, a buried volunteer victim in the debris pile, as a series of experienced and less-experienced search dogs work across the rubble to find me. I will be here a while, still. I've been well hidden below the crush of rock, and from where I lie, I can see little in the dim light — cement, a piece of what appears to be plywood, and, if I turn my head slightly, a few tufts of wild grass stretching up through rebar. The air that reaches me is warm and spongy with drizzle, but the cement itself is still cool from the night before. Over time, some of that cool has seeped into my bones. My left foot, wedged sideways in a ballerina's turnout, has gone numb. The rest of me feels plenty, though. Some of the cement beneath my back is jagged. There's a hard chunk of something pressed against two ribs. One piece of cement against my forehead is mercifully smooth, but if I turn my head to the left, a raw piece of metal snags my ear. This is not the most comfortable hiding any of us does for the search dogs, but it is some of the most realistic.

Between dogs, there is a debriefing for the previous handler and a briefing for the next one. Sometimes, if the wind is right, I can hear the handler's command and the occasional eager *woof* of the responding Lab or Border Collie or German Shepherd. Other times, I can hear nothing more than the whistle of draft side-winding through shattered cement. I have been here only a short time, but in the gaps between dogs it's not hard to think I've been forgotten even in this soft little while. I've started the day with a good breakfast and a quiet walk to the debris pile, and though I am in this place on a voluntary basis and I have no injuries, it's not difficult to imagine the fear and hopelessness of a victim caught, much worse than I am ever caught, for hours, even days, in the rubble following catastrophe.

Dog Number Five is ready to run, and from far away I hear the "Find!" command and a few distant thumps that may be running feet. The voice sounded like Deryl's, which means the dog searching will be Sadie, a German Shepherd. The wind has lessened, and within moments I can hear Sadie's progress around the pile and Deryl's footsteps after her. I hear the scrape of her claws as she scrambles upward, and then a moment of silence, as though she's poised to make a decision — this way or that way in the sticky air. It's an instructive moment, listening to the rhythm of the working dog in progress.

I hear Sadie's definite change of gait, beginning with a soft lope that quickens, a pause, and then the scrambling sound of the dog moving upward. It's a little difficult to be sure where she is as I hear her moving across the pile, until I hear her pad into a nearby vertical structure. Its floor is smooth, though littered with a scatter of heavy dust and bits of concrete. I am close, and I can hear the softer movement of Sadie circling inside it and then the quicker sound of her exit. She has rejected that space for a possible living victim. I hear the closer scrape of her climbing paws. Plywood lying nearby creaks, then makes a shuddering sound as it bears her weight. Above me, I hear a huff of breath, a mutter, and as I wind my hand up to touch her forepaw, a *woof* as she signals to Deryl she's made the find.

Though I have hidden in the debris pile countless times across the past five years, I still feel a surge of relief each time one of the dogs find me, here or any other place. Their successes increase my conviction and confidence in the work.

Two nights later, wedged into a closet between a wall and three stacked fire mattresses as we work on urban searching, I sit in the dark and listen to first Shadow and then Misty find me. Though I am two rooms away from the "Find!" command and do not hear it, Shadow's easy tread is so distinctive that she's unmistakable. I always think of Shadow searching with the precision of a surgeon: opening a space and making decisions as she moves, with great efficiency. As her pace quickens, she begins talking to Jerry long before she reaches the closet, where she puts her nose to the crack beneath the door, huffs, inhales, and huffs again. Then she talks — a long string of dog syllables that have an almost human cadence. She's got me. Jerry knows it. And when he opens the door, Shadow peers in at me and gives me a little *hmph* — like *is-this-the-best-hide-you've-got in you?* It is.

I take Shadow's apparent condescension as a challenge. For the next dog, I decide to lie between the fire mattresses in the same closet. They are heavier than I might have guessed, and little air gets through. It doesn't take long to break a sweat lying there, and I hope this isn't one of the brand-new dogs — then I realize: I have the brand-new dog, and she's out there and I'm in here. I hear the distant "Find!" and the sound of a dog on the move, and so I lie still, wondering how sweat adds to the overall composition of my scent. I can smell me, and I am not impressed, but I wonder if the coming dog notes only the chemical change: *Susannah freshly glazed with fresh water, salt, glucose, ammonia, and lactic acid. Oh, and she's lying on mattresses that have had fifty-six — no, fifty-seven — other humans on them. Two of them wore Old Spice.*

The coming dog is Misty, the Collie who moves through the large room like a thoroughbred on light feet. I can hear her steady gait quicken, then a pause as she picks her way through a series of ladders lying flat. At the door of the closet, I hear her breathing change from a pant to the rounder *huff, huff, huff* of a dog drawing scent into the cavern of her muzzle. She paws at the closet door, scratching and huffing with excited certainty. I hear a single little squeak. When her handler, Fleta, opens the door, Misty makes short work of finding me between the mattresses in the dark. I am a lovely, living human sandwich lying there. She is a tall, beautiful dog with a long nose, and she snakes between the mattresses to give me a joyful kiss on the mouth.

Months later, the sun is merciless on us one morning as the dog teams work scenarios involving debris, damaged cars, and the "burn building" — a concrete, one-story house routinely filled with wood and hay and set ablaze for training firefighters to put out. Today is more like summer than spring, and the burn building is stifling. A recent training burn has left it sooty and rich with the scent of charred wood, and with the iron windows latched closed, the structure has little air movement, making it harder to search. My eyes tear immediately when we enter. I imagine Puzzle's overwhelmed nose. Is an environment like this the olfactory equivalent of eighth-row center at a Metallica concert?

We need to work quickly too. We have volunteers sweltering in there, despite their gel-filled "cool down" neckerchiefs. The burn building is no place to be slow. Handlers and victims come out from that hot space bathed in sweat; the dogs make their finds and dash free of it as though their tails were afire. I have a bandanna tied around my forehead, but its cool is long gone. Perspiration has soaked through it and run into my eyes. On our last search in the burn building, I have to follow the vague, light swoosh of Puzzle's tail out of the darkness, the sweat having literally blinded me in the short time it took to clear six rooms and extricate a single victim.

We sit in rehab for twenty minutes, drinking water. I swab Puzzle's paws with cooling alcohol, then wipe my face and put on a new kerchief for the next round of searches. Puzzle lies in the shade of the fire hose rack and lifts her nose as the other dogs and handlers work across the various scenarios. Hard work today, but she twitches each time she hears the word "Find!" the command and its response now a reflex of muscle memory.

The heat from the debris pile radiates so powerfully that my face stings as we work it. I wonder about the dogs' paws as they scramble over its jagged, tumbled surfaces, but they give no sign of discomfort. Puzzle loves working debris, and she watches as the certified dogs circle the pile thoughtfully, choosing the tidiest way to a find, or dash across it with the precision of a tennis pro's return volley. A youngster still, she searches debris with a technique somewhere between the two — a mad gallop around the pile to what seems to be the best point of scent for her, then a happy scramble across its surfaces. She is still a little small and clumsy. Some leaps onto rubble require a second or third effort. Some finds must be achieved a different way. We work several debris searches, then stand down to rehab again, crossing the long stretch of green grass toward a shady area with more water and, for Puzzle, a couple of pieces of watermelon, a favorite post-search refreshment in the heat. The watermelon is no longer cold or even cool, but the deep pink chunks are sweet, and after a bite or two, we both feel energy begin to return.

Border Collie Hoss isn't feeling well today. He sits in the deep shadow of the ladder tower, watching the team work. He's alert, but his expression is tired and there is a sense about him of overall malaise. Hoss is a hard-working dog and compulsive about it too. He has worked a couple of searches at the training site, but Terry has noticed he's "off" and knowing that Hoss will rarely stand himself down, Terry has decided to let him rest for the remainder of the session in the shade in the back of the truck. His dog is obedient, but from his tucked posture and watchfulness across the training field, it's clear Hoss is at odds with himself. He feels sick but still wants to search. The truck is a good vantage for this boy who misses little. Over the course of the morning, he watches the FAS team rigging extrication systems and supervises the dog-and-handler teams working at a distance.

Hoss has always been kind to Puzzle. The few times she has been too obnoxious, hop-hopping at his side or pawing at his muzzle, Hoss has simply put a weighty paw over her shoulders and pressed her down to the ground in a decisive statement of authority. She's learned to accept this correction at the moment it is made, though

I sometimes wonder if the lesson will ever carry and if she will, in time, stop all the puppy stuff that requires dog-to-dog discipline in the first place.

Today she is a little bewildered that he's five feet above her. Trotting idly away from the rehab area, Puzzle stands beneath the truck and looks up to Hoss as he looks down at her. At the sight of him, she play bows in petition for a game, then stands looking at him bemusedly, apparently aware that he cannot come down from the truck to play, no matter how much both of them might like to. I watch the two dogs study each other.

Then Hoss disappears for a moment inside the truck, returning quickly with his ball in his mouth. He puts his head over the side, gazes at Puzzle briefly, and with a flip of his muzzle, drops the ball, where it bounces across the parking lot. Puz is off like a shot to fetch it, bringing it back to the truck and, on command, releasing the ball to me. I hand it to Hoss, who tosses the ball again for Puzzle to fetch. I can't quite believe what I'm seeing, and the three of us collaborate on the game for a few rounds before I call in a low voice to Terry, and say, "Don't move, but look at this." Terry stands still and watches his dog throw the ball for my pup, who brings it back for Hoss to throw again. "I'll . . . be . . . damned," Terry says, and signals to a couple of teammates to watch the game in progress.

Hoss and Puzzle are inexhaustible. Over and over, Hoss throws the ball from the bed of the truck, Puzzle brings it back and hands it to me. I give it to Hoss, who throws it again. Hoss has always been a ball dog, but he has always been the one on the receiving end of the throw. He has also always been a smart dog and, clearly analytic, he recognizes now that though he's in no position to fetch, he can still play ball just fine, thank you very much. Puzzle is glad to play with Hoss. If she didn't have so great a stretch to reach him, I get the sense that neither of them would need me there at all.

Perhaps every team has its smart dog stories. I've heard plenty of them and witnessed a few. These high-drive dogs, given a job very young, quickly learn they are valued for the ability to interpret a situation and make a decision about it. They use these skills in the field, but they are equally likely to use them off-duty. Underestimate a search dog at your peril.

Shadow has never been fond of leads. Her loyalty to Jerry and her confidence combine to suggest that she's going to stay near him wherever he needs her to be, but no way does she need to be tied to the man. In fact, she intensely resents it. She's a pack-oriented creature with her own agenda, who accepts being tied with limited patience. During the years of her training, when she was learning to work on a long, braided length of webbing, she systematically chewed through it a handful of times when left to her own devices. Jerry patiently spliced and knotted the lead each time, which gave it a beaded appearance from a distance.

One cool Saturday morning at the fire academy, the handlers all temporarily tied their dogs to the A-frame, a rooflike structure designed to teach firefighters how to chop and vent a house fire. The handlers left their dogs sitting happily in shady grass, heading inside the academy for a quick class before returning to scenario training again. About halfway through the class, a security guard knocked on the classroom door, asking the group "if they knew the dogs were outside and wanting to come in." He gestured over his shoulder, pointing to the building door. The handlers left what they were doing and saw five dogs with faces pressed to the glass. All of them dragged the remains of tattered webbing. The security guard reported that Shadow had been the first to chew through her lead, and then she moved from dog to dog apparently instructing or assisting them as they chewed through their own. When all were free, they moved as a pack to the door of the building, where they stood now. Some were grinning and wagging. Shadow's expression was conversely haughty: *we do not take kindly to being left outside, thank you*. When Jerry walked out the door, she gave him an earful in fully articulated Husky. An "equal-opportunity release artist," some of the team old-timers call Shadow. And they never leave her alone with a dog secured on a lead.

Hoss the Border Collie is another famous opportunist. One summer day during the debriefing after a search, Hoss, who had been beside his handler, suddenly disappeared. It was not like him to stray or to leave Terry for any extended length of time. When the group noticed he was missing, the dog had completely vanished: he was not with the search dogs, not with the other handlers, not with any of the law enforcement officers he might have schmoozed to throw a ball.

The search had generated a crowd of bystanders, and some grew concerned that perhaps Hoss had been dog-napped. There had been precedents; high-profile search dogs sometimes attract unwanted attention. And Hoss is a friendly, sociable boy, trained to walk on a lead beside strangers in emergency situations. He would not have snapped at someone who led him away. The search for him grew tense and hurried before someone noticed that one of the handlers, whose car was running in order to cool her own dog in the back of the vehicle, had left its front door slightly ajar. It had been ajar before too, when Hoss had prized the door open with a paw and leapt inside to stretch out across a seat, his belly positioned to the air conditioning vents. He pirated a candy bar and relaxed. When discovered, Hoss seemed oblivious to the worry he'd caused, a smart dog unto himself who saw an opportunity for comfort while his people rushed around in the 100-degree heat, waving their hands and yapping.

12

THE FAMILY STORY

EVEN JUST STANDING on the front lawn before we head out to sectors, it's difficult to find the missing woman at the center of this family argument. Her daughter Nora says Miss Celeste has always loved leaving. Nora's voice makes a hard little wobble when she raises it to talk over her father, who tells us all there's an open jar of peanut butter in the kitchen, and she struggles to be heard over two neighbors debating the year Miss Celeste moved into her daughter's house. Nora's so tired it appears the gray skin of her face hangs from the bones. She left work early, has been out looking for her mother all day, and now it is dusk going dark, and she is discouraged, frightened, and, she admits this, shot through with anger toward the living ghost of her mother that has no place to rest. Nora cannot blame her father, who is also frail and worried about the peanut butter and thought he'd locked the door. She cannot blame her thirteen-year-old son, who was already at school when his grandmother took it into her head to go. ("I didn't do it!" says the boy to anyone who will listen, "I didn't let her out.") Miss Celeste's daughter is afraid that in the heat of the afternoon, her disoriented mother dropped down dead in some space she couldn't get out of, lost in the tangle of old memory and new neighborhood and lacking all sense of time or orientation to save herself. Miss Celeste was diagnosed with Alzheimer's disease four years ago.

She is five foot two, 115 pounds, and only a little arthritic, a former dancer (a Rockette we hear from one bystander, a Vegas showgirl, says another). She still carries herself well: shoulders back, a slight turnout remaining in her walk. Salt-and-pepper hair she sets in rollers nightly — the same style she has worn for years. She knows her name, and though she could not recall meeting you an hour ago, she will recount the full detail of a trying day forty years before, when she had to leave a dress rehearsal because her first-grade daughter had forgotten her lunch and could not be consoled. Miss Celeste had boarded two buses wearing spangles and tights. It's the famous family story. Nora has heard it all her life. She repeats it to us, repeats that she's tired as a sort of apology. It's ironic, she says, that now she's the one leaving work to chase her mother down. Nora has produced photographs and a plastic bag with a nightgown folded inside it: a scent article for the dogs, the only thing of Celeste's not straight out of the wash.

A pair of house painters across the street told the police they saw Miss Celeste go, and they wondered a little about the elderly woman out alone on a hot day in her long coat — but they didn't wonder enough to approach her or call for help. Just a little after ten this morning, she went right down the sidewalk in her dress and coat and Mary Jane walking shoes, carrying a purse and brown paper bag in her hand. She went east around the curve of the sidewalk and from there, both witnesses say, passed right out of view.

Two dogs have already scented the nightgown and have gone out with their partners to confirm Celeste's direction of travel. Once we have word from them, search management will assign sectors for each dog team. We double-check our gear for extra water and first aid supplies relevant to Celeste's possible falls, dehydration, and hyperthermia.

Neighbors and family circulate among us, a crowd of twenty or more. One brings a stack of paper cups, a campsite Thermos of lemonade and coffee in a carafe. There are a lot of what-ifs and if-onlys said to one another and to us — *If only I had mowed the lawn today instead of yesterday, I would have seen her. If only she'd gone the other way, she would have passed right by me reading the paper on the porch. Normally I'm in the front room that time of the morning, but this time I was on the phone* . . . You hear sometimes about bystanders co-opting a family's emergency, wanting to share the drama, but there's a sense among these neighbors of failed responsibility. They replay the morning as though they could intervene and stop Miss Celeste before she disappeared.

The group on the lawn parts suddenly, like little fish scattering in advance of a big one. Daughter Nora steers her father aside by the elbow. Celeste's twin sister, Aunt Charm, has arrived to assist the family crisis. She looks like Celeste caught in the soft bend of a funhouse mirror. Her first words to me are about herself: she has Bell's palsy, contracted years ago when she put her face too long against the cold of an airplane window. Aunt Charm is a psychic with a husky tenor voice who graduated from a table in New Orleans's Jackson Square to more private consultations in a velvet- and sequin-draped room not far from Bourbon Street. And from there she had retired. *Retired well,* she tells me, there apparently being a good living in clairvoyance. She has charisma despite the comedy/tragedy conflict in the muscles of her face. Her glasses droop on the affected side, giving her a somewhat rakish expression, and her voice suggests both a smoking habit and a wise connection to unseen things. At the precise moment Celeste went missing, Aunt Charm says she felt her go — a little rift in the soul while she stood in the shower. As she bowed her head to rinse her hair, she felt Celeste too slipping quietly down a long, dark hole.

That doesn't sound so good to me, but Aunt Charm seems unworried by the image.

Celeste is always looking to escape, she says, present tense.

Even before she got sick, she was never really with us, explains Nora, as though she lost her mother long before this morning.

Aunt Charm adds an insight about her sister: Celeste will never speak in a voice above a whisper, if she speaks at all, and when she walks, she bends forward and rocks slightly on the balls of her feet as though to tiptoe. *Bullshit,* mutters Nora about the whispering, which Aunt Charm ignores. Aunt Charm describes their troubled childhood bound to a shattered father who never recovered from his experiences as a prisoner of war. He had refused to buy a television, had ripped the phone free of the wall. All their play had been some variation of the Quiet Game. She says it made his daughters good and sneaky.

Nora tells us that the elderly Celeste has wandered before, returned home by the mailman once, by the neighbors twice more. She came home each time flushed and unhappy, unable to describe her plans but clearly frustrated by the interference of others — and eyeing the door for next time.

I have heard Miss Celeste's description repeated so often that as we take additional information from the briefing, I seem to see her at the edge of every shadow. I've read of searches where the vague lost person stood among her rescuers unnoticed, and though Celeste isn't here, I see her standing in the yard nonetheless, considering, turning left as she headed from the house this morning. An estimated 80 percent of people who still retain directional skills will turn right when they are lost, but the Alzheimer's patient does not, necessarily. Celeste's condition has rapidly deteriorated. She has no more directional skills, no more right and left, even, no spatial orientation, no ability to recognize landmarks she has passed. She is all urge to go, but Celeste does not know she's lost.

Would she have taken help from someone she didn't know? Her daughter and Aunt Charm deliberate. Nora says yes. Celeste's sister closes her eyes and says no. Aunt Charm's voice has acquired a shortness, an edge, as though she senses old skepticism about her psychic gifts. The two of them spar a little at the edge of an argument. Forestalling an unspoken "prove it," Aunt Charm says Celeste gleams like a lost thing at the bottom of a drain. Nora pushes her lips forward and looks away.

The first two search dogs have confirmed Celeste's direction of travel. She's been gone more than nine hours, and while a strong woman her age could have walked one to two miles per hour and made some serious distance in that time, heat and Celeste's condition make it likely that if she had remained afoot, she'd be found closer to home. It's time for us to head out to the most immediate sectors. We wear gloves as we handle the plastic bag with her nightgown, and we do not touch it at all, but the dogs do, their curious noses snuffling over the cloth for a moment, memorizing her signature scent before they turn away.

"Find *that*," say four handlers to their dogs. Collie, German Shepherd, and two Labs spring forward in their separate directions, and the sector searching has begun. We hear a scatter of applause from the crowd on the lawn — the kindly, spirited presence of the dogs always injects a little hope. The windless air is thick with mosquitoes. As I jog away behind Johnny and Buster in the twilight, I can still hear Nora and Aunt Charm proving to each other which one knew the missing woman best.

We move quickly along the streets of our sector, dog, handler, field assistant, and a young police officer beside us who has never worked beside a search dog before. We are urgent with the sense of lost time and the extreme vulnerability of an Alzheimer's patient who may have gone all day without water. We look to Buster for some sign that he's caught any scent of Miss Celeste. We call her name hoping that she might call back to us. (*Yes she would*, says her daughter. *No*, says her sister, *but she might wave a little*.)

Miss Celeste seems to wander with intent, sometimes called "goal-directed" wandering, but she has also demonstrated the aimless path-following, or "critical wandering," that caused her to once get stuck in the tight space between a neighbor's garage and fence line. Today she could have begun with an agenda in mind and then lost it, following a travel aid — a sidewalk, road, or path through the grass worn flat by passing schoolchildren — until unable to go farther and unable to turn around and go back. In such cases, a search dog is an invaluable asset, charged only to find her scent without the constraints of human logic. And Alzheimer's wanderers often operate outside the margins. Any space a human searcher might reject is a possible find space to a search dog. If Miss Celeste lies huddled behind a row of garbage cans or is squeezed in the crawlspace beneath a playground slide or has stumbled from a park path into a ravine, the dogs will find her.

Intent. The coat, the purse, the brown paper bag all speak to me that Celeste had some kind of plan, at least for the first few steps down the sidewalk, but it's anyone's guess. I think of my own neighbor of twenty years ago, a neighbor who, at ninety-one, would sometimes walk out of her house in her good dress, pearls, and apron — dressed as though she were hosting a church social — and begin to rake the gravel in the alley behind us. She would rake with great determination deep along the alley, sometimes for blocks, until her son would drive down it and pick her up to bring her home, happy to have done so thorough a job all day.

We press on, moving fast, dripping muck sweat and attracting a lot of attention. Doors open and residents lean out to openly watch us. Others pretend not to watch us while they do something else. Some locals trot forward to ask if we're looking for the "lady they saw on the news." *We are*, we say at a jog while they move along the fence line in pace with us, *and have you seen her?* They have not. They promise to keep their eyes open.

At one point, I turn around and see an assortment of children following us half a block behind, their eyes locked on Buster, waiting for whatever magical thing it might be that a search dog will do. And Buster looks magical. It's dark now, and to the delight of the children we have clicked on our hazard lights: lights on us, lights on the dog. Some pulse red, others flash an alternating blue and white, some glow neon green. "Don't shoot me lights," I call them. They are meant to caution passing drivers, but I wonder how a frightened, lost woman might view us at night, glowing and blinking and descending upon her like aliens.

Miss Celeste's story has been well broadcast, and the farther we get from her home, the more neighborhood energy seems to shift from personal loss to a general excitement. *Celeste,* we call. *It's time to go home now.* Down the street the children's treble echo: *Celeste. Celeste. Celeste.*

We hear no answering call — and with every cry, Celeste seems a little more lost.

It's a busy night at the neighborhood park. There's a game going in the softball diamond, a pack of young men thumping and scudding across the basketball court, families in the brightly lit playground area, a party of some kind at the pavilion end of the green. The park is part of our sector, and Buster diligently sweeps across it in broad, generous strokes. He is uninterested in the hundreds of human scents available to him here, new scent, older, and oldest, his head up and down as he works the air for any trace of Miss Celeste. Buster works his way across the park, all concentration, and perhaps it's because of the crowd or perhaps it's because we are intent on his focus among all these people, but none of us quickly sees the charge of a large, off-leash dog who barrels through the crowd, teeth bared for Buster. He's a young, strong mixed-breed, and he clearly means business, but as he springs Johnny reflexively falls over his dog to protect him and grabs the attacking dog in midair, flipping him onto his back on the turf as though he were roping a calf. The dog makes a startled *huh?* sound and goes immediately passive where he lands, regressing to almost a puppyish wiggle beneath the flat of Johnny's hand on his belly. Muscular Buster, who in other contexts might have taken on the attacker, has stayed put where Johnny pushed him.

"*Shiiiit,*" says the officer, who finds his voice first.

I'm silent, still a little stunned — and feeling guilty because identifying hazards for the dog team is my job, and I didn't see this one in time.

A middle-aged man in running gear emerges from the shadows, his movement a little cramped, a little crablike, like he's not sure whether he wants to own up to this or not. There's a lot going on in his face. He doesn't have a leash, but it is his dog inverted in the grass, and there's a police officer with us who may or may not write a citation about the incident.

"Sorry," he murmurs, as he takes his now-simpering dog by the collar. The dog has his tail between his legs, his mouth also open in an apologetic grin.

"Better get control of your dog, sir," says the officer.

Man and dog slink off together.

"That was . . . that was . . . *something*, Johnny," I say, inadequate, in my mind years away from having that kind of confidence with a dog.

Johnny stands up, Buster rises and gives himself a little shake, and we are back to work.

By midnight, we have all gone out to multiple sectors. The closest have been cleared, farther ones have been searched, and the dogs have demonstrated interest in only two areas. Buster paused in the doorway of a local school building, and a few blocks away three of the dogs in blind verification all exhibited significant interest near a bus stop beside a busy road. Nothing across the street. Nothing at the nearby convenience store. The police ask us if this abrupt loss of scent indicates the woman got on a bus, and Fleta tells them that any number of factors could cause scent to disperse on a busy road. That she got on a bus is certainly possible. But there has also been foot traffic, car traffic, radiant heat, the day's earlier wind. It would be great to be able to say that when scent stops beside a road it's certain a missing person left by vehicle, but we cannot claim that absolute. The dogs jointly indicate that Miss Celeste was here. What we also know is that from this point, the dogs have nothing else.

Operating across several scenarios, the police will pursue the bus possibility further, while search management has developed sectors even farther from the neighborhood, including target areas where local buses might stop en route. We're about to go out again.

"How long will you search?" asks an officer.

"Until you tell us to stand down," says Fleta. "We're prepared to search as long as you need us."

The crowd too is steadfast. The gathering at the house has diminished only slightly. Neighbors sit in the grass or on the edge of raised flowerbeds. Nora stands alone beside her mailbox, head bowed, her arms folded across her stomach as though it hurts. I can hear the rasp of Aunt Charm in the huddle somewhere. Miss Celeste's husband is nowhere in sight. A few neighbors come forward toward the dogs, asking to pet them or to help them in some other way, wanting news. Bottles of water are poured into dog bowls, pressed into our hands. One nice fellow tells us he's hidden a pizza just for the dog team in his car.

"She's dead, isn't she?" I hear Nora say to a policeman. She has said it to several neighbors, to a couple of us, less a question as time passes and more like a truth she needs to acknowledge. The late hour and the dogs' return have discouraged her.

"Ma'am . . ." he says, shaking his head, then stops when another officer runs up to him, murmuring something. They walk away together, then come back with quick steps, not quite a run. "We've got her," he says quietly to Nora, who is now supported by friends who've rushed forward, but the words and his changed, relieved posture snap the news across the lawn. The crowd converges where they stand.

"Alive," I hear Nora say to the friends who are holding her.

"Of *course* she is," says Aunt Charm. She says it to those standing nearest, but loud enough to give Nora a little smack.

Alive, but in what condition? Even the authorities aren't sure, but they do know she's coming here.

It takes half an hour for a police car to arrive, and Miss Celeste has an audience when she is handed carefully from the vehicle into the headlight beam of a waiting ambulance. The dogs' heads instantly come up, and their tails wag. They do not have to be told. This is their person. Oh, definitely their person. She does not appear to see them, but they strain where they stand, wuffling pleasurably. Handlers exchange glances. Miss Celeste is too frail for a meeting, and the dogs remain where they are. Their partners bend quietly to them and praise. "Good *that*," they say, crackling open sleeves of beef jerky. "Good dog!"

Word travels fast: Miss Celeste had indeed caught a bus to a shopping center miles away. From there the driver had reported her disorientation and continued on. But before the bus dispatcher could communicate a description and location to police, she had vanished again. Further details are fuzzy. There had been at least one, possibly two car trips afterward. A Samaritan finally left her where he thought she wanted to go: an elementary school in an adjoining suburb. The police of that town found Miss Celeste lying on a stone bench in the doorway, wearing her coat, purse at her side, clutching a sack lunch — a peanut butter sandwich and apple juice. Now she appears pale and bewildered, but she is smiling a little as she stands in the light, nodding politely to the surround of loving strangers.

"Goddamnit, Mom," says Nora, like a tenderness. She throws her arms around her translucent mother and weeps, rocking her, one hand covering her eyes, the other clutching the brown paper bag.

13

THE SEARCH YOU'RE CALLED OUT TO

DOG TEAMS ARE RARELY the first emergency response resource on the scene. For us, most pips of the pager represent a chronology — someone has been determined missing, caregivers, family, and friends may have searched first, perhaps for hours, before calling 911. Police or firefighters (or both) arrive and make the search an official incident and, having deployed according to their own procedures and having not located the victim, call additional resources if available: air support, ground-walking search teams, and dog units. This chronology may seem agonizingly slow to anxious families (and to dog teams themselves — fresh scent is always better), but many searches result in possible crime scenes that should be overseen by law enforcement before additional resources could contaminate the environment.

Many of our team's calls occur late in the evening — some for immediate deployment, others (particularly when the victim is believed deceased) for early morning deployment the following day. The pip and its text message are cryptic, with little information beyond the nature of the victim — missing toddler, Alzheimer's walk-away, suspected drowning — and the search location. When the pager goes off, we respond immediately to the team manager if able to search.

Because these calls frequently come late at night, a first priority is to have a pager with a sound so distinctive it's likely to wake us. Salespersons are never quite sure what to make of me every time I buy a new cell phone (several of mine have come to grief in the water on searches). My priorities are odd. I need a phone large enough to hang on to, ideally with an available rubber cover — Day-Glo orange would be a plus — and I'll always trade sleek and pretty for solid and sturdy. But I also spend a lot of time reviewing each prospective new phone's standard ringtones, annoying other customers by repeatedly beta-testing an electronic version of *The 1812 Overture* at max volume next to my head as I lean over a counter, feigning sleep.

Would that wake me up? I wonder, and move on to the next phone, which lacks *The 1812 Overture* but may have the advantage of a particularly discordant *Beethoven's Fifth. Dit-dit-dit-BLAAAAT!*

My current phone is set to a pager ringtone that while melodious, goes on a long, long, long time, then follows with a nagging pip every few minutes if you fail to acknowledge the text. Though Puzzle is unmoved, something in this pager's electronic song rouses and infuriates the Poms, who bark as it plays. And plays. And plays. If the song doesn't wake me, the little dogs certainly will. Bonus!

The pager supercharges all activities that follow. When I was first qualified to go on searches, I made the mistake of preparing to deploy in tidy stages. It was an organized process, like an aircraft checklist, but too slow, and without a dog I still took twenty minutes or so to get out of the house, assuming I started off in pajamas and half-asleep. ("What's your best bare-ass to haul-ass time?" a colleague on another team once asked me. His own best time was astonishing, though his teammate did confide that the guy showed up to one search with his shirt on backward and Scooby-Doo boxers showing out of his unbuttoned trousers.)

In those early days, I was eager to better my time out of the house. Eventually I learned that I could call in my response to the team manager at the same time I put on my uniform, an exercise of balance and coherence. I would shimmy into the T-shirt with the phone in my left hand, then speed dial while I balanced on first one leg, then the other, pulling on my pants with the phone cradled beneath my chin. Lean against the bed, still cradling the phone with my jaw, pull on, lace, and strap down boots. By the time I had the boots on, the call had rung through and I'd have hands free to copy more specific instructions not available on the text message. This call-and-dress method has served me well in following years, as long as my foot doesn't somehow get caught in the pants. The unbalanced fall, the hot language, the dropped phone easily adds another two minutes to my departure.

Hair in a ball cap, glasses on, and I'm ready to load a little cooler with ice, water, and a couple of breakfast bars in case the search gets long. My gear is already in the car trunk — I never take it out except to repack or restock.

This all assumes a call-out in warm weather. Winter calls, with their necessary thick socks and long johns and turtlenecks and long-sleeved T's — and Thermos of hot cocoa for the rehab period — add time. But I keep my search clothes ready in one place. The cocoa and the Thermos are in the same cabinet, the electric kettle just three steps away. My best clock out of the house, sans dog, is eleven minutes — curiously, a winter search with the added clothing. Worst (a fall in tangled pants, failed speed dial, misplaced car keys) is about twenty-eight minutes, which may not seem too bad until you realize that most calls are to a location involving at least a half-hour drive at civilian speeds — we have no lights and sirens — and a slow departure plus drive-time means that you don't get in the search field for an hour or more. If the missing person is presumed alive and weather conditions or his own health is precarious, that hour comes at a price. Regretting the Keystone Kops quality of some of my late-night departures, I trade notes with teammates and try to learn from their strategies — particularly the dog handlers, who have to not only get themselves out the door, but also get their dog and the dog's fresh supplies out too.

Some of the dogs help at this, and some hinder. Max and Fleta's partners Mercy and Misty react immediately to the sound of the pager and the putting on of uniforms, blocking the door to prevent Fleta and Max from leaving without them. Jerry's Shadow gives him room to maneuver, but he notes that she pays attention to his changed movements. When she's on the way to training, she lies quietly in the back of the SUV, but while on her way to searches, Shadow senses Jerry's different energy; she hangs her head over the seat at his shoulder, as if scrutinizing the route, as if to ask, "Are we there yet?"

We are sure the dogs know the sound of the pager and antici-pate what's coming next.

The Poms have learned that the pager's long chime means I'm going to be moving through the house very fast. Excitable Whisky likes to stand in the hallway and bark *Wow!* every time I pass through a doorway, which feels like my own private cheering sec-tion. The other dogs tend to stand off to the side silently, watching my back and forth like polite observers at a tennis match. Not yet certified to deploy, in the early days Puzzle also watched from the back of the couch, then would cheerfully move to her crate when I gave her the "House, house, house!" command, curling up in it and waiting for her peanut butter Kong. But she has since learned that the pager means search gear she recognizes, gear I frequently wear at training, and as she approaches certification, I see her expres-sion change when I gear up and do not ask her if she's ready to go to work. She's made the connection. Sometimes, Puzzle gives me a baleful look as I gesture her into the crate, turning her nose up at the Kong. Sometimes, she gives me the look, adds a mutter, and then flops down in the crate with an elaborate sigh, turning her back my direction. *Go ahead,* her sullen posture suggests. *Search without me. And good luck with that.*

The road to a search has its own surprises. A fair percentage of the time we begin the drive out and the pager pips again, indicating the missing person has been found — a turnaround/stand-down page — which is universally good news but can do strange things to your biochemistry, the earlier flush of adrenaline now with no place to go but home. On one pair of back-to-back searches, I got to exactly the same place on the freeway when I heard the pip of the turnaround page. Two night calls. A turnaround page at exactly the same place on the freeway. What are the odds? I drove home calculating whether this might influence the likelihood of my getting struck by lightning or winning the lottery. So far, neither has happened.

I've never known a colleague to grumble about the interruption of a callout followed by a subsequent stand-down page, but we trade a few stories afterward. Without the hard activity of a search, blazing out the door only to return minutes later can take a bit to unwind. One colleague plays solitaire on the computer. Another watches *Fresh Prince* reruns in the small hours. I sometimes weed the rose garden at two in the morning beneath the light of a security lamp hanging off the garage. There's a strange Proustian moment of connection every time I prune back the mint growing among the roses. I now associate the dark, fresh scent of crushed chocolate mint with the good word that a toddler missing from a lakeside home — feared abducted, feared strayed, feared drowned — had been found asleep in her parents' laundry hamper before we got there. Two years have passed since that callout, but I think of that little girl every time I pinch mint for iced tea. She would be four now, or five, and I wonder if her nap in the basket has turned into the kind of family story that will be told on holidays, told to her fiancé and eventually to her children, just as she remains a figure on our side of the narrative — as a late-night call, a missing child in winter, an early find — *alive* — and a universal reprieve.

Some morning deployments tell a different story, particularly on weekday mornings, when a close search location can still take an hour or more to reach. One drowning call on a lake across the Metroplex was challenging enough to reach as depicted by map, the route served by a spider web of freeways that tapered off to county roads that fed to undeveloped residential streets that wound down to gravel paths and a boat ramp. Teammates were heading in from all directions (not one of us lived close to the search site), and on that particular winter morning every major freeway had a problem of one kind or another, from overturned eighteen-wheelers to burning cars to spilled green stuff from a produce truck made slick as it was overrun by traffic. Most of us left home before 7:00 A.M. for a 9:00 A.M. deployment. But by 8:45, we were all immobile and scattered wide across the two cities, unable to contact the officer leading the search, who was probably already on-site, and whose cell phone seemed to be out of range. Crazy-making conditions, but as I crept over the glaze of smashed tomatoes that had caused a few cars to spin out and into each other, I was grateful this was a recovery call for someone long deceased rather than a call for another strayed child or missing elderly patient, where every minute lost to traffic was potentially fatal.

Sometimes we have a little help getting there. Several years ago, a traffic jam on the major artery leading to the site of a search for a missing second-grader threatened to slow our arrival by an hour or more. Somehow local police got word and intervened, leading three cars of us out of the congestion via the shoulder of the freeway, one police car ahead of us and one behind as we drove in trail, passing a mile or more of motionless vehicles. So many frustrated drivers shot the bird at us as we passed that my memory of that drive bristles, as though the long row of cars had quills.

The dogs in general seem to handle the journey better than we do, perhaps because they're free of the deeper implications of each call. But no mistake, they are intensely aware of the job they are heading to. Some dogs take the travel a little harder than others, the adrenaline rushing straight to their digestive systems, resulting in nausea or diarrhea, or both, conditions they seem to shake off once on-site.

A handler acquaintance from another team once told me the story of his first dog, a chocolate-kiss-colored Lab, who would lie quietly in his crate on the way to training, but behaved differently on his way to searches, where he would stand in his crate and nuzzle the catch that latched the door shut — repetitively, rhythmically, *bang-bang-bang* — so much so that sometimes he emerged from his crate with the skin of his muzzle rubbed bare and bloody. By the time he retired, the old Lab, a veteran of many searches, had a callous on his nose. *How did he know?* the handler still wonders. *Why did he only bang the crate on callouts?* The gear was the same, the crate was the same, the car was the same. The only difference was the beep of the handler's cell phone and his own hasty motions to get them out the door. And of course, we both hazard, the changed scent from a human who just got a biochemical jumpstart in the middle of the night.

Some searches are short. We've had a handful of them in the history of our team. Jerry, first to arrive on a morning search for a missing adolescent believed suicidal, was briefed on the boy's description, the chronology of his previous actions and his current disappearance, and the cryptic messages the boy left across the sidewalk, words that could be variously interpreted as a suicide note or an homage to a popular rap song of the day.

"Did you . . ." Jerry asked the officers carefully, "check the girlfriend's house?"

Head shakes all around, and while the rest of us were en route, an officer found the boy at his girlfriend's house, where he'd been all night. The remaining dogs arrived just as the team was being stood down, a dogless search with a happy ending.

Another search for an Alzheimer's patient who'd been missing more than half a day had an ugly prospect. Fleta, Jerry, and

Shadow arrived at the facility where the elderly woman had gone missing. After the initial interview, they went upstairs to scent Shadow on the woman's bed and clothes, hoping to determine the woman's direction of travel. Jerry and Shadow went ahead, and Fleta remained behind to get a more portable scent article for the other coming dogs. While in the elevator returning to the ground floor, she heard Jerry say over the radio that they had the victim. Shadow had gone from the room, down the hall, out the front door and had found the woman less than thirty feet away from the facility entrance, lying wedged beneath a stiff row of bushes. Alive, just stuck. No broken twigs or disturbed leaves marked her presence, and the calling officer said he'd personally passed the hedge where she lay a number of times. Total time on the search from start to finish: less than ten minutes.

Some searches are just weird. An urgent out-of-state call to a remote location was the proposed scene of a homicide. The bones of what appeared to be a human foot had been found by hikers, and local authorities called in dog teams to find the disarticulated bones of the rest of the body. After a long journey to the location, the team arrived at a small area cordoned off with crime-scene tape. But on-site, none of the dogs indicated any interest in the foot, and none of the dogs seemed to find anything amiss in the deeper wood.

"Something wrong with your dogs?" drawled an officer testily, to which a handler responded, "I think something may be wrong with that foot." It was a potentially tense *oh-yeah-sez-who?* moment, but not long afterward, a forensic team arrived and quickly assessed the bones as bear, not human. A small bear, an adolescent bear, perhaps, with bones remarkably similar in construction to a human foot. *Understandable,* they assured the law enforcement agency that had called for search dogs. *These things happen all the time.*

A few officers graciously hid for the dogs, giving them a motivational find as a reward at the end of their long journey. Afterward, as the team loaded into cars for the long drive home, the calling agency deconstructed the cordoned area and opened it back up to hikers, a quiet aftermath save for the *pup-pup-pup* of the crime-scene tape as they tore it free.

People sometimes ask what kind of search we do most frequently. It's a question I've asked other teams myself — curious about the intersection of geography, calling authorities, population, and need. Some of their responses are what you'd expect. Teams located near the edges of national parks or major ski areas may do a lot of searches for lost hikers or strayed children in the woods, while those serving areas popular for water recreation — boating, fishing, swimming — may have a high percentage of drowning calls. Some responses were harder to predict. Two Californians from the San Francisco area once told me the majority of their recent winter calls had been for Alzheimer's walk-aways, while another handler from a picturesque town on the East Coast said he and his dog were most often called to suspected crime scenes in the thirty-mile stretch of woodland that separated his little town from the next.

Because our team is based in an urban area surrounded by wide stretches of ranchland and prairie and peppered with popular lakes, our calls come in for any number of reasons. Though there are exceptions, we typically work more drownings in late spring and summer, walk aways in the autumn and winter, despondent potential suicides after the turn of the New Year — and of course sit standby or deploy during tornado season and during the hurricane months summer through autumn. Weather causes many of our searches, and every changing season reminds us of the coming needs of the next one.

And still we get surprises.

Years ago, Max and Fleta deployed with Hunter and Saber to south Texas after a long period of hard rain and extensive flooding. Damage was widespread, and lives were known lost. Many residents were still missing. Served by the SAR dogs of a state task force, the search area seemed unending nonetheless. Max, Fleta, Hunter, and Saber worked for days across flattened, mud-bound farms and small towns.

One day's search required a helicopter transport. The waterline had risen far upland and roads were so completely impassable that the only way to get to the search site was by air. Handlers, dogs, and support personnel deployed to the top of a rise, their search sector an extensive area of flood debris field below.

As they prepared to begin their formal search, Fleta's Saber pulled away from the group and bounded uphill to a scruffy area of low mesquite trees. He pushed his way through the surrounding brush to a spot just beneath one young tree and began worrying at the dirt, pawing at it urgently. Though this was not the direction of the sector and she had never seen Saber behave this way on previous searches, Fleta knew from his intensity that something was up. She crawled awkwardly into the thicket after him, talking to the dog, looking for recognizable signals from him as he pawed the thick, heavy ground beneath the tree. The accompanying officer asked what was going on; Fleta could only answer that she wasn't sure, but that Saber was on to something he couldn't seem to get to. She gave Saber a few minutes working at the dirt, and when nothing quickly surfaced, she pulled him from the thicket and tied him to the base of a tree, where he sat and howled with frustration.

Max and Hunter went in for verification purposes. They approached the scene from a different angle, and like Saber, Hunter immediately pressed for the area beneath young mesquite. He too began to work the dirt in the spot where Saber had pawed his shallow hole. Seeing his dog's similar intensity, Max crawled into the area beside him as Hunter deepened the hole and Saber continued to protest yards away. Soon the shallow dip was deeper, and after a particularly furious spate of Hunter's digging, Max caught the first scent of cadaver: faint at first and then stronger as the dog worked.

A body in the brush, buried beneath a young tree that had partially grown over it, high above the flood's debris field. The disaster response crew with them offered to begin to dig, but Max shook his head. This, he said, was likely a crime scene. Better not touch. The group called the local sheriff's department, who asked if the handlers were sure the dogs hadn't caught the scent of dead animal.

They've been ignoring dead animals in the debris field for days, Max and Fleta responded. The scent was undoubtedly cadaver, and they believed the scent was undoubtedly human as well.

Overextended or skeptical, the sheriff's department didn't pursue the matter for a couple of days, long after the dogs and handlers had cleared the area and had been deployed to search another one. When law enforcement did dig beneath the tree, they found the decomposing remains of a man who'd been shot between the eyes. Dead and buried long enough for a young tree to grow over him, his death unrelated to the flood that brought the dogs there in the first place.

There's a saying in the SAR community: the search you're called out to may not be the one you end up on. Being prepared means being ready for anything.

14

HOME AND HEARTH

I'VE GOT TWO PUZZLES: the emerging search canine, confident and capable, and the adolescent family dog at home, beautifully housebroken, but in other behaviors unpredictable. I've read five training manuals, and the dogs have a trainer we all value, yet in the private hours, I'm clearly floundering — without guidebooks for steering a young dog along the fuzzy line that separates a well-behaved family pet and an independent leader in the search field. Puzzle must learn to be both. I need her obedient to me but not overly dependent, disinclined to jump on people who walk through the door, but stubborn enough to insist when I have made a wrong choice on a search and the scent we need is in another direction. She should be assured enough to search ahead of me, and I should have trust enough to let her work apart from my micromanagement.

And in all of this, I need to believe that dog peace will somehow return to the household.

Collaborative is the word I think of when I watch the other handlers with their dogs, the relationships long-defined and trust between them evident. I know things didn't start out that way. I've heard the puppy backstories and the way this handler or that one had to mediate between the new dog and the older ones in the family. I've heard about the wrecked landscaping at home and the dog-to-dog posturing and the squabbles over favorite toys. I know there are occasionally days when one of the senior search canines has an issue at home, then shows a little attitude at training — shooting the paw, we call it — and dog and handler have a stern exchange. I have even seen a mature search dog take it into his head to vanish in the middle of a training search — off on his own *yabba-yabba-woo-hoo!* — abandoning his handler for the first time in his dog life to go walkabout. I take a little comfort that I'm not the first handler to struggle with dog dynamics at work and at home, but right here, right now, the job sometimes seems a lot bigger than I am. And behind my frustration is the loom of coming failure, that somehow despite all the reading and note taking, despite wanting this as much as I do for both of us, I do not have it in me to effectively partner this dog.

At the house, we have forged a little order. The universal "Sit" command serves us well. Puzzle seems aware — and happier — that she's not the only one expected to behave. Sometimes the dogs are rewarded with treats for the obedience; sometimes they receive only praise. Though I watch Puzzle carefully for signs of resource guarding against the smaller Poms, when treats are doled out during a community sit, she politely waits her turn and concentrates on her praise, her treat alone. She is aware that I'm watching. Sometimes she looks back at me with a teenager's deadpan expression: *What?* she postures touchily. *What?*

Yay! Six dogs, six sits, six treats, no throwdown! But I can't take anything for granted. Puzzle is always ready to engage. Verbal Sprits'l's energy excites her, and Whisky's flash-paper hysteria escalates that excitement. If Whisky and Sprits'l squabble, Puzzle will launch into the thick of it. Worse, if Jack grumbles at Whisky for getting too close to his food bowl, Whisky's returned growl will provoke Puzzle to jump in and settle things, invariably landing on Jack, who squawks with terror, which escalates Puzzle's aggression — a situation I cannot allow.

Peace in our house during Puzzle Year One requires a constant presence of mind on my part. Like flying an airplane: this is where we are, this is what's coming next, and this is what we do ahead to prevent bad things from happening. The dogs all eat at a distance from one another, and Puzzle eats in an area where no presumptuous Pom can challenge her and where she, in turn, cannot stalk a dog with his head in the food bowl and begin the stare-down that precedes a fight over the dish. My job is to get the bowls up before Puzzle has access to the smaller dogs' eating area. After eating, each goes outside for a little constitutional, and Puzzle — a slow, dainty, dispassionate eater — is always the last. They go out separately, they come in on their own timing, and after dinner they all meet up in the kitchen, where a sit is expected on my part and an after-dinner dental treat is expected on theirs.

The routine is consistent, the system works very well, and denied the situations that lead to problems, Puzzle and Jack get along with quiet reasonableness. Jack is cautious and wary around her, but I'm pleased to wake one night to find him huddled against Puzzle for warmth and Puzzle lying belly-up next to him in sleepy companionship.

Puzzle's early aggressiveness toward Jack still concerns me. What was that? Why did it happen? Though I believe the original conflict was about power, I can't be sure if Jack's wariness and fear send off "weakling" signals that arouse the bully in her, or if she reads his sidelong gaze and stiff posture (or his thick, stand-on-end coat, according to one behaviorist) as a direct challenge that she is willing to address. After Puzzle has similar skirmishes with Whisky and with Sprits'l, also relatively young and relatively strong, over high-value items, I hypothesize that my smart but immature Golden is determined to rise in pack status and is willing to take on any dog that she believes stands in her way. Clearly, the senior, special-needs dogs don't stand in her way. Apart from the occasional play bow, Puzzle ignores wobbly Sophie. Scuppy she defers to, following him in the yard, examining what he too pauses over, lying near him when he settles.

• • •

They do not cuddle together, but the oldest dog of the pack and the youngest one have forged a connection none of the rest of the dogs share. In January 2005, when twenty-three-year-old Scuppy begins having occasional seizures, Puzzle is the dog who first shows me he's in trouble. One cool evening when they have been lying together on the day-warm sidewalk, I hear her thump the back screen door and whine a single urgent note to get my attention. This is not usual behavior from Puzzle, and when I push through the door to her, she immediately jumps away to the center of the yard, looking at me as though waiting. It's the same wait I have seen from her in the search field when she has raced ahead to a space I must catch up to. As I move to her, she jumps away again, heading down the long fence to the base of a pecan tree where Scuppy lies on his side, one leg contorted and trembling. He is conscious but bewildered, the foreleg drawn up awkwardly. His mouth is open, and he is panting rapidly. I touch the leg, which seems intact, and in a few minutes this first focal seizure releases him and he sits up, dazed and withdrawn. I carry him to the house, but once inside he walks gingerly on his own. The paw is down, but he seems dissociated from it, as though he doesn't trust it or isn't sure it's there.

He is terribly thirsty. Scuppy drinks deeply from the water bowl and removes himself to one of the dog beds by the hearth, where he lies quietly the rest of the night. Puzzle lies next to him on the floor, and a few hours later, Sprits'l joins her there. Neither stretches out. They sleep in cautious poses, on their chests, chins on paws. When I walk in the room, their heads raise. Scuppy is deeply asleep on his side and does not stir.

The seizures continue. Infrequently at first — weeks apart — but they appear to be worsening, as our vet thought they would. Puzzle shows the greatest concern of any of the dogs when Scuppy has a seizure, sometimes waking me in the night when he has begun to go rigid but not yet to howl, a new byproduct of the seizing. We sit together by the old dog on his soft bed next to the fireplace, waiting for the episode to let go and for him to return to us. Each time, he comes out of it a little more slowly.

Across the next few months, Scuppy retains his voracious appetite and his impeccable sense of 7:00 A.M. breakfast and 5:00 dinnertime, but grows weaker. He takes shorter walks in the backyard, where self-involved Puzzle forgets herself and supervises from a distance. She has ceased to play anywhere near him, as though recognizing that he is fragile and will easily topple. In time, the old boy begins to wobble to the back door and mutter — a signal to me that he needs help out to the yard and back in again. He grows content to remain on his cushion beside the fire; Maddy the cat occasionally cuddles him and Puzzle lies not far away. Sprits'l tends to visit and briefly hover, then goes away to return again later. The other dogs watch from a cautious distance. They are uneasy with his frailty. But Scup continues to eat and wags his fuzzy, upturned tail at the first scent of peanut butter, his favorite treat.

Lab tests show no treatable condition for Scup, and our vet advises that the best we can do is keep him comfortable, spoiled, and happy to the end, which the vet believes may be coming soon. The seizures have become more frequent, and Scuppy is losing weight, but he still retains an interest in the household, a pleasure in the outdoors, and a passionate attachment to his dinner.

The old dog brings out a maturity in Puzzle that she has not previously demonstrated at home. She moves slowly and quietly around Scuppy. Beside him she is a different, softer, wiser dog. I do not understand it, but I'm grateful he has her warmth on cold evenings and her canine companionship in addition to human affection. As he grows more introspective and slips farther from us, sometimes Puzzle alone will perk his interest in the goings-on of the house.

In time, he moves beyond even her reach. One Monday afternoon in late March, Scuppy has a seizure that runs abnormally long, recovers, and within hours has two others. I gently bathe the urine from him, and he groans and nuzzles into my hand when I rub his ears, but by evening he has begun refusing food. As does Puzzle. As does Sprits'l. In the night, he has another seizure, and by morning is too weak to even raise his head. Though I had hoped

Scuppy might die peacefully in his sleep, he grows feebly nauseated, retching up bile as his kidneys begin to fail.

I cannot allow him to suffer. I wipe his coat clean and comb him
lightly, stroking and talking to him very gently before wrapping
him in a towel for a last trip to the vet. Puzzle watches us from a
slight distance, but when Scuppy makes a little mutter, she gets
up to wash his face. She sniffs him thoroughly, curiously; her face
is anxious, and I recognize that by the scent of him she may know
far more about his condition than I do. I allow them this time together, and then I bundle Scuppy close to my chest and make my
way with him out the back of the house to the garage and to the
car. In my arms, he feels light as spun glass, his bones hollow as a
bird's. At first, Puzzle seems to think I'm just taking the old boy out
for his toddle around the garden, but as I turn with him to pull the
garage door closed, I see Puz at the door of the screen porch looking out at us. Her tail waves slowly as I look back at her, and then
it stops.

Have a friend long enough, and in time he or she is going to have
to break bad news to you. Ellen has been the bearer of bad news
more than once. Some of it dog-specific. In 1989, when my husband and I were on a trip to Minneapolis for the Twin Cities Mar-
athon, Ellen dog-sat our Bogie, a Shetland Sheepdog and my first
dog. High-energy Bogie had taught me valuable lessons about the
perils of puppyhood and boredom, lessons that my husband and
I believed we had mastered by the time we went to Minneapolis.
Bogie was about eighteen months old at the time.

On the first evening of our trip, I called Ellen to check on
Bogie.

"How's it going? How's Bog-dog?" I asked.

She said "Fine," but the word had a tightrope quality to it. A
little extra fricative on the *F*, and the long *I* sound slightly drawn
out.

"Everything okay?"

"Yes." The second yes almost seemed convincing, but when

I hung up the phone, I turned to my husband and said, "Something's wrong at the house."

We gave it a few minutes, and then I called her back. Ellen came clean. She hadn't wanted to worry my husband the night before his big run, but the truth was . . . Bogie ate a chair.

"Ate a *chair*?"

I had heard correctly. Bogie had stripped a bentwood rocker completely free of its wicker seat and back, leaving only the curved wood behind. The chair looked, she said, like what cicadas leave behind when they slip out of old skin. Maybe it could be upholstered. The wood was pristine. He had not actually eaten the wicker, though it was gnawed into a pretty fringe — piled up in a soggy little stack in the hallway. And he had done the whole job with an assassin's silent efficiency. One minute, Ellen was watching TV and Bogie was asleep in the hallway. The next minute, the dog was asking her for a game of tug, and the chair guts lay where he had been sleeping.

This was the first piece of furniture Bogie ever ate, but in the course of his extended puppyhood, he also stripped a bathroom of carpet from the comfort of his crate and kindly disposed of a set of mauve hand towels we had received as a wedding present and had loathed for years. When Bogie got through with them, there wasn't enough left to successfully wipe a dipstick. Bogie was a voracious and indiscriminate destroyer of furnishings, whose tastes went everywhere. But he had a private standard. He never once touched a houseplant, a roll of toilet paper, or a shoe.

Fifteen years later, I thought I came to Puzzle wiser. But Ellen's voice on the other end of the phone suggests otherwise. She has been dog-sitting the crew on evenings when I teach a night course. When I call her to let her know I'm on my way home, I hear the guarded tone she'd used with Bogie all those years before.

"What?" I say.

"Your dog," she replies. And though I have six dogs, I know which one she's talking about straightaway.

"What?" I repeat.

"She ate the fainting couch." Then she clarifies. "Well, first she dug the stuffing out of it, and then she stripped off the rest of the upholstery, and then she ate . . ."

"What?" I imagine a Golden Retriever full of foam rubber and upholstery tacks.

". . . all the treats Sprits'l had been hiding between the arm and the seat cushion."

I sputter a little, trying to frame this, and then I remember all those "Sit" commands in the kitchen, and Sprits'l trotting off with his treat and his small, superior posture, and I think of the early search games I had done with Puzzle, hiding treats in the house — yes, God help me, even in pockets of the furniture — and I can't do anything but laugh.

When I get home, Ellen shows me what's left of the antique couch, and I peer down at what's left of the treats too. Puzzle has left a few crumbs that are fresh, but other untouched biscuits are discolored and hard as rocks. Sprits has claimed that couch since puppyhood. Sprits has been hiding his treats in the deep fold of that upholstery a long, *long* time.

I'd thought I kept a tidy home. I remember his other favorite spots, and before Puzzle can do a thorough shakedown of the entire house, I search under his preferred dog bed, the spot beneath my dresser where he likes to lie behind the curtains. I don't find biscuits, but I do find his collection of stolen leather things: a key fob with one of my old office keys, a cell phone cover, the luggage tag off my briefcase. Sprits'l has long been given to thieving and now, I realize, to hoarding.

The disemboweled couch has ended his career, and I go back to look at what remains of it. Unlike Bogie, who chewed wicker from a chair for the sheer pleasure of worrying it free, Puzzle has gutted the couch not for its own sake, but in order to find the treats she could smell deep within the folds of its upholstery, deeper than my vacuum cleaner ever reached. It's too late to punish her, and what would I punish her for? Initiative and success at a game I had originated?

Ellen comes in with all the dogs. Sprits'l knows immediately that something's up with his couch, and he is outraged at the violation. He huffs over the crumbs, circling and chattering. Puzzle watches me study her handiwork. She has no interest at all in the fainting couch now, but she leans against my knee, her tail faintly waving, as though to say *yes, it was quite the job, but I got through it.* I make a mental note to find an upholsterer tomorrow, and I consider the digging and tugging Puzzle must have gone through to get all the way down to the couch's wood frame. Making the best of a bad thing, I throw a coverlet over the couch, and I hope Puzzle will search for the source of human scent with the same conviction.

Goldens are soft dogs, I was told by more than one person in the days before Puzzle. *Goldens can be easily wounded. They're so eager to please that a sharp word can destroy them. It is so easy to break their hearts and spirits.* Some of this seems melodramatic to me, and counterintuitive, since plenty of Goldens are working dogs of all kinds. Puzzle has not yet shown me any great fragility — in fact, quite the contrary. I have let loose a few sharp words, and though she seems to recognize the knock-it-off meaning behind the tone, she has certainly never cowered. But I move forward with her thoughtfully. Behind the puppy willfulness and general blockheaded egocentrism could be a soft, sensitive dog in the making, I suppose, though you would still never know it at this point while on a walk with her.

As our walk saga continues, I have tried various collars, harnesses, and the Gentle Leader, a check device that wraps over the muzzle and, when the dog pulls ahead too hard, turns the dog's head due to the inappropriate tension on the lead. The idea is that most dogs will learn that pulling too hard results in a self-generated check. Puzzle strains against all collars; she disregards the changed locus of control with a harness. She responds well to the Gentle Leader for a few, optimistic steps, then suddenly porpoises in a spasm of dislike, landing on her side to paw at her muzzle or try to wipe the hated Gentle Leader off in the grass. The more elaborate the device, the less progress we make. For a number of reasons, I do not use a prong collar on Puzzle. Her puppy and adolescent testing suggested that her threshold for discomfort is very high, and there's the possibility that I could do her genuine harm with a prong collar before she ever truly perceived the check.

"Why does it matter how she walks?" asks a friend. "Won't she do most of her SAR work off-leash?"

I try to explain that a good walk is at the heart of obedience, and that obedience is at the heart of good search partnership. The controlled cross of a busy highway, an emergency stop when I shout that command from a distance, a responsive "Down" in the presence of structural instability — all these demands in the SAR field grow out of respect and accord begun on something as basic as a walk.

Trainer Susan weighs in on my two Puzzles. "At search," she says, "she seems more mature than she is because she loves the work. She likes the challenge. And you're following *her*. But on a walk, you're telling her to do what she doesn't necessarily want to do. To her, obedience is boring. Remember," she adds, "she may look like a big girl now, but she's still a puppy in the head."

Puzzle and I walk twice every day, an event I try not to dread. She is remarkably strong, fully capable of going from a nice trot to a doggy broad jump in moments. Walks have left me exhausted, bruised, and sore a few times, and though I pride myself on a long fuse before I get angry, walks have also occasionally left me purple with frustration. *The leash is a telegraph line,* I'm told by more than one trainer, and I know any tension I have at the outset of the walk communicates directly to her. At this point, she is rarely *on my walk,* as Susan would put it, and I wonder if Puzzle feels my tension down the leash in the same way she picks up on Jack's guard-up wariness in the kitchen. I wonder if she perceives this as a similar advantage to be pressed.

We walk on, regardless. I try all the tactics suggested by trainers, dog whisperers, competition obedience instructors, and sympathetic friends with senior dogs who ruefully remember their early days with leashes and "Heel" commands. One Golden owner, who repeated puppy class three times with her beautiful, reddish male, tells me it's just a matter of patience.

"Walks were hell for the longest time, and then at one point I looked up when Pico was two years old, and I had the perfect dog. People would stop me and say, 'I want a dog like yours,' and I would think, 'Like *mine*?' My commands for Pico weren't any different. They just finally sank in."

Two years old, I think, and gulp. Puzzle has just had her first birthday. Even though passersby often comment that she's remarkably mellow for a young Golden, I'm privy to all the shades of Puzzle on a walk, and *mellow* is not the word I would choose.

We head out one cool afternoon following a rainstorm, and Puzzle is charged with excitement after being housebound the majority of the day. She's an especially pretty, spirited dog on this walk, glowing in the muted light after the storm, splashing happily through the occasional puddle. People smile passing us. I smile back, huff-huffing. We wrestle for the first block until she settles into the walk by the second. *A settle by block two may be some improvement*, I think as she trots ahead of me on a "Wander" command, where she is free to explore ahead in an easy lope, stopping and sniffing and occasionally rolling in soft grass, as long as she doesn't pull on the lead and obeys when we pass a dead squirrel or dog poop and I say, "Leave it."

"Wander" is getting better, but "Heel" is still awful. In heel, she continues to veer away on a diagonal, as willful a disengagement as she can make while still attached to a lead. We work on "Heel," "Stop," "Sit," "Turn," "Wait," "Leave it," and "Stay" as we walk, with modest success. "Sit" is pretty strong; "Leave it" seems to be the only command with 100 percent obedience. Puz is happy to ignore anything I say no to — an excellent behavior for the search field. "Heel," "Stop," "Stay," and "Wait" need a lot more work. Today I'd be happy for improvement on even one of these.

This is a dog who will tell me she has found a person tucked in a pipeline beneath three feet of rubble. *But, Puzzle, why won't you just walk with me?*

I muse on strategy as we turn another corner and head for a busy intersection that borders a park where we often train. Puzzle pads ahead easily, but she must heel while crossing streets with me. I'm preparing for the inevitable struggle across the approaching four-lane when I step on a loose piece of sidewalk that comes up the moment I put weight on it. I come down, smacking my forehead against cement, my right wrist snapping hard beneath my weight. There's a roar in my head, like the rush of decompression out a hole in an airplane, and though my eyes are open, I realize that for the moment I can't see. I have dropped the leash and hit my head, and when I try to turn to look for my dog, I can't see her. I'm aware that I'm near to blacking out.

"Puzzle, *wait*," I say, and with a heart sink that I'm probably going to lose her, it's the last thing I remember for I don't know how long.

I wake to the huff of her breath in my ear, and I open my eyes to see Puzzle in full alert above me, her leather lead dragging free behind her. *How long have we been here?* I wonder. The daylight seems changed, but my vision is still not right. We are a few yards from the busy intersection, and my dog has not, apparently, left my side. I sit up. The right wrist is bad. My cell phone is shattered. I use my left hand to touch my head for blood and find a chestnut-size lump. Best to sit a moment. Puzzle sits beside me and attends, offers once to lick my face and then waits quietly minutes later when I try first to rock to my knees and then to stand.

Five blocks from home on a weekday afternoon. I'm not in great shape, but I have no idea who in this neighborhood would be home at the moment to help us and who would not. I take Puzzle's lead in my left hand, and on the "Wander" command she moves soberly forward without pulling. I'm still dazed, but Puzzle heads for home as though she recognizes the reverse course or intuits our walk is done. She moves gently, ignoring the challenge of two barking Dobermans in a backyard we pass. Here is the obedience we've been working on for almost a year, and I cannot know what provokes it — only that she obeyed a "Wait" command while I lay unconscious, either as a form of obedience or a concern that I had fallen, and now she walks ahead as if chastened by the experience.

"Good girl," I say to her when we get back in the house. She follows me to the refrigerator for ice and to the phone as I call a friend for a ride to the emergency room, and to her credit, she saves me from additional embarrassment when she puts her muzzle to my backside and I feel the cool wet of her nose against my skin. It's then I realize that not only have I blown out the seat of my jeans and my underwear, but I also walked all the way home mooning anyone who cared to note the tall, shattered woman walking behind a very good dog.

15

THIS BOY HERE

WE THUMP ALONG the shadowed lanes of a mobile home park, awkward behind the steady grace of a moving dog. Heavy in our boots, prickly with sweat, we've been out only a few minutes, and we're chafing already beneath the unforgiving rub of packs — packs in which we've crammed every possible thing we might need in the rescue of a six-year-old boy who's ten hours gone. He is asthmatic, diabetic, allergic to bees, frightened of punishment, inclined to run.

Braden has light brown hair and blue eyes. Earlier today, he wore blue shorts and a red T-shirt, green and yellow athletic shoes, and glasses. Two front teeth are missing. He was last seen with other children, older neighbors, squabbling over a Game Boy. Up to this year, he's been a city child, but now he lives in this mobile home park that is rural in three directions and suburban only if you look out the front gate and stretch your eyes toward a gated community across the freeway. Braden was not reported missing until he failed to show up for supper.

Near midnight, his young mother can barely get a word out, sitting on a picnic table beside her boyfriend, also silent, who has an arm around her shoulders. Her head is down. His is up, attentive, watching each addition to the search. Three, four, five police cars, two fire trucks, and now the dogs. A clutch of other family members stand in the strip of yard beside the missing boy's home. They pulse red-blue in the flash of police-car lights and stand disengaged, watching the search but apart from it. There is an open animosity among some of the group that carries out to where we are. Comments are made, derisive laughter even. Some nod while others shift slightly away.

"Oh, *hell* no," said one woman at the earlier arrival of the dogs. She shook her head, went inside, and slammed the door.

"Now this boy here," says an uncle who has come forward, "has a history of this." The uncle is a tall man standing in the cold pool of a street lamp with his hands in his pockets, head bare, his face flecked with leaf shadow from the hackberry tree that crowds the light. He is the designated family representative, and he has not moved from the place where he stands the entire time we've been here.

Place Last Seen, Direction of Travel, Containment, Attraction: these terms can direct a missing-person rescue, allowing responders to choose the place to begin and the first direction for search, to prevent a moving victim from traveling outside the immediate area, and to provide attractors that can lead a missing person to safety. In a perfect scenario, the PLS is consistent among eyewitnesses, the direction of travel known. The missing person doesn't fear responders and is excited to see the flashing lights or hear the quick, light chirps of a siren. He is physically and cognitively able to head for help.

We rarely get the perfect scenario — I cannot recall *ever* getting it — and on this search, our understanding of Braden wavers. Runaway, abduction — or something else? The PLS is in a constant state of revision. Witnesses disagree on his direction of travel. What seems to be a common theme is that Braden is deeply afraid of getting into trouble with adults, and there is a changeable story about this afternoon that describes a fight over a favorite toy — that may or may not have been dismembered by another child — a broken window at a friend's house, a pair of soiled pants, and then a hard run away from feared punishment. One version of the story leaves out the fight and concentrates on the toy that Braden may have tried to walk to a supermarket to replace. Other stories detail Braden's two previous runaway events. Once, because he was mad about a broken promise to go swimming. A second time when he was left behind with a new babysitter he didn't much like.

The uncle says, "Braden doesn't make trouble, but he brings trouble on."

In the smoke of conflicting stories, anything may be possible behind Braden's disappearance. His medical needs are a concern among us. The time gone even more so. When a young child has been missing for more than two hours, successful rescue probabilities drop. We know today's high temperatures. We all sense the time passed and quickly passing, and though we never think it's possible to move any faster, somehow in the search for a child, we do, pushing hard behind the dogs. They also seem to feel the extra urgency, so much so that even the quiet ones bark before they gear up to run.

The earliest dogs out could not confirm either of the directions Braden was said to have traveled, but this isn't really surprising, considering the relatively small area, the passage of hours, and a great deal of foot traffic in every direction. Braden could have been here, or here, or here, his scent now lost in the blanket of other scents dropped more recently. The other possibility is that something else has happened to him, and he was never in any of these directions at all. We search as though either condition is true.

I run behind a handler whose dark dog lopes easily down the narrow streets, threading his way between trailer pads. Missing Braden is public knowledge here. The police have already questioned local residents, and now we move house to house among watching bystanders. Some homes are dark at this late hour, others flicker blue and yellow with the glare of television screens, and others still are ablaze with light. Venetian blinds bend a little, exposing people looking out at us as we look back at them, their movement catching our attention. A couple of teenagers come forward to ask if they can help, clutching a photocopied picture of Braden police had given them earlier. They are the only ones to do so. Other residents watch silently from porches, their expressions withdrawn, some with arms folded, flicking cigarette ash onto cement. One man calls from a porch that his baby is sleeping and that we'd better not set the alarm off on his car. When our passing search canine causes a housebound Chihuahua to bark, we hear the bang of a screen and another man shout that he's "gonna fucking kill me a goddamn dog" — sharp words flung our direction that make my stomach knot until our pace jars it free.

This community has not softened to Braden's trouble, and it strikes me that maybe it cannot. We have been on searches where local police offered us Kevlar vests, and though this isn't one of them, I feel our vulnerability here as well as his, a twitchy awareness as we jog behind the dog, calling for the child within a neighborhood that seems . . . something. Hostile? Wary? Frightened?

It seems a hard place for a little boy to get lost. I think of diabetic Braden, who is last known to have eaten a bologna sandwich at lunchtime. I have two energy bars, beef jerky, and a juice box in my backpack. With every step I hear the slosh of it, a little chug like *I-think-I-can.*

I am childless, which is not to say I never had a child. In the decade of my marriage, I almost had five of them — pregnancies reflecting the fitful stages of our good years together and twice, our duress. Because I never knew them, I think of these children now by the placeholder names we briefly gave them then: Baby 1, Baby 2. We called them this not for want of better names, but because we learned to hold our collective breath and carefully round the corner on each trimester. My sensible, hard-working husband with a wild streak was a closet conservative. He valued an even keel. When our first loss came six months into our marriage, an early surprise and a devastating blow, we would not be jinxed again. So we didn't get too hopeful, too excited about another pregnancy, ever. We didn't actively try, and we instinctively knew it was harder to lose a baby already named than one affectionately known by the order of conception.

After the first miscarriage, we conceived again a year later, then a third time after I graduated with my master's. Again two years later, in a moment of feeling flush enough to send a baby to college (Baby 4). And finally, after three years of job losses, financial struggle, and temptation in various forms, again. Baby 5 was the child I carried into a car accident and out of it, the pregnancy that held the longest, and the baby whose miscarriage began while I was piloting an airplane. Physically stunned by the sudden, catastrophic labor and the loss fully formed enough to see, to hold, we fell to earth — my husband and I — within the year, and that would be the end of us.

He took the cat, I took the dog. We separated nightstands and divided dishtowels. We argued over bills, taxes, apartment deposits. And then it was done. We moved to separate cities and licked our wounds in private.

Those babies return to me as yearning when I least expect it. Sometimes, all these years later, Baby becomes an individual, and I see the cut of my ex-husband in a boy at the supermarket. Or a girl on the street stops to ask directions, and the flash of her form in the glass of a moving door is something like me.

I've been asked if these losses are why I work search — some Freudian byproduct or act of reparation, of denial. I don't think so, of course, but friends say I might be denying that too. It's a well-worn concept and a repeated one. A few kind souls suggest a nobler motive: on searches involving children, perhaps I'm saving some other mother the grief I've known myself. That sounds very good, but I don't think about motive much. I work search the way I plodded through the muddy aftermath of miscarriage and divorce: one foot before another, hoping for good but prepared for grief, and following the dog ahead anyhow.

• • •

There are a hundred or more mobile homes here, but the community sits tight enough that occasionally I see the flicker of other canine units on their neighborhood sweeps. We call out to the little boy, telling him he's not in trouble, that it's time to go home. Our flashlights silver the underbellies of trailers, the interiors of cars. After a time, the bystanders retreat to their houses, and we're left with only the glittering eyes of crouched housecats, their gazes hard on the dog as we pass.

Near the farthest reaches of our sector, the dog we follow rushes suddenly forward to the door of one mobile home. He thumps so hard against it that the door pops open, revealing a half-dressed man bent down to the bins of his fridge, fishing for something in the crisper. The man yelps with surprise at the sight of the dark, powerful dog, almost falling as he rights himself. Lights come on in the neighboring home, shouts back and forth. The handler apologizes and pulls his dog from the doorway. We step cautiously back as the man slams his door onto its latch and then locks it.

"No radio," says the handler quietly, aware that anything we say broadcasts widely across team radios and could be audible to bystanders near other dog teams. "I think we'd better walk this one back in."

That strong indication in a doorway, two other dogs responding markedly on the trunk area of a car. This is what the dogs have given us. It can be a strange moment describing tangible responses to trace evidence that humans cannot smell — you always hope the authorities understand what the dogs are truly doing. This time, when handlers relay their separate information to police, investigators confer together and tell us the indications make sense. The doorway marks an area where the boy often visited, where in fact he may have played today. The car, owned by a friend of the family, was one Braden had ridden in a lot. That the dogs indicated strongly here, in a neighborhood where the child has also been in other houses, other cars, and on the playground swing set seems significant to us. Why so much fresh scent here? Perhaps it's significant to investigators too, though we are not included in their deliberations. We stand by at a distance as they bend over the hood of a police car, pooling the known information from interviews and the interest of the dogs.

A mutter in the distance, then loud and louder still: a police helicopter passes low over the mobile home park and outward to the fields beyond it, pilot and spotter flying an airborne version of the tight sweeps we have made on the ground. The intensity of the helicopter searchlight and the heavy *whup* of rotor blades have likely wakened every living creature in the area. And for the time it is with us, the helicopter now makes dog work virtually impossible, the downwash from the blades creating a scatter of scent worthy of a small tornado.

Now we stand with the dogs that lie flat in the cool grass along the street. They are less interested than we are. They have seen and heard helicopters before, and this rest with their water bowls is welcome to them. We humans watch trees whip and objects blaze in the bright circle of light that slips easily from the helicopter across the neighborhood, and though I have no reason to fear that scrutiny, something in the nearness and approach of it makes me want to run.

I wonder what sense Braden makes of all this, if he is alive and conscious, if he knows the helicopter's there for his sake. I say as much to a young officer standing nearby, who shakes his head. He says over the noise that the residents of this mobile home park are pretty familiar with that helicopter. There's a lot of crime here: bad drug deals, abuse cases, robberies that turn to assault and, occasionally, to murder. Many of the longtime residents are too poor to move away. The officer's voice is matter-of-fact, but he says with some compassion, "They never know anything about anything when we show up, because they've got to live here after we've gone."

We count twenty-two passes before the helicopter rises easily away, slides winking into the darkness. When it's gone, I feel my knees begin to shake. I'm tired and more than tired — heartsick with certainty that Braden isn't here. I don't say anything. None of us says anything. With a gesture, an officer stands the dog team down. He tells us that tomorrow we'll search more widely: the surrounding fields, the farther places where bodies have been found before.

Seven hours later, I'm rested and well-juiced with coffee, in the left seat of a Cessna 152 a thousand feet above the ground, while a spotter gazes down from the right seat. I'd expected to run with the dogs again today, but at check-in, the Incident Commander said, "We'd like to send you up, if you're willing. It would be good to have you overfly areas that might be tough for the dogs, so that we can sector and prep the teams appropriately before they go out." Twenty minutes later, I was at the airport renting the Cessna. Twenty minutes after that, we were aloft.

This morning's heat is already surly, and the little plane is battered by thermals as we circle potential points of interest and fly gridlines over empty fields. I'm grateful the spotter is a fellow pilot from the flight school, unlikely to get airsick from the heat, the maneuvers, or the turbulence. He is a calm young man with sharp eyes, and he calls what he sees to me: the arrival of additional resources for today's sectors: horseback riders, ATV drivers, and a large crowd in a supermarket parking lot that could well be intended to walk certain areas a few feet apart, scanning the ground for any physical evidence that might be tied to the missing boy. At least a hundred more volunteers will join the search today, and it won't be an easy one.

We see unmowed fields. Plenty of creek beds surrounded by heavy brush. Several construction sites and a junkyard. A ribbon of road that was once a main thoroughfare from country to town. As we fly, the spotter jots terrain details on our photocopied map. We take turns flying, alternating who spots, our eyes straining for some sign of Braden on the move below. Now at five hundred feet above the ground, we should be able to see the missing boy in open areas, but there is nothing of him in the tall grass or flat spaces. Nothing in grass verges beside the road. What we do see is terrain it could take days to thoroughly cover.

We land, call in the information, and take off again. By the time we are airborne, ground searchers are on the move. We overfly their sectors for the rest of the day, hoping the presence of searchers will provoke some kind of movement from the missing child. And if they can't see him, we might be able to.

It's the call we understand but never like to hear. Whether out of ideas or having information they have not shared with any of us, investigators stand down the search in the late afternoon. Every sector has been covered — some by separate resources — and no trace of the boy has been found. "Abduction" is the rumor floating among the assembled company, always a possibility, now widely believed if not confirmed. Many of the searchers offer to remain here on standby, despite the 105-degree heat and the injuries already among some of the volunteers: heat exhaustion for several, a sprained wrist, a horse that took a bad fall crossing a ravine. The authorities decline. They too are pulling out. The case isn't over, but the ground search is.

The exhausted dogs load quietly into their cars and their crates, drooping over their water bowls, some of them dozing before they take the time to lie down. We're a subdued group, leaving with a few pats on the shoulder between us and little to say.

On my way home, I drive through the mobile home park a last time. Not much adult movement there in the heat of the day, but on one of the empty trailer pads, four shirtless boys play Keep Away with a deflated basketball. They stop and point a little as I pass, a *who's-that?* gesture and a brief stare before they turn away. A few streets over, an elderly woman sits with a small child in a kiddie pool. She nods as I drive by; the little girl waves wildly. In the unapologetic light of this summer afternoon, in a mobile home park half a century old, last night's search for Braden seems unreal. There are no cars in front of the house where he lives. It is quiet, cloth awnings collapsed against the windows to better block the sun.

A few hours after the search stands down, a park resident walking her dog smells smoke, peers into a ditch not far from the community, and finds a roll of smoldering carpet wedged into a drainage pipe, carpet from which a child's foot protrudes. He is found just feet away from the verge where investigators had parked, in a pipe that had been searched several times, penetrated by flashlight the night before. Days pass before we learn what is thought to have happened. There's word of a playmate's accident with a gun, the collaboration of adults to hide the matter, a transport somewhere else — and the return of Braden's body only after the search had terminated. The dogs' indications were relevant. The recovery raises questions we will never know the answer to. What was the message behind his return — a desire for discovery? A belief he would not be found in a place already searched? Or a more pointed message to authorities?

When we debrief the search a week later, several of us acknowledge the nightmares and insomnia that have followed it. Some of us are angry, some so sad we can barely speak. Rescues that become recoveries are never easy. Recoveries involving children — whether we are there at the moment of find or not — may be the hardest of all. In time, we go on to other searches and other sectors behind the dogs. But I am never far away from Braden. For months, he remains a figure in the corner of my dreams, with a wound to the head and a wound to the palm, as though he saw what was coming and put up his hand in the moment of flash.

16

FEAR STAGES

I FEEL THE THUNDER before I hear it. Five-pound Pomeranian Sprits'l is on the bed, tap-dancing on my chest. He senses a line of storms approaching from the south. Early morning storms in Texas are often the worst, especially during shifts of season, and I never know if Sprits hears them, smells them, senses the drop in pressure, or hears the change of wind, but for the last two years he has become increasingly storm phobic. He isn't hysterical or destructive during storms, but deeply anxious, panting rapidly and kneading his paws on any available human who will hold him. Now he is squeaking and gibbering in my arms. Four A.M., and if I squinch my eyes shut and block the ticking of the alarm clock, I think I can hear thunder miles and miles away. He always knows long before I do.

Sprits is the only dog that's nervous. I have three others on the bed — I can make out Fo'c'sle Jack and Sophie at the foot, their heads pressed together as they sleep, and Puzzle, whose snores I hear and whose dead weight I feel against my back. She is sleeping hard. I lie in the dark and idly scratch Sprits'l's chest, which seems to help him a little. He stops the tap-dancing but stares out the window toward the southwest, rigid and expectant. He is not my first storm-phobic dog, and I wonder if he learned to fear storms from our late English Setter who was afraid of them in a big way—an eighty-five-pound dog circling, pacing, and wedging himself under chairs, digging frantically in the bathtub, his head down as though he were receiving blows. Sprits as a puppy was never nervous about bad weather, but I have to wonder if he watched old Chevy and learned what it is to be anxious, or whether he evolved to this on his own.

And I wonder too about Puzzle, who has never yet been disturbed by storms. Will she in time come to dread them? The condition is apparently common in Golden Retrievers—so common that acquaintances who find out about Puzzle often say *Oh-you-have-a-Golden-Retriever-and-is-she-scared-of-storms?* in one breath.

If Puzzle is going to have a problem with storms, it isn't this morning. The wind rises, and the cross-draft in my old house makes the glass in the windows rattle with each change of pressure and thunderclap. Jack and Sophie have raised their heads and grumbled a little before settling back down. Storms hassle their dream cycles. I roll to my side and let Sprits tuck himself in the *V* at the back of my knees. He settles there, and I lean toward Puzzle's warm, sleepy presence. I have always loved cuddling a dog during bad weather, and she's a good size now for a full-body hug. I press my cheek to her forehead and drape my arm across her middle. Every crash and bang of thunder makes Sprits squeak a little, but Puzzle refuses to rouse. *What a steady girl,* I think. She rolls belly-up and sighs, and the storm's bright crashes have resolved to the occasional flicker and boom.

A free-floating statistic you hear in canine SAR states that 80 percent of would-be search dogs wash out. They can't do the work or won't do the work or too many things stress them to overload and they shut down. Aptitude testing for puppies gives an initial idea of a puppy's overall assurance, but there are no guarantees which way the maturing dog will go. I heard the statistic long before I got Puzzle, and I went into our partnership knowing there was more than just *can-she-smell-it-and-tell-me* involved: a search dog's drive and confidence are as important as good gifts of scent and smarts.

I watched her go into and out of the first puppy "fear stage," when she suddenly was averse to wheeled things and to toddlers, a condition that faded with desensitization as weeks passed. Now Puzzle's due for another one. A second fear stage is common between six and fourteen months. So far she hasn't reacted strongly to anything, but knowing the speed of her changes, I try to calmly show her the whole range of bizarre stimuli that for a search dog is common ground. I hope this can be a bonding opportunity: a *here is this thing we respect but don't need to fear — trust me.*

This morning, young firefighters are learning how to drive the big trucks. Two fire engines round a corner and flash past us at the fire academy. Sitting with me in the grass five feet from the curb, Puzzle could be nervous. That's a lot of truck and very close. There's much for a dog to be afraid of as the engines tilt and blaze through their paces — turning corners, braking suddenly, navigating through tight lanes, backing up. But Puzzle doesn't seem to be afraid at all, regarding the fire engine maneuvers with calm, unmoving benevolence. When the trucks stop and the firefighters jump out, she occasionally wags her tail as she scents one who is an old friend.

Puzzle has grown up with big noise, living in a house that sits next to ongoing construction. If houses aren't being torn down to the left or the right of us, the city is tearing up the streets, repairing aged infrastructure. The daily noise and dust have made me cranky, but — credit where it's due — the cement mixers, dump trucks, and backhoes may have accustomed Puzzle to big vehicles and the noise they're capable of making. I have seen her belly-up sleeping in the backyard grass while jackhammers pound asphalt twenty feet away.

For all she accepts storms and fire trucks with equanimity, this is not to say Puzzle is fearless. She is of two minds about the firefighters themselves. From puppyhood, she has schmoozed the men and women of local fire departments for petting when they are in civilian clothes. (We joke that she simpers, "They're big and strong and lightly smoked!") But a recent experience with a firefighter in turnout gear has dampened her enthusiasm a little.

The firefighter is Max, a team colleague and a thirty-one-year firefighter, the subject of Puzzle's deep devotion. On a bright, windless training day, out of sight from the dogs of the team, he puts on full turnout gear and oxygen system. It's an important part of their training. The youngest dogs of the team have never seen (or heard) a firefighter in full gear up close, and today is the day we hope they will make the association that the lumbering yellow creature with the shiny visor, indecipherable expression, and raucous breathing is a human underneath. Many dogs dislike their first experiences. Puzzle has seen quite a few firefighters in full gear from a distance, and in the engine bay she has sniffed curiously at long rows of pants and boots dropped in a neat, vertical, waist-open stack for quick gear-on — but this will be her first up-close experience with a firefighter in full gear.

Max rounds a corner and approaches the group of young dogs, all of whom shy, most of whom bark. His own search dog, Mercy, backs and barks in alarm for a few seconds until she connects the changed form with the scent of her handler. Two others are pointedly wary until Max gets on one knee and speaks to them. Whether his scent or posture tell them this guy's okay, they come forward with hesitance, then greater confidence.

Puzzle, however, is having nothing of him. She went skittish the moment she saw Max, and as he stands near her, speaking to her in a voice distorted by the mask and rasp of the SCBA, calling her by name, she cowers and pulls away, trembling. When he extends a hand down to offer a treat to her, she huddles behind me and submissively pees — something I have never seen her do before or since. In time, she takes a tentative sniff of his gloved hand and offers a tentative wag, but there seems to be nothing about this experience that comforts her.

Max wisely moves away — no sense in making the first experience a permanent problem. Puzzle watches him go, calming as he turns his masked face away from her and heads back the direction that he came from. I cannot make out if she failed to recognize the scent or sound of Max in the gear, or if she knew it was him and was terrified by his great change. I don't have to wonder long. When Max returns in his civilian clothes, Puzzle shies from him for the first time in her life. She presses to me for protection and looks briefly up at him with a betrayed expression on her face. She clearly knows what's what: the funky, stomping guy with the shiny face and distorted voice was Max. Her Max! It is not difficult to see the friction of her cognitive dissonance: *Max is a friend. Why would he scare me like that?*

It is a grudge she holds for months. Though every interaction with Max warms slightly, we all notice her subsequent hesitance in approaching him, as though she thinks in a flash he might change into the monster that first offered a treat, then scared and shamed her into peeing herself.

"Puzzle," Max says six weeks later, "are you ever going to forgive me?"

One thing's certain, Puzzle needs more turnout gear experience. I take her through the engine bays every training session, allowing her to walk the room's periphery where all the gear hangs, and after a moment of wariness, she thoughtfully sniffs the trousers, boots, coats, and gloves as we pass. "Own this," I say to her. "And this . . . and this." "Own," in our language, means *check this out, get comfortable with it.*

We acquire an old turnout coat and pair of trousers, and I bring them home, first throwing them haphazardly on the porch for all the dogs to sniff. Sprits'l to the rescue: from the first, he stomps over the gear fearlessly, his small, curious nose working it over, punctuating the inspection with an occasional snitz. The other Pomeranians follow, and a friend remarks that this process looks a little like a science-fiction movie, where fuzzy, fox-faced space parasites somehow swallow a firefighter whole without making a mark on the gear left behind.

Days later, I move both coat and trousers to an outdoor chaise longue, draping them over the frame as though it were a human lying there. Again the outfit looks like the person inside has been sucked right out of it by tidy aliens. Nevertheless, I hide treats in the thick yellow folds. Puzzle is somewhat curious about the change of position, only mildly interested until Sprits'l jumps on the chair and bounces across the coat and pants to find the hidden treats; then suddenly competitive Puzzle wants in on the action.

For the next week, I putter around the yard wearing that turn-out gear and yellow ladybug galoshes. This firefighter rig once belonged to a large man — the pants are seven inches too long and the jacket could hold three of me — and I wonder what that long-retired fellow might make of me toddling around the rose garden in his bright yellow pants and coat while holding a pair of clippers and a watering can. The ensemble has a makeshift crazy-lady air. Once, when I carry a bag of clippings to the compost heap at the side of the house, two neighbors laugh aloud before shifting to the other side of the street to avoid me. The next time I cross their path, they stare. They seem disappointed I don't have my little outfit on.

In time, my gardening, lounging, and taking tea in the turn-out gear have the desired effect. Puzzle comes to accept it calmly during training exercises, particularly when firefighters go about their business uninterested in her. I watch her watch the rookies suit up. She tilts her head and brings her ears to bear now and again when a person she recognizes slides into the heavy coat and trousers, looking speculative when their heads disappear beneath a helmet with a shield and mask. When it's someone she's fond of, I see the characteristic Golden furrow of the brow, an almost maternal look of concern, like *Oh, I wish you wouldn't do that.* On several training sessions, we hide volunteers in a turnout coat and pants, face-down in a tumble of wood, and — good news — Puzzle shows no qualms about finding them in it.

But her memory of Max in the suit remains fresh. Long months after he approached her for the first time fully suited in firefighter gear, he hides for her one day in the engine bay, wedging himself in the space behind a rack of the heavy yellow coats and trousers, helmets, masks, and boots. Puzzle has happily found other victims similarly hidden, but this time she runs into the room, clearly orients the scent in one corner of the bay, and screeches to a stop about six feet away from where Max is hidden. From that comfortable distance, she alerts to me, she alerts to the head trainer, and just to make sure we get it, she alerts to us both again. I encourage her to move closer to Max, but there is no way this time she's going to breach the space between them. *Fool me once . . .* , she seems to say, staring hard at the spot where Max crouches behind a row of turnout coats. She is sure and she is stubborn. She knows it's Max hiding back there, and — nothing doing — she knows what he gets up to when he gets a little access to that gear.

I make a note to myself: hide Max in turnout clothes more often. And I add a second note: maybe invite him to suit up and come over to pull a few weeds.

Thunderstorms, fire engines, jackhammers — not a problem. Toddlers and turnout gear, getting there. Puzzle moves forward, but I too have issues that I need to get past. Puzzle's a year into her training and doing well. She has more than two hundred successful scenario searches behind her. Urban streets and buildings, wrecked cars and mangled aircraft, debris fields, dense wilderness. Now, because half or more of the team's searches take place at night, we train accordingly.

I'm not at all afraid of the dark, but some night spaces make me a little uneasy even by flashlight. This is particularly true of building searches. It's my own clumsiness at issue: I don't want to fall over things I can barely see. I've had a few missteps with and without my dog, falling once face-first onto an oxygen tank. Puzzle, however, is comfortable in dim light, padding through dim warehouse and furniture-tumbled apartment spaces, climbing stairs with easy confidence.

Wilderness night work is her particular favorite. The Golden grows more joyful as the light fades, as though the diminished view intensifies all the things available to her other senses. Not that her night vision is necessarily bad: though information on canine sight is sometimes contradictory, contemporary research suggests that dogs have much better night vision than we do — more rods than cones, an assist to night hunting, while our cone-rich eyes give us better color vision. Puzzle and the other dogs seem to bear this out, bounding forward at the "Find!" command with the same ease they demonstrate by day.

While the dogs take darkness in stride, volunteer victims are relieved when the search canines work quickly at night. It can be an interesting hour, hidden somewhere in deep brush without a flashlight, waiting for a series of dogs to suss you out in the brambles, even as the nocturnal wildlife comes forward to make sense of you in the stillness. Our volunteers have come back a few times with their eyes wide and neck hair prickling. They've brought back stories of creeping sounds and snapping sounds and unblinking eyes that flicked once or twice in the moonlight.

It isn't hard to feel lost out there, and it's not difficult to be joyful when the dogs make the find. I've hidden in the brush for every dog on the team except my own, peeking through vines to watch them sweep their sectors, imagining how a stranger would see them — the light dogs ghosting along in the moonlight, the dark dogs unreadable, their easy trot almost wolflike in the dimness. The volunteers know what's coming — from the dogs, anyway — but I think of those who are genuinely lost and realize again the importance of people-friendly dogs out doing this work. I'm glad of my light-coated girl with the whole body wag and the smiling puppy-soft face.

But she scares me sometimes, does Miss Puzzle Boldly-Go, who seems to trot from light into darkness without pause. What I've learned across this year with her is that I can face my own fears at this work, light or dark, and push through them, but I am much more anxious about Puzzle. It's the parent's conundrum that I have sidestepped in my childlessness: that conflict between love, protection, and a young one's developing independence. It lands on me in full force now.

In familiar territory, we work primarily off-lead, and though Puzzle is well past her flight impulse, and her willingness to check in with me doesn't vary from day to night, I find myself stiffening before I take off her lead and give her the "Find!" command. This is particularly true in wilderness or debris fields where I have little ability to be a second set of eyes for her, to see what might be a threat from yards away. Coyotes. Stray dogs. Vagrants with a grudge. Anything could be out there, and sometimes is. Puzzle wears a set of blinking lights on her collar that helps me plot her movements when I cannot hear them. That helps. But in the dark, I seem to quiver with protective antennae. It's hard not to hold her back.

A trainer I know says that some of those 80 percent dogs wash out because of their handlers, and now, in the latter stages of our training together, I'm first aware that I could be the weak link between us. This is not a job for the merely well-intentioned. I have the training, the head skills, and the physical and emotional stamina for this, but Puzzle provokes my vulnerabilities.

One night at the fire academy, our trainer hides a victim on a high A-frame built to simulate a roof for training firefighters. The victim clings by his hands to the roof's peak, his body dangling out of sight down the other side. Puzzle and I are working a sector that includes mangled cars and railway tankers, and on this clear, cool night, the victim's scent is sweet and strong for her. After a couple of sweeps through the area, my dog rejects the tankers and the cars and dashes for the A-frame, lifting her head once at the bottom of it and then racing up the incline to the top, wagging and alerting on the victim draped down the other side, licking his hands. "*Woop!*" she says, the joy of the find making a little pop like a consonant at the end of her croon.

At the base of the A-frame, I'm about to climb to meet her when she dashes down the incline to get me and lead me back. "Good girl," I praise, and she bolts up the roofline again, alerts again, then scrambles down the roof to meet trundle-bug me only halfway up. She's made a good find and a great alert, and though I'm pleased at her insistence, she's terribly excited, scrambling from the victim back to me several times as I climb. Every dash down the roof seems closer to the edge of it in the dark — a ten-foot drop at its greatest height, a drop onto cement and training equipment she seems oblivious to. Or perhaps she can see that edge clearly, has it all under control.

"Puzzle," I call to her at the top of the roofline. I hear my voice quavering. "Good girl. Good girl. But 'Stay.'"

She does — oh, beautiful stay — balancing there with the victim at the top of the peak, wiggling her great joy of the find, tongue lolling. In the darkness, she is all light coat and dark eyes and *ha-ha-ha* exhalation.

"Hi," I huff to the volunteer victim at the top.

"Hi," he says back.

"Ten bucks says she makes it down from the roof before we do."

"Not gonna take that bet," he replies. I see him grin. With one hand hanging on and the other free, he gives her a scritch on the cheek before we begin our careful slide down the incline to the ground. On the release word, Puzzle, with her lower center of gravity, skitters easily down the slope. She stands on the asphalt and smiles up at my slower progress, her tail waving idly.

As I make my way down, I decide to teach Puzzle a "Creep" command, a word for "go slow beside me" in cases like these. I can imagine other scenarios where such a command might be useful — crawling under barbed-wire fences, making our way through damaged houses — anywhere slow progress might be the safest course. *Woo*, she says to me cheerfully when I arrive, a little encouragement for the human from the dog.

Night work is good for both of us. I have lessons of confidence to learn in this uneasy space between Puzzle's puppy foolishness and adulthood. Across the coming months, we train on, and I begin to understand how she makes sense of her surroundings at night. She's not heedless. With her nose in motion, her paws outstretched, her gaze extended, and her ears brought forward to bear, Puzzle is capable of making good choices. But I watch her light form flash over debris in the darkness, and because I love her as well as respect her gifts, I hold my breath when she slips out of sight. It's a hard-won peace, this letting the dog do her job outside the scope of my protection.

17

SNAKE-PROOFING

I AM UPSTAIRS, tapping away at my journal with the stereo on, and Puzzle has been whining at the puppy gate for several minutes. She's come in from outside, and now she wants to come up.

"*Wait,* Puz," I call, using our words. Trainer Susan would be proud. "Let me finish this, and I'll come down and let you in."

She whines again. Nothing doing on the *wait.* I hear her somehow pop the latch and press through the puppy gate, bounding up the steps to find me. She pushes her way between the hassock and my chair to sit nearby. Without looking away from the computer, I reach my hand to her face and feel her snuffling there.

Okay, I shouldn't be pleased. She didn't wait. (Trainer Susan would *not* be proud.) But this is a cozy, friendly connection, and for the division of a minute, I am first bemused by a dog who has figured out how to open the puppy gate and grateful also for the adolescent Golden who has finally begun to seek me out for companionship. We've had a number of little breakthroughs recently. Partners at last.

Stroking her idly while I reread today's journal entry, I'm only half paying attention to my dog. It takes a moment to realize that her face feels misshapen, and I recognize that the snuffling I heard against my hand didn't stop when she pulled away from it. I look down to Puzzle, and a Puzzle in trouble looks up at me, the left side of her head swollen twice its size, her eyes terrified. She is struggling to breathe. Saliva she cannot seem to swallow runs from the sides of her mouth, soaking the fur of her chest.

I drop down beside her, turning her face in my hands. This looks like anaphylaxis, an allergic reaction to something she'd eaten, gotten into, or the result of a bite or a wound. Her head seems to be swelling more even as I touch it, and when I find two small puncture marks just below the edge of her mouth in the soft flesh that joins face to throat, I know this is an emergency issue. Somehow I lift her up, get her down the stairs, and into the car. A neighbor agrees to drive while I hold Puzzle upright. She is gasping now, the inside of her mouth tinged blue.

The emergency vet is just a few miles away, but this Friday night the direct route is choked with restaurant and club traffic. Puzzle is propped in my arms, trembling as I lift her chin with my fingertips and hold up her head, the only position that seems to relieve her labored breathing. My friend drives carefully. We try not to further distress the dog, so we speak in low voices about whether we tough out the traffic or try longer, alternate routes. I wonder if Puzzle feels my racing heart against her shoulder. It takes only minutes but seems forever to get to the vet.

The receptionist at the emergency clinic takes one look at her and triages us into an examining room quickly, where the on-duty vet examines Puzzle at once, noting the double puncture wound. Rodent, possibly, but snake far more likely by the look of the injury, and this is the season for them. I think of my house's proximity to water and of the undisturbed woodpile in the backyard, both attractive resources for a snake even in a residential area. Still, it's hard to believe. *We're out working in all kinds of wilderness, and she gets a snakebite at home?*

"These bites are very painful," the vet says. He disinfects the area, gives Puzzle a shot of Benadryl and another of antibiotic, and starts an IV. She doesn't growl or resist, tilting her chin up to rest on my shoulder as I lean down to her. And then I hold her and we all watch, waiting for the swelling to come down and her breathing to ease. Long minutes of no change at all. She struggles to get comfortable. The random scrabble of her feet against the table is so helpless a sound I fight tears.

After a time, she stops drooling, and a little while after that she swallows. When Puzzle opens her mouth to pant, I no longer hear a labored rasp, and I can see the flush of pink tongue. "Things are looking up," the vet says, and he leaves us to attend the other emergencies that have crashed through the door. Across the next hour, we hear the click of nails on the lobby tile, bright thank-yous in the corridor, and later, a young man weeping. I stand in the examining room with my head bowed to Puzzle. I too have lost loved animals at this clinic, even in this room. But not this time.

We drive home more slowly than we'd left it. Whether sedated from the Benadryl or relieved that she can breathe easily, Puzzle no longer trembles in my arms, but lies awake and occasionally gulping. I can feel her pulse beneath my fingers, the motion of her swallow against my arm.

She is strong enough to walk, but we carry her gently into the house and put her across my bed, where she lies without protest. The little dogs yap and chitter, and lifted to the bed, they give her the obligatory vet trip sniff-over. And then they settle, all of them, the way she had once settled near Scuppy. Jack, shy and wiggly, gives Puzzle's face an experimental lick. She seems unaware of all of them, her eyes following me as I draw the curtains and change into my pajamas. When I leave for a glass of water, she immediately tries to jump to the floor.

Puzzle is needy — a condition I have never seen in her. I prop us both up on pillows and curl beside her on the bed, feeling the press of her spine against my chest. In time, she sighs, a relaxed heave and an exhale that suggests all is better, if not well. She sleeps easily, but I do not, realizing how serious this could have been had she not come to me. And I wonder what went through her dog mind as she bumped free the puppy gate separating us and bounded up the stairs to put her face into my palm.

I can easily imagine Puzzle putting her nose to something rustling in the woodpile. Was the snake a resident or a transitional character? How long after she'd been bitten did she come to me? I think of the Poms, equally curious and one-fifth of Puzzle's body weight. Tonight's situation, already bad enough, could have been much worse.

The next day, wearing boots and leather gloves, friends and I disassemble the woodpile with much noise and crashing, and we move it behind a gated fence inaccessible to the dogs. And I make a plan to disturb that woodpile daily. Come winter, we will burn it all up.

Puzzle is eighteen months old and has not yet been "snake-proofed," in the traditional sense. Snake-proofing is a common procedure for field and search dogs, involving a shock collar and thoughtful, controlled access to a living snake, which is not harmed. From a considered distance, the dog is allowed to get the scent of the snake and see the nature of its motion, and at the point the dog exhibits any interest, a mild shock is applied via the collar — ideally teaching that the snake has a painful potential and is to be avoided at all costs. Some dogs get the point with little provocation from the collar. Even the tiniest shock elicits a start and a *yike*, and a second view of a snake causes a backpedaling motion worthy of Wile E. Coyote. One of our handlers laughs that his dog, generally calm and relatively fearless in the search environment, leaps straight up at the sight of a snake in the brush, landing in his arms with Scooby-Doo's "ruh-roh!" expression on her face. Other dogs require greater deterrence. Belle, a yellow Lab with a high pain threshold who has grown up around snakes, would not be put off no matter how high the setting on the collar, a shock she did not even seem to feel.

I wonder how Puzzle will respond at her own snake-proofing session. She's a dog of great curiosity, but also a dog of deep grudges against things that have frightened her. This could go either way.

Puzzle's regular vet examines her face the next day. He is an upbeat, confident man with an easy laugh that fills the room, and no matter how many times Puzzle goes to the vet for one injection or another, she adores him, tolerating any number of pokes and prods and sharp sticks to be with him. Now she stands quietly as he examines her, trembling a little with the intensity of our joint scrutiny. Dr. Yzaguirre confirms the snakebite — probably copperhead, probably juvenile. The swelling has diminished this morning, and the neat double-slash of the bite is clearly visible. He shakes his head a little, then gives Puzzle a stroke and a playful tug of her ear. A lot of venom in these young snakes; a little lower on the jaw, and this could have been very bad. I mention Puzzle's future snake-proofing session, and the vet laughs a little. He would be surprised, he says, if she needs it.

Puzzle seems to agree. Across the following weeks, she watches our regular disturbance of the woodpile, raising up on her hind legs to peer over the fence at what we are doing, and though she has always loved stealing kindling, she has little interest in joining us.

We go to formal snake-proofing as soon as possible. I'm not sure what to expect as Fleta fits the shock collar around Puzzle's neck in the parking lot of a wildlife rehabilitation facility near one of our local parks. A wildlife handler brings out a large, lidded plastic tub carrying a de-venomed diamondback rattlesnake. The lid has holes in the top of it, and we begin the training procedure by simply allowing Puzzle to approach the tub in the way of any curious dog. As she approaches and her nose begins to work the scent of it, Puzzle has already stiffened and become wary. Her path forward has altered to a cautious half-circle. I watch her nostrils work, and though she is receiving small, increasing shocks, she doesn't seem to notice them. At the most downwind point to the tub, Puzzle veers abruptly away.

Fleta and I deliberate. Initially, Puzzle was a little too curious about the tub, but the moment of strongest scent and strongest shock seemed quite clear to her. She had no interest in approaching the tub again. The snake handler suggests that we move to the next stage, allowing Puzzle to both see and scent the snake in order to gauge her true response. This takes little time. The handler places the snake on the ground, where it begins its graceful side-slither to the north, and Puzzle backs up to the fullest extent of her lead, circling wide away from it, every muscle stiff with alarm. Though she had received the associated shock, she did not react to it — not even a flinch — as though every part of her awareness was focused on the snake.

The snake pauses a moment in its own meander, splendidly poised, then slopes into motion again. Puzzle responds with another half-arc away from him.

Good choice, I think, and because I'm too often from the if-a-little-is-good-more-is-better school, I ask if we should double-check Puzzle's aversion with another exposure to the snake, another shock.

Fleta shakes her head, grinning a little, watching my dog counter-curve away from the snake on tiptoe, her fur on end and tail rigid. "No shock on that last one," she says. Puzzle's expression is so tense she appears walleyed. "But I think we can safely say this is one dog that's snake-proofed. And then some."

18

A HANDLER'S GUIDE TO RISK MANAGEMENT

THE ELECTRIC FENCE isn't live, authorities tell us, just minutes before Buster brushes against it at the edge of our sector, catapults back, and yelps from the shock. Snow has been falling heavily for the past hour or more, and the fence has become almost impossible to see in the first place, especially where it threads through overgrowth and seems to disappear. The farm we search on this midwinter day is decrepit; the three houses sitting on the land haven't been lived in for a long while, but the property is in use. The fence is certainly live — perhaps to discourage predators or trespassers, or to keep the livestock out of what once would have been the farmhouse yard.

Buster shakes off his shock and, after a word of encouragement from Johnny, continues working his sector, stepping deliberately over a woundless dead rabbit, so newly dead that when I pull off my glove and hover my hand over its fur, I feel the rabbit's residual warmth. Snow has fallen thickly in past minutes, and now the dead rabbit appears to be made of lace, her dull eye frosted over. Soon she will disappear entirely, as the ground has quickly disappeared beneath our feet.

Our search here, two states away from home, is just as ambiguous. There could be the remains of one teenager on this land, or two, or none. The authorities are guessing, pursuing a lead from a lead from a lead that has led them in unexpected directions on a case almost a year old. The area is remote. Where once this farm might have been on the far side of the small town it adjoins, hard decades have caused the town to recede and the outlying farms to fall to ruin or give over to other forms of enterprise.

The three houses here reflect generations across a previous century. Unbound by city code or ordinance restrictions, they are placed in a haphazard clutch on the land, as though to take advantage of utilities connected to each house on the property before. The oldest of them — a modest structure with a wide front porch — was probably built in the early 1900s, the smallest of the three looks like a 1950s ranch with its red brick and wide windows, and the last of the group, closest to the road, appears to be the newest of the homes, built perhaps forty years ago at the height of a neo-Mediterranean era. It is a light brick house with arched windows and iron burglar bars, black scrollwork on the porch railing, and a rusty iron Don Quixote lying face-down in the dirt. This would be a quiet, uninterrupted place to hide someone — living or dead — which is the possibility now. I'm working a sector beside Johnny and Buster that involves the Mediterranean house and a long, narrow stretch of land behind it that includes pasture, outbuildings, a burn pit, and a row of stables leaning over to the point of collapse.

Though the snow gives the scene an air of gentle benediction, we are all tense here. We came to this search after a two-day briefing that warned about possible dangers in the area. The calling agency has been frank: in the places we are to search, there are likely hazards. There may be meat-baited, cyanide-laced coyote traps, the so-called M-44s that can look deceptively like pieces of old pipe or sprinkler heads. These could be an obvious danger to our dogs and even to us. Before we deployed, we studied pictures of the devices and a whole series of warning signs required to be posted on property where the traps are embedded — and then we were told that plenty of ranches have the traps but not the signs, worn away by weather or never posted in the first place. Several of our handlers shook their heads at the briefing, unwilling to risk this danger to their dogs. The calling agency answered with a promise to have the search areas swept first by grid walkers trained to identify and dismantle the devices.

The coyote traps are not the only possible problem. There are meth labs deeply hidden in some pockets of this terrain, protected by homemade explosives on tripwires. Some of the labs may be abandoned, but the explosives could remain. Day two of our briefing included pictures and samples of the devices and tripwires, often more difficult to see than the coyote traps. There seemed to be a thousand ways to blow up unwelcome strangers, and that would be us. Any search is better with a good prebrief, but despite the promise of trained ground sweepers clearing the way ahead of our work, we ended the briefing session pensive. We made the long trip to the search area subdued.

Today, the farm where we search has been swept and theoretically cleared of all dangers, including the electric fence, supposedly off, that shocked Buster. This does not inspire confidence. After apologies and assurances, we work forward, hoping the fence is the only surprise we'll get in the field. Johnny and Buster move carefully ahead while I sweep sideways back and forth beside them, looking beyond them both to anything that appears to be a threat. Lovely as it is, the snowfall doesn't help matters much as it obscures the ground before us. I see livestock moving easily a distance away — perhaps this suggests the area is safe.

There is a small herd of pygmy goats on this land, and a few donkeys. We've been warned that the donkeys are probably not dog-friendly. It's hard to know what to make of their stares as they approach the fence that cuts our sector in half. The fence is live, and they seem to know it. They are cautious not to touch the posts and strands, but they crane their heads carefully over the side. They gaze at us steadily with an air of expectation, their fuzzy faces sugared with snow, and one occasionally extends his jaw forward and brays. The hard, metallic screech of the animal echoes less now than it did an hour ago, softened by the snow's accumulation. When we approach the fence as part of our search sweep, two donkeys bring their ears forward and one lays his ears back. I don't know much about donkeys, but my money bets the one with the big brown spot on his forehead and the laid-back ears is the dog hater of the group. The others just seem social. One pretty chocolate-colored creature extends quivering lips toward the pocket of my jacket as I pass, which suggests someone else has been feeding her treats from pockets. Every time she does it, the tender expression in her eyes looks like she just wants to give me a little taste.

The goats are even more aggressive. Not one of them is taller than my knees, but what they lack in height, they make up for in confidence. They are not shy, rushing forward as though we are the bearers of food or god-sent relief from goat boredom. Two of the smallest, twin silver and black Agouti doelings, seem to have something of a crush on Buster. As we leave one part of our sector and enter the next where the goats wander, these two rush forward to sniff at his haunches. There's a funny, complicit little tremble between them that shudders snow off their coats. They begin to follow him as he works. Buster's a farm dog and used to barnyard animals, but he's not sure what to make of his growing entourage when the rest of the herd follows these two from a respectful distance. When he stops, they stop. When he turns, they pivot also, plodding his new direction, their small heads bobbing.

"Shoo — go on now," says Johnny, clapping his hands and waving. The herd skitters slightly sideways a few steps, but their focus is on the two females who are love-locked behind Buster and who have ignored Johnny entirely.

I know less about goat dynamics than I do about donkeys, but it's interesting to watch the rest of the goats defer to these two small females, who seem to be the power players here. Who are they to the herd? What about them makes them leaders? Charisma aside, they don't make this sector easy to search, and Johnny and I confer a moment. As Buster and Johnny move forward, I begin stomping and waving every few feet, singing off-key to distract the goats enough to give the dog some room to work. Some of the herd isn't sure what to make of me and scatter a little farther. Buster's two smoke and silver girls shoot me cynical looks from the slit pupils of their golden eyes, and then they ignore me too.

The herd follows us to the white brick house with the burglar bars, but they pause at the edge of what would formerly have been a yard. They come no farther. We step onto a bare cement porch that has a fragment of a woman's shirt lying a few feet away from the door. It was once part of a western shirt, red yoke and sleeves, white from the yoke to the waist. One pearl and metal snap remains. It looks too clean to have been here long. Buster is uninterested in it. I note the scrap of fabric but don't touch it, writing down its description, and we enter the house, which smells of moldy shag carpet and cat pee.

Someone lived here and someone left here with little thought to resale. There are empty, yellowed fast-food sacks on an abandoned dinette table, overturned cereal boxes speckled with rat excrement, and old, old food in the refrigerator. Dirty dishes in the sink, the remains of several meals dried and crusted over. The bathroom has so strong a smell that Johnny and I recoil, breathing through our mouths as we walk down the hallway. Though his nose is more sensitive than ours, the heavy air doesn't dissuade the dog. Buster lifts his nose thoughtfully in the fug — a whole host of rich, human smells — but he turns away, indicating nothing suggests a violent human crime here.

I stand at the edge of what would have been a living room and watch him work, relieved to think that the dog found no death and no evidence of recent life in this space, that perhaps this house didn't hold missing teenagers for the last days of their lives.

The dog pads out of the house and we mark it as cleared, making our reverse way back through the waiting goats, who caper a little with excitement as we separate the herd and cause them to regroup and hustle to follow us. Buster's two little goat friends join him, breaking into a trot as he moves out of the pasture as quickly as possible. We slip through the gate, frustrating their follow, and we leave the goats behind. They press against the fence line, their expressions wistful. The Lab shoots us a disgusted look and something of a dog shrug, then sets back to work.

We enter a long field, where a flock of peacocks joins us in the farthest part of the sector. They follow in a stately progression beside us, replacing the goats that have been left behind. The birds are unafraid of us, unworried about Buster. We search and they move quietly in trail, picking their way with great care, without fluster or gibber. The vivid males and speckled, elegant females are remotely beautiful against the falling snow, creating the surreal impression of a search sector embroidered in brightly colored thread.

"Is it just me," says Johnny, ever understated, "or does this search just get more weird?"

Buster seems relieved to be rid of the goats and unworried by the peacocks. He works quickly, crossing the area in four easy sweeps and rejecting it of any interest. We leave the birds to their field and the goats to their pasture and enter the leaning, shabby outbuilding that lacks a door. The first room is full of feed bags and smells of dust, grain, and bird droppings, but the second room is curiously empty apart from a cushioned rocking chair sitting in the center of the floor. Buster moves to the chair, circles it thoughtfully, and as he is sweeping the little room, suddenly yelps softly and backs away in haste, winking his eyes and snorting. We smell nothing, but Buster certainly does. Not a response to human scent, it's as though something burns.

Johnny looks to his dog that's now pawing at his nose, and we move away from the building as Buster's eyes begin to water and he begins to breathe heavily.

"What the hell?" says Johnny, bending down to examine Buster's face. He has never seen his dog react so. I circle the outbuilding and peer into the room that gave him the problem, and I can see nothing but the battered chair and dusty floor. Our tracks in. Buster's circling paw prints. Our tracks out.

I make a note of Buster's curious response, call it in on the radio, and rejoin Johnny. "How's he doing?" I ask.

"He's okay."

"Not a good day at the office for Buster."

"No," says Johnny, still bending down with a careful eye to his dog.

Buster recovers in moments, but he's eager to move away from that outbuilding, and he's quick to go back to work. The dog scrambles across the field, lifting his nose in the direction of a row of adults watching from an adjoining property, yards and yards away. Three are standing. Two sit in lawn chairs and gaze in our direction over the backs of several abandoned cars. They are swaddled in parkas and hats; some of them cradle a Thermos. I flick a nod of acknowledgment, but they do not respond.

We finish the sector and head back to Incident Command, where we are introduced to two men and a woman who are, we are told, anthropologists and archaeologists here to potentially protect any find of human remains that may be irrelevant to our search and have historic or tribal significance. One of the young men had seen Buster's contact with the fence and heard about his experience in the outbuilding over the radio, and he bends over the dog now, talking to him kindly and rubbing his ears. The three have come prepared to watch and to wait.

Several local officers walk across the snow in the field near the oldest house, probing it gently with a pike designed to penetrate dirt and allow buried scent to rise. There's a chance that this current search sweeps over old, old graves. The anthropologists watch, their eyes on the officers but their conversation directed to us. The dogs fascinate them, they say; they have never seen this kind of work before. While I write up the sector report and sketch a map to attach to it, Johnny and others talk with them about the use of dogs for the recovery of human remains from ancient sites. One of the anthropologists jokes that what they really need are "dig dogs," trained to keep archaeologists and anthropologists from picking at the dirt too hastily. A good dog alert could make all the difference. Sometimes, he says, a single strike of pick and mallet can bring up things you weren't quite ready to see.

There is nothing visibly amiss in the oldest of the houses, but a police canine and Saber have shown strong interest in a bedroom windowsill and upward along a wall beside it. They have also shown interest in a dark spot on the floor. On a blind search after the others had emerged from the house, Belle, working in the basement, went "straight up the wall," according to her handler, stretching toward the same floor area from below. *Human scent here,* the dogs separately suggest, though the house is remarkably neat and still bears the faint scent of cleanser. Blood spatter from an attack, semen, or old blood from a commonplace injury? Learning that two of our dogs confirmed the police canine, the officers overseeing the search stand together in the snow with their hands deep in the pockets of their black leather jackets and their shoulders hunched forward against the cold. Though the search has recovered no bodies here, the floor, wall, and windowsill of the oldest house merit forensic examination, and we are far from any place with those resources. Several officers continue to confer while one goes to release the anthropologists and another tells us they have nowhere left for the dogs to search.

Our work is done, and after the calling agency releases us, we begin to pack our equipment and prepare the dogs for travel. They are tired and withdrawn, ready to go off-duty and sleep in the protective warmth of their cars and their crates. We're ready too. This kind of work needs to be done, and the team exists to do it, but the possibility of poison and explosives on this search made the already difficult work even harder. None of us knows what to make of Buster's response in that outbuilding. Nothing about it looked good.

Thick snow still falls, and we push through it shin-deep, some of the dogs wading through drifts that brush against their bellies. Despite protective footwear and heavy socks, many of us can no longer feel our feet. The dogs' paws are icy between the pads. Icicle beads have formed like tribal necklaces around the ruffs of the ones with long coats.

"God," says Cindi, shaking off the search and its dangerous possibilities, "I'm glad that's over." I breathe deeply and rub my eyes, feeling a little winded afterward, suddenly aware of how often I'd held my breath through that sector, how hard I'd stared forward into the white of the snow.

As we load the vehicles and Buster, Belle, Saber, and Hunter are defrosted and made safe for transport, I look across the fields where we searched, now completely blanketed with snowfall. The human audience is packing up, retracting lawn chairs, their bright Thermoses tucked beneath their arms. The peacocks have taken to branches of low trees, to the dividing fence that separates them from the goats. They huddle beside one another silently, their graceful heads bowed and the trailing plumage of the males counterbalancing their forward weight. The little goats have carved a trail for themselves to the leaning shed. One of the females has jumped onto an overturned trough. She gazes toward the truck Buster leapt into, but the rest of the goats don't seem to notice our departure. They saunter idly along the trail to the shed and back again, the untouched snow that borders their route so deep that from where I stand the goats appear to be swimming, only their dark, bobbing heads visible above the white.

I am home very late from the search. It feels strange, light, and heedless to walk easily through my backyard without scanning for cyanide traps. The dogs have been long asleep when I come in, and they rouse a little fustily, the Poms briefly deliberating whether they should riot when the door opens and then, seeing that it's me, deciding not to. They rise, stretch, and wobble forward in greeting while Puzzle, who cocked an eye in my direction when I came in the door, remains belly-up on the back of the couch.

Too tired to sleep, I sit beside her, stroking the fine line from her throat along the jaw to her soft ear. She has always seemed a sturdy dog, but tonight I think of tripwires and coyote traps, and I'm aware of her fragility. Had this search been mine to choose as a handler, would I have made the choice to work her, despite the known risks and failed assurances? I don't know. But this is no reprieve. The decision could come up again, and soon. Puzzle is only weeks from her certification tests.

"Here's a handler's guide to risk management: don't live vicariously through your dog," an experienced handler from another team once said to me, "and for God's sake, don't get attached." The best handling, he said, is done from a distance. He had dogs at home that he loved, but his search dog was not one of them — a working dog in a different place with him. He had to keep her there. They were functional partners only as long as the handler held real affection for her at bay.

I wonder what he would have made of this search and its potential hazards. Would he have been hesitant at all? Would he have been cautious only due to the investment risk? Or were those long-ago comments to me made in a moment of posturing, and did his colleagues know him as a man who split his hamburger in the truck and let his search dog sleep on the bed? The fellow had been insistent. He had worked several dogs in his search career, and when he told me that "loving a search dog screws with your priorities," I understood his perspective. But I couldn't agree with it. I wondered then and I wonder now if I could ever be capable of that kind of remove.

19

SHOW AND TELL

AT THE END of a long corridor smudged dark with recent smoke, Puzzle stands with her nose to a door, her tail waving faintly. Six rooms, six closed doors, and behind one of those, a single volunteer victim buried in rubble. We are in the fire department burn building, and today Puzzle is telling me which closed door to open and which others to ignore. She was given the "Find!" command yards from the building, and in she ran, smiling, her tongue out sideways. I am steps behind her, running from bright into immediate gloom. The air here is thick with soot and the dust of spent hay, and in the flashlight's beam, I can see the swirls of Puzzle's slipstream wash up against the wall like an airplane's wingtip vortices. If she were to disappear down some dark passage, for a time at least I could track her path through dusty air. I sneeze, then sneeze again.

The airflow here is tricky. The burn building's outside windows are open to today's southerly breeze, while all its internal doors are closed. Here, the scent of a human hidden in a single room can easily slip out the bottom of one door and wash up against neighboring walls or onto the closed door opposite, sticking there in the dust and damp. "Scent traps," these are called, and scent can be deceptively strong there, misleading the dog trying to pinpoint the source. In this exercise, Puzzle's got to know better, and she's got to show me how much she knows better.

These closed-door drills are some of the hardest, most intuitive work a dog team can do. In a damaged office building full of locked doors, a dog that can indicate the right door to kick in for rescue is a tremendous help to the firefighters who have to break through them. In past training, we've not been entirely successful. Because I didn't yet know how to read my dog, when scent was faint, I was inclined to open every door. And Puzzle was glad to let me do so, smiling there and sometimes moving idly into the empty room and sometimes not, as if uncertain how much to humor me. With closed-door drills, I had to learn to hang back, to stop doing the work and stop opening doors just as a given. When I frustrated Puzzle with our slowness, she began to make her cues bigger: a little scent there, A LOT OF SCENT HERE.

Today she has her nose to one door and stands expectant. It's clear which one she wants. Last door on the left at the end of the corridor. As I approach it, her wagging tail wags faster: *oh-yeah-oh-yeah-this-one-oh-yeah*. I decide to test her loyalty to that door, and at the last minute I put my hand to the latch of the door opposite, a *wrong* choice. Puzzle's tail stops wagging, and when I grind the latch slightly, I hear a little *pffft* snort out of her that could be a sneeze but sounds like disgust. She does not turn away. She sticks to the door she prefers.

I stop and turn to the door where she stands. "Is *this* the one you want, Puz?" I ask her. There is the briefest brow-furrow, an expression of incredulity at my indecision (like a doggie *Duh!* — I'm not kidding), then a harder wag when I put my hand to the right door latch. She is all encouragement. When I pop open the door, Puzzle gives her two-boing hop as she bounds across the threshold toward the victim for the find. And then she turns and beams at me, giving me so thorough an *atta-girl* that I laugh out loud.

It is a perfect moment of joyful understanding between us. From the depths of her total dogness, Puzzle is pleased, and she knows that I am pleased, and after I help the victim from the rubble, she spins and capers down the corridor, smudging herself liberally with soot.

And what of snakes? In the months after Puzzle's snake-proofing, I realize her experience with the snake in the woodpile was profound. Clearly Puzzle saw the snake before the strike to her face, and its shape, coil, and movement made an impression she remembers.

After the bite, she immediately became wary of coiled rope and occasionally jittery on walks when we passed someone pulling a garden hose through tall grass. Once, when strong wind catches a length of black rubber tubing and blows it into the street in front of us, Puzzle freezes and barks furiously. I maneuver her downwind of the object, where she wuffles her cheeks for the scent of snake, relaxing only when the scent isn't there.

And she is willing to generalize. On one training day at the fire academy, Puzzle and I cross a parking lot to get to the training area and approach a fat, hay-stuffed silt filter placed over an open gutter. Puzzle catches sight of the silt filter in her periphery, starts, then presses her body against my legs, refusing to move forward and refusing to let me move forward, either. Her eyes are dark and wide. She barks furiously where she stands. The silt filter is about four feet long and perhaps ten inches in diameter, and to her dog eyes I suppose it looks like the tubby mother of all snakes. Puzzle looks up at me where she has frozen, her expression dumbfounded, as if to say "Look at *that* mama-jama!" We are upwind, so we circumnavigate the object, and she works her nose downwind of it. A couple of good inhales and Puzzle seems a little sheepish when she recognizes her mistake. She immediately saunters over to the silt filter as if to hide her earlier alarm. There are times when Puzzle's face-saving maneuvers remind me of a cat.

I look back at the silt-filter episode with interest. When Puzzle had been afraid of Max in turnout gear months ago, she had hidden behind me. When the silt filter first appeared like a snake to her, she instead froze in *front* of me, unwilling for either of us to go forward. I appreciate that double caution. Is my dog becoming protective of me as she matures?

Though her sight response suggests what may have happened that night in the woodpile, I don't want Puzzle afraid of every snake-shaped object that we pass. There are too many hoses and ropes in our future. At the fire academy, I lead her past every coil of rope and hanging line, every type of fire hose in motion with the rookie firefighters. The acclimatization works. Puzzle gives these things an eyeball in passing, and that nose works rapidly both on approach and departure, but she no longer spooks as she once did. The garden hose at home she ultimately forgives. She no longer scuttles away, but she knits her brow every time I move it, as though she sure wishes I would smell it first.

Puzzle has other opinions she's happy to share. On a warm evening, she has stopped in the middle of a training search and has deliberately taken her long lead in her mouth, growling and tugging as though to pull it from my hand. We are searching for a single victim in a mixed sector — partly urban, bordered by scruffy, unimproved "wilderness" acreage — and after I've had to stop and untangle her lead from mesquite thorns three times, my dog is clearly telling me I'm slowing her down.

"She wants to work off-lead," I say to Deryl, who runs with me.

"So take her off," he replies, swatting at a mosquito.

It's a simple solution, but I hesitate. Tonight she's on-lead because we're training in an area we've never been to before. If Puzzle were to take it into her head to run, to let go of this training search and flee on some whim of her own, it would be almost impossible to find her. It's an uneasy moment, and one that plenty of other handlers have experienced before me. The 100 Percent Recall: the dog who always comes back when called. When do we trust a dog's emerging commitment? With a search dog it's got to be solid. It should be solid for Puzzle now.

It's not hard for me to remember the puppy that ignored my "Come" commands in our own backyard, but Puzzle has become more than that dog. In environments we know well, she commonly works off-lead. And her long wait beside me after my recent neighborhood fall demonstrated loyalty or obedience or a mixture of both. I know I should trust her now. But I dither. *I don't know this area,* I think. *Anything could be out there. And it's getting dark.* I make plenty of excuses not to trust her, not to take the chance.

While Puzzle stares at me with challenge, Deryl waves away the mosquitoes that have surrounded us in so thick a cloud I can hear them singing against my ears. We're getting chewed to bits while I deliberate and, worse, whoever the poor soul is out there hiding for us in the mesquite and poison ivy has been chewed even longer.

"Has she ever run away from you before?" Deryl asks.

"Not since she was a puppy. And never from a search."

Deryl is a military man of quick decision, but he says gently, "You've gotta let her go."

I take off the lead, and Puzzle doesn't have to be prompted. She's off with purpose — moving quickly while we run behind her. I'm better now at watching my dog and not falling into holes, but this terrain, with its universally high brush covering uneven ground and dried creek beds, is still a challenge. We crash and huff and stumble, chest-high in the scrub that Puzzle presses through. She moves without pausing, and though I only occasionally see an ear or the flip of her tail as she winds her way between the trees, the sound of her suggests she's on to scent. This is not the intermittent, tentative snap and crackle of a dog casually nosing around. I have begun to learn the sound of my working dog as well as the sight of her.

We are losing light. The deepest part of the brush has already gone gray, and as I cut myself free of brush, I realize that I've lost sight of Puzzle altogether. We stop, and in the distance to our right, I can hear my dog's rapid scrambling through the thicket, maybe thirty or forty yards away.

"She's got him," I say to Deryl. "Or at least she's got *someone,*" I mutter. The team has had a few surprises in the wilderness, finding people who'd sought out private spaces and, surprised (and naked), were not prepared for the launch of a joyful search dog in their midst. Now we are veering right and pushing hard to make our way to the dog, and now we're in the strange nether of light between dusk and dark when flashlights don't help much, but the ambient light is too faint to distinguish low branches and braided vines covered in thorns. *I'll start falling any minute now*, I think, just as a branch flips my glasses off my face and over my head, where they land like a horseshoe around the upturned limb of a young tree.

"Do you hear her?" I ask, blundering forward again.

Deryl shakes his head. In the distance, probably from the direction of a housing community on the other side of this land, I can hear two dogs barking frantically, and I have to wonder if Puzzle has thrown off the search out of boredom or disgust with my slowness, and if she's now a football field or more away, pressed to some fence and taunting those dogs.

I'm about to call her name when I fall hard, landing face first in a thick clutch of poison ivy thrust upward from the base of a tree, twisting my pack off one shoulder and losing my glasses again.

"You all right?" asks Deryl.

I am not all right in any sense, I think to myself, feeling impotent, swallowing frustration — and worse, weak and nauseated after the fall. I am gathering my glasses, shredded gloves, and twisted backpack when I hear the snapping of branches just ahead and Puzzle moaning her victory *wroo*, a sound which unfailingly means she has found the victim and is proud of it. And because I was not right behind her, this time she has come back to get me and take me to him — a "re-find," we call it. Re-finds can be a trained technique, but Puzzle, never one to let her achievements go unnoticed, does not have to be prompted to go back. She pushes her cold nose to me and quivers a little.

"Where is he, Puz?" I ask, as her movements into the brush quicken. She crawls through some low spots and bounds over vines in others, and a few minutes later I hear her *wroo* again, see the light flash of her tail as she alerts on our patient volunteer, lying supine in a tangle of thicket.

"Good find! Good girl!" I shout to her, fumbling mangled treats from my pocket as Deryl helps the volunteer out of the brush and Puzzle bounces and preens. It was a good find. Direct, purposeful, independent, and — loyal. Loyal to the victim, loyal to the work, loyal to me. It was not enough to find the fellow once. In the absence of her handler, tonight Puzzle understood the job wasn't finished until she came back and showed him to me.

"See?" said Deryl. "She told you. And know what else she's telling you?"

"What?"

"She's telling you she's ready. And you better be too."

We are days away from the first of three certification tests — Wilderness, Urban/Disaster, and Clear Building — and now is when our strengths and weaknesses will show. In the plus column is certainly Puzzle's great enthusiasm for this work, our joint tolerance for discomfort, our experience together across all kinds of scenarios (now more than 250 training searches with the team or apart from it), and the fact that neither of us gives up easily. In the minus column is certainly that this dog is much faster than I am. We're not a slow team, but I can't help imagining Puzzle with a younger, stronger handler — an even match for her speed. I have seen her pause just so that I could catch up.

Puzzle, just a few months shy of two, is in that marvelous place where puppy energy and adult strength and coordination intersect. This is a happy time for her, and it shows. After training with the team or after training sessions at home, she is talkative and cheeky, full of dog mutters for me and play bows for the Poms, tossing toys their direction for a game. Her engagement with the world is a pleasure, her energy a challenge.

One afternoon, she finds a swatch of my discarded red SAR shirt, torn by thorns in the day's earlier training, and she runs outside with it to taunt the Poms: *I have this and you don't*. Dog Keep

Away is a very real game. Sprits'l is easily incensed and begins to chase her; Whisky's provoked to chase them both; two new little foster Poms get in on the action; and then Jack has to follow, his signature bark like a rooster's crow. The backyard is in an uproar, and when I go out to investigate, I find all the Poms chasing the Golden. They're galloping and barking and chasing her in great circles around the yard. They are amused to be furious, and Puzzle canters before them, tossing her head, the bit of red shirt waving from her mouth like a flag.

No video camera on hand. I sit down on the stoop and think, *Watch this and remember.*

I look at the Golden and feel the challenge of her. I was forty-four when Puzzle came to me, and I'm forty-six now. I keep reading that forty is the new thirty, and I don't want to acknowledge that a body slows down, but I've already noticed a change in my own stamina just in the time Puzzle's been by my side. *I should be getting stronger with all that running after her,* I think. But even the neighborhood walk with the forty-pound SAR pack has become tough sometimes. Other days after training, I'm so tired I go to bed with the six o'clock news. What is up with that?

I'm a healthy eater, get plenty of exercise, am not overweight. I scrutinize my diet with the help of a nutritionist. I take more yoga, more dance lessons, walk farther with and without the pack. I've never been a fan of elevators, but now I try to jog rather than walk up every set of stairs. This dog is ready to run, and I want to run this dog.

"Getting old," says my father about both of us when I tell him I've been tired lately. He is maybe joking, maybe not.

She's ready, Deryl said. *And you better be ready too.*

There are plenty of dog handlers who are older than I am, running young dogs and making very good work of it. I'm determined not to give in to this — even if I have to eat daily bowls of Wheaties in Geritol, or whatever the modern equivalent is.

20

THE WILDERNESS TEST

I MAY BE the one who pulled up a satellite image and the local weather data, studying them over coffee I couldn't taste, but Puzzle is the one who, on a bright March morning in 2006, looks far more prepared to run a certification test than I do. She strains impatiently at the end of her long lead as she waits at the edge of a nature preserve. She can already scent people on the trails. In a few minutes, we will be given a wilderness sector with zero to three victims and an hour and fifteen minutes to find them. The weeks just before Puzzle's Wilderness cert test, some days I felt ready, and other days completely vulnerable, like those dreams about exams you haven't studied for that you somehow end up taking anyway, stark naked.

Today I feel thoroughly prebriefed, which should inspire confidence. I know the area, the terrain, the weather conditions, and I know how my dog works. But I also know the wicked, thriving brush that fills the off-trail areas of the lowest parts of this preserve, which is built on a set of rolling hills. No examiner is going to give us a sector as easy to walk as a city park. And I'm betting my sector will include the low spaces. This is brush with teeth that in some areas grows as high as my chest. Not just uncomfortable. Not just impassable in some places. Scent muddles and meanders through it, and Puzzle and I must get through it too. There is my chief concern.

Puzzle will push her way through anything if it's physically possible to do so. She never seems to feel the thorns and slows only when a web of vines is thick enough to trap her. I'm not as quick to follow, though, and if there's a graceful way to get through this kind of terrain on two legs — even with a knife or small machete — I haven't yet mastered it. The brambles here can check me at every pass — snagging my boots, gaiters, pants, shirt, pack, hair, and hat to the extent that I have to cut myself free. It's the snagging and the cutting I'm not too sure about. (Maybe I *should* take this test naked.) I am concerned that Puzzle might find scent and push to it beyond my ability to follow. I'm now confident she would wait with her victim, vocalize his presence, or come back to return me to that place; what I don't know is how my slowness might eat up our total test time. There's every chance I could be the one to fail us, and I know it.

I've been warned by the examiners who set up the test. All victims are camouflaged. And all victims have been instructed not to make a sound in reward to Puzzle until I make contact and acknowledge finding them.

Matt will run FAS team for us and has been similarly told to do nothing more than define the odd-shaped edges of the sector and radio call the finds. He is ready to go too. He stands a little apart, and Puzzle wanders over to nuzzle him, wagging as he strokes her head. Puzzle loves Matt. He was her first volunteer victim and is one of her favorite field assistants now. Matt's in his twenties. Puzzle is not yet two. They look capable standing together, very much up to the task. I close my eyes and hope to channel a little of that.

In the presence of modern technologies, there are those who suggest that the canine wilderness search will become a thing of the past. Some canine teams already seem to feel the change. At a conference in Baltimore, I spoke with a woman who had once been on a search team that had primarily worked wilderness, a team that eventually folded because they no longer got calls. "Everyone has a cell phone these days," she said. "And a lot of people have GPS units," added another. Some care organizations serving Alzheimer's or dementia populations have expanded their own protection initiatives for patients — shifting from identifying patches on clothing to GPS locators that make it possible for caregivers to track a lost patient via satellite, even in the woods.

Yet lost children on camping trips and hikers who fail to come home are still a part of the news, as are the disoriented elderly, many of whom are found not far away from the care facility or the home they left, but are found hidden in the undeveloped land that surrounds it, having fallen or strayed into terrain they can't escape. Cell phone batteries die, and it may be a while before every individual in a kayak or out for a hike has a GPS locator around his neck. We train forward. In an urban area like the Dallas–Ft. Worth Metroplex, our wilderness searches are not confined to Boy Scouts who got separated on a field excursion. The chain-link fence behind a housing development may be all that separates civilization from an expanse of owned but unimproved land, rapidly changing a so-called urban search into a wilderness search that can stretch on for miles.

A potential suicide case we worked years ago centered on the deep brush surrounding a steep ravine and the creek that wound through it — all sandwiched in the middle of a fully developed city. Working across that area, we sometimes couldn't see teammates standing eight feet away — the brush was that thick. Yet there was evidence of human traffic and in the most remote corners, for those who knew the way, wild and sometimes beautiful spaces. A winding stream, untouched bird nests, yellow wildflowers peering over the edge of the ravine, a little waterfall. But if you stood still and the wind was blowing from the right direction, you could hear the distant sounds of organized life: traffic, certainly, and a girl shouting to a friend, "Don't be that way!" Someone with an open window calling his child to come in for the night.

And so we continue to train wilderness, knowing an hour from now we could be called to work a state park or the scruffy back forty behind a multimillion-dollar housing development. Easily half our searches result in some sectors that require compass navigation, GPS orientation, and an ability to watch your dog and where you're going at the same time.

The first two I've got. The last one, not so much.

A word from the test coordinators and we are off, heading eastward along a road to the most downwind point of the sector. With any luck, on the way out Puzzle will get a little scent against the wind and either find a victim outright or forecast hot search spots when we come the other way. The breeze, warm at the front and cool at the trailing taper of each gust, invigorates her. She trots out along the cedar trees that border the sector with her head up. She's not pulling on the lead, but I can feel her excited tension on the line. I always think of the poet Robert Herrick's phrase — "that brave vibration each way free" — when Puzzle quickens before a search.

At the edge of the sector, I give her a brisk rubdown to stimulate her circulation and rev her charge even more. I ask if she's ready to go. She is. Puzzle flips her head around with a grin, and I feel her shiver pleasurably beneath my palms. "Find!" I shout, releasing her from the lead, and off she dashes, nosing immediately into the brush to begin our series of wide sweeps perpendicular to the wind. She is quick as I thought she'd be, and in these early minutes I'm having a better time of following her than I had forecast. The woods here consist more of young trees than brush, and as Puzzle winds her way across the area, I see her stiffen, her head pop up, and she makes an abrupt change of direction, nosing through the wood without a sidestep, working a scent cone. In just a few minutes, she has found the first victim, Don, huddled against a tree beneath a camouflage jacket.

Six minutes.

"Good girl!" I praise her. Don laughs. Tight nerves and a mild cedar allergy make my voice a little warbly, and from a distance I can see Matt also grinning. I sound like a squeaky eighth-grader. Puzzle takes her treat and gives Don a second kiss, and when I call "Find more!" in the most masterful voice I can conjure, she heads back to her sweeps.

We make several difficult presses through the woods again, but I see no sign of scent from her until the fourth sweep, when she leaves the woods entirely and crosses to the path in the middle of our sector. I watch her make a little arc with her muzzle and her eyes narrow with thoughtful appreciation. It's like watching dog radar. By all the signs I know from Puzzle, this dog is about to lock in and run.

I push out of the woods after her and raise up a few feet from the clearing. But I raise up prematurely, just in time to be caught by the low branch of a tree — a right sharp smack to the forehead. "Ohhh —" says Matt, in the way crowds go "Ohhh" after a hard hit on the football field. His face is red. I think he's trying not to laugh. My hat has gone, but before I can retrieve it, Puzzle gathers herself for a leap into the opposite brush. I see her head come up, and she is off and running uphill before I'm clear of the woods she had left.

I ignore the hat, which I can come back for after the test, and run after Puzzle, desperately trying to follow her course through the woods. Puzzle chooses a path that bends to the east before it curves back southwest, and behind me I hear Matt call that we may be crossing out of the sector. I can't be sure, moving as fast as we are, but my dog is certainly onto something human. She scrambles upward along uneven stones, and at the top of a rise, she pauses, as though the scent she'd been certain of had suddenly disappeared. For dog and handler, it's a peculiar "what the —" sensation when a dog runs out of a scent cone. Like being in the middle of a deflating hot-air balloon — a moment of great *hoosh* and then, *now what?*

It's a critical point for the handler too, but I've learned that in the wilderness, Puzzle never seems to fret over the *now what*. She's good about working her way back to the last point of scent. Today, all jumped up in the hard light of the cert test, I'm as likely to misdirect her as to do anything useful for the search. So I just shut up and watch. Difficult to do. Hard not to hurry her. But I've pressed Puzzle in previous training, tried to do the job for her, and have seen the exasperated confusion that followed. Sometimes to be faster, you have to be absolutely still.

Puzzle stands quietly, turning her head slightly to the left and the right. I see her mouth open slightly and her nostrils work. She reminds me of a boy I once played Hide-and-seek with as a child. He was fast and intuitive about all the good places his playmates would hide, and at the moment he ran out of good leads, he'd stand perfectly still and wait for someone to betray themselves by sound. It always worked, and stillness will work for Puzzle too, with her nose lifted to catch the thinnest strand of human scent on the wind. One wayward little gust or one movement out of her victim will confirm it.

Her pause gives me a moment to recover, and behind where she stands, I peripherally try to determine if we are still in the sector or not. Difficult to tell with no map and only a set of directions to go by; the area looks different up here, some of the marking tape is obscured by brush, and I can no longer be sure of our boundaries. Matt, twenty yards away, is also considering, but we don't have long to deliberate. Puzzle suddenly twitches, and she's off again, taking her chosen path west-southwest to a low valley while Matt and I, on intercepting courses, meet behind her. At the base of a hill, she leaps suddenly upward, taking in air with merry, greedy gulps, as though she's wading through a bowl of scent soup. She ignores paths and scrambles through low brush to the top, where a young woman is hidden beneath a camouflage tarp. Puzzle alerts, beaming at the victim, at me, at the victim, at me as I make it to the top.

Twenty-two minutes.

Matt calls in the find, and we all return to the place where Puzzle had first bounded away from our sweeps. We'll begin the sweeps again, working our way through the last third of the sector systematically, looking for evidence from Puzzle that someone else is there. This last area is the tough one, however, a right bastard third of an acre, the stuff of my misgivings. In we go. Even Puzzle feels it. She struggles to work her way through the thicket, and from feet away I can see bloody streaks on her haunches and another on her ear where thorns have caught her. Our pace slows as moving forward becomes a matter of kneeling, crawling, and cutting in some spots.

I am on my hands and knees working my way around a tree when Puzzle's head pops upward again, and I hear her thrashing in the brush as she shoulders her way to the hottest point of scent, about fifteen yards away from me. She's got someone, and I can hear the foliage rustle with her wiggling happiness, the beginnings of her victory croon. I blunder forward and a branch snags my glasses and twists them half off my head with enough torque that the frame bends and one of the lenses pops out. The offending branch swings back to pop me in the eye.

The timer ticks forward.

We're down a hat and a pair of glasses, but ahead, Puzzle has found a third victim: Sara, heavily camouflaged and trying not to giggle as Puzzle wriggles around her in a sort of happy orbit. When the dog cannot easily get to Sara beneath the tarp, she woofs twice in frustration, turns to me, and woofs again.

Thirty-seven minutes. Matt attempts to radio in the find, but in this low spot, there seems to be no clear signal, and we get no response. He tries to call a teammate on a cell phone, again getting no response. I feel the passage of time, and though we are well inside the test window, we've got further brush to clear. On the third attempt, the teammate answers and promises to relay the message.

We've connected to the team at forty-two minutes, and though I know the test parameters suggested no more than three victims, I give Puzzle the "Find more" command anyway, just to make sure. This is more than the test for us. In this wood, it's quite possible someone else — a hiker, or a parent and child out for a walk — is in here. If they're in here, I want Puzzle to find them. I want to report that we found every human in our sector, whether a part of the test or not.

No, she indicates. No one else. She is very sure. She pushes through the last small section of the sector with her head up and her tail swaying lazily, aware she's done a good job and that it's over. When she catches the scent of our teammates in the parking lot, she dashes to them with great show, wagging and circling and *wroo*ing. And hobbling. She's got something in her paw, and when I arrive to debrief, she grins up at Johnny while I kneel beside her to examine it. There's a broken thorn stuck deep in the largest pad. *When did she pick that up?* I wonder. *She never showed me.* I clean the wound, marveling at the power of adrenaline. My own arms and hands are crisscrossed with bloody scratches that, at the time of the search, I didn't even feel, but this thorn is large. I certainly would have felt it.

"Good dog," says Johnny.

"Good search," says Fleta.

"Nice hair," says Johnny, and the rest look at one another and laugh.

Yes, I can see in a car's rearview mirror, the hair has gone every which way, some of it braided with tiny leaves, some of it sticking straight up. And the branch that cost me my glasses also left a cut on my forehead that looks like a second eyebrow. When I smile in the mirror (and I can't help smiling — we passed!) the cut shifts upward a little, giving me a slightly demonic look of surprise.

Puzzle puts her soft muzzle in my hand. She's drunk some water and blown a few bubbles in the bowl. There are droplets across her nose and forehead. Never a tidy drinker, she dribbles across my palm. She's good on the hurt paw, but she's cut across the face, and one ear's a little ragged. As I clean her wounds, Puzzle seems content. She lies beside me, both paws extended across my leg as I disinfect the cut on her face. I see her ears pivot; she's aware that other dogs are working other sectors. At the sound of distant "Find!" commands, she looks up at me with sudden question, and her shoulders quiver. *Let's go! Let's go! I could do another sector easy!* her demeanor suggests, but this is our cooldown period, and whether she needs it or not, I do. My legs are shaky with fatigue.

One cert test down and two to go. We sit together at the edge of a clearing and listen for the sounds of other searches borne by intermittent wind.

21

CLEAR BUILDING

FOR THE FIRST TIME in twenty years, I dream of tornadoes again. Tornadoes and running and uncertain spaces in the dark. One week not long after the Wilderness test, I have a storm dream every night, dreams vivid enough to wake me straight up — not frightened, but breathless and full of wonder — like Alice with the Red Queen, running *Faster! Faster!*

These aren't the helpless nightmares of childhood. In these dreams, I have choices — this room or that one, leave the car to hide in a gulley or run downstairs to huddle over my dog. And I'm not alone. Puzzle is always with me. I love that she is with me. Sometimes the whole pack of Poms is with us too, their little hedgehog shapes racing over dark fields. I'm amazed how fast we move together. And in the same direction (that *is* the stuff of dreams).

"Wow," says a friend who loves to talk dream symbols. "Tornadoes mean upheaval, destruction, fear of separation." She waves a teaspoon at me. "Your life must be in a whole lot of turmoil right now."

No more than usual, I think. But it's spring, and the civil defense sirens have already sounded a couple of times. And then there is this coming thing with the search dog. We're all about tornadoes these days. We've got the Clear Building test on us soon.

The Clear Building test simulates search in structures damaged by explosion, or tornado, or flood — structures that may become rapidly unstable. Some call it the Triage search, which thrusts the implications upfront: In very little time, a dog and handler must determine where victims are located in a building or if an at-risk structure is "clear," which would allow responders to turn their attention to other places where victims may be trapped. This is urgent, accurate canine searching against the clock. There's a special command to start the search and a special reward at the end of it.

Sister to the Clear Building search is perhaps an even harder one — where dog and handler must circle an unstable building and make the victim/no victim call from outside it. In the catastrophic conditions following disaster, this means the difference between a building being shored, stabilized, and entered by first responders, or not. There are so many variables for dog teams here: Where are the open spaces that allow scent to escape? From where to where does the air move within the building? After storm or before another one oncoming, which way does the wind blow, if it blows at all? And in the dark and in the wind, if my dog makes a slight signal that indicates faint scent from some remote, internal part of a building, will I be able to see it?

These are the searches that wake handlers in the middle of the night. These are the searches that reset priorities in the weeks before a cert test — when the drive to succeed on a test can eclipse the greater duty to the work. The idea that my dog's signals and my subsequent call may be a life-and-death decision for victims and the first responders who serve them is chilling. The trick is to attend this responsibility without stressing over it. It's easy to feel too much, to think too hard — which for me are first-cousin behaviors to second-guessing and failing to trust my dog.

Puzzle doesn't carry the weight of such knowledge with her, and she'll work most efficiently if she gets no uncertainty from me.

Handlers say that if she really enjoys this training now, she'll commit to the job in situations where it is no longer fun. So on the Clear Building scenario I've got to ramp the dog up, let her do her job, and pay attention to her signals while she's doing it. I've got to be upbeat. She's got to be fast, confident, brief, clear. And we both have to be absolutely in sync.

We've got this, I think, the first time we try the exercise. Even in the dark, I'm better at sidestepping debris than untangling thorns. And Puzzle loves live finds. She loves to run.

Puzzle has never been that interested in treat rewards, but the other handlers tell me that zapped weenies really keep dogs motivated on Clear Building exercises. I have a brand-new bag of cut-up microwaved chicken wieners as a special reward for doing this fast, hard job. They are greasy, wizened, disgusting. But I'm suddenly very popular with every search dog I pass.

We take our first Clear Building practice session on so beautiful a day it is hard to imagine disaster is even possible. Puzzle quivers with excitement near the building we are to search. Part of the building simulates an apartment complex. Part of it simulates a warehouse. Part of it simulates a high-rise. There are a lot of rooms here, a lot of corridors and closets. In many rooms — debris. We'll be running from bright light into dim. I cup my hands around the edges of my eyes to make my eyes adjust.

Though my head is full of midgies I can't quite ignore — little flustered thoughts about light, and time, and the pair of us failing to find victims, the specter of a real search where failure could mean a death sentence for someone else — Puzzle seems assured. I wish again for a thirty-second sync to the workings of her mind at the edge of all of this. Standing here with my head bowed against the light, I know only that she seems ready to enjoy her work. She likes the wind-up. She sparks like a firecracker at the moment of command.

The instructor gives me the signal. "Search and find!" I shout to Puzzle with a quick unclip of her lead. She flashes quickly into and through the nearest room, disregarding its tumble of furniture, jumping over an overturned couch that half blocks the door. While I hopscotch after her, and Rob follows as FAS team in trail, Puzzle dashes into the next room. She finds Melody crouched in a corner beneath a desk. Quick work. A good start.

"Good girl!" I cry (*oh, we've so got this*), and hand her the brand-new high-value treat to eat on the run. "Find more!"

Except she doesn't eat on the run. For the first time in her search training history, Puzzle sits, and takes the zapped weenie, and rolls it around in her mouth, and drops it on the ground, and sniffs it and takes it again, where she chews it blissfully, passing the half-inch morsel from one cheek to another with her mouth open slightly, as though to catch every nuance of its taste across her tongue. She has her head tilted back and her eyes closed in a little where-have-you-been-all-my-life? squint of pleasure. It takes her six times as long to eat the treat as it did to find the first victim. Forty-seven seconds. I clock the treat time and groan.

"Find more!" I cry as she thoughtfully licks her lips. She bobs her head and canters out of the room to another warehouse area where Johnny is hiding behind a door. Johnny inspires a huge alert in triplicate, a *Johnny-Johnny-Johnny* ecstasy. They briefly connect; he gives her a scritch; I fumble for a smaller chunk of mini-weenie, the size of my littlest fingernail. Puzzle takes it with a modest smile and to my dismay sits down to enjoy it as the timer continues to tick. It's a small bit of wiener that one of the Poms would have downed in a gulp, but not Puzzle. She makes a full meal of the experience, tilts her head from side to side, working it. At one point, she seems to push her lips forward a little, as though to send the weenie's delicious scent up into the sweetest part of her palate. *Oh baby!* She seems to smile up at me afterward — *is this what searching really fast tastes like? A hard run and then can-apés afterward!*

Twenty-eight seconds on the second treat.

"Find more!" I call again, and Puzzle springs up cheerfully, dashing down the stairs and through a first room, then a second, pivoting from her nose and leaping over an air tank to find Teresa crouched behind a coil of fire hose. The room is dim, but I can see Puzzle working her way into the corner. I see the wave of her blond tail and her dark eyes shining up at me when Teresa is revealed. Puzzle glances to the treat bag and sits with a give-the-doggy-her-due expectation. This is the last room. I tear apart a tiny bit of cocktail weiner and give it to her. It's portion-sized for a Barbie doll, but Puzzle seems prepared to savor it, finishing with a little sigh of pleasure.

We exit the building, me stumbling squint-eyed into the bright, at five minutes, twelve seconds. An early run, not a terrible time, but almost half of it was devoted to chicken wieners.

"How'd she do?" asks Terry.

"Was she motivated?" asks Deryl.

"She did well," says Rob, while I fumble for words to describe the quick finds coupled with the snail's-pace consumption of weenie. With characteristic understatement, Rob looks down at my dog and says, "But I think maybe she needs a treat she can eat a little faster."

What would that be exactly? Having set a high standard with the chicken wieners, I've painted myself into a corner as far as treats are concerned. Puzzle has quickly learned that this, her fastest duty ever, comes with one heckuva reward. But weenies are slow eating. When we run the Clear Building exercise again, I try a variety of smaller, crispier treats that the other dogs seem to inhale in motion. Puzzle takes the not-wieners, shoots me a look, then dribbles them to the ground — as if to suggest I'm just having an off day in the treats department — before she dashes off.

Treat or no treat, at least she dashes off, I think. Our times are improving. We're coming very close to the required three minutes or under. As her skills solidify here, I want to keep her motivation high. In time, Puzzle may not need any treat at all during this kind of work, but for now, I want the new activity associated with very good things.

Zapped wieners seem to be the reward of choice. She loves best what she loved first, but they are killing our time. One day, I cut them up into Chiclet-size morsels — quick for her to eat, but difficult for me to get hold of in the bag, I realize, when she's speedy to a find and I reach for a reward, coming up with nothing more than wiener grease on my fingers.

Which is enough, apparently. I make a little abracadabra movement over her head; Puzzle gives my fingertips a quick lick and races off again with the "Find more!" command. At the end of the three-minute drill, we come out with all victims in 2:52. I cheer and praise and feed her three legitimate pinches of shredded wiener during her mad samba among bystanders. She is very proud and has added a popping smack of the lips to her whole *woo-dig-me* vocabulary.

Success at last! We've worked out the routine. She runs and finds full tilt, and I pound through the building after her, one hand with a flashlight, the other in a bag fondling weenies.

By the time we take the Clear Building certification test, the vague scent of grease on my fingers is enough to reward Puzzle for the moment. On the test drill, she gallops through both floors of the building, chivvying out a victim in a stairwell, another behind a door, one in a wooden maze, and another beneath a stack of sawhorses, then canters outside and down the stairs and sits to wait for me, her head high (two floors, eleven rooms and a stairwell, four victims, 2:43). I follow cautiously, squinting and winking and feeling for steps down in the bright morning light.

I talk with the evaluator. Without requiring a command, Puzzle sits at my feet. I can feel her quivering there, barely able to contain her great joy. She is a grown-up, polite girl, but I have forgotten to reward her for this search well done. As the evaluator and I agree that all victims were found within the timeframe, Puzzle begins to nudge the treat bag hanging from my waist. I hear another handler laugh.

Rob says, "I think you better reward your dog."

I look down and she looks up. *Ah-roo-wow-wow-wow,* Puzzle says, smacking her lips with such vigor her bottom scoots a few inches in its required sit. The message is clear: *Good search. Quick search. Some fun was had by dog.* She noses the treat bag again and eyes me speculatively, as if to say, *But you, my dear, could be a little faster.*

22

TRUST THE DOG

TWO THINGS I THINK I know about the debris pile at this moment: 1) there's human scent but no human here, and 2) there are also no snakes in the rubble, warm from the sun of this midmorning in May. In these opening minutes of the most downwind point of our Urban/Disaster certification test at a fire training academy, Puzzle has circled the debris pile and climbed onto it with the confidence of a dog that has issued her own all-clear about the snakes. She moves quickly, her mouth open and her tongue already out sideways against the day's rising heat. Her tail, always a barometer of what she's sensing, sways with the rhythm of her movement. I've finally learned to decode the sway of tail that marks Puzzle wandering off-command and the sway of the tail that says she's working, and she is working here.

Rubble work is a curriculum all its own: a safety risk with its unstable surfaces, angry, fissured edges and twists of rebar, and a scent challenge due to its fitful air currents. In warm weather, heavy debris may double as a happy habitat for snakes. A tornado or hurricane can change neighborhoods into miles of such rubble, and genuine disaster adds additional problems for the work—the presence of hazardous materials within the debris, the potential that a poorly coordinated search can be fatal to the living victims trapped there.

With their lower center of gravity and the virtue of four feet, search dogs negotiate rubble much more swiftly than we do. I've tried to learn from them the virtues of staying low, distributing my weight widely, and climb-crawling rather than trying to walk upright over it. I cannot follow Puzzle step-for-step across the rubble, and part of the necessary skill requires working apart from the dog, decoding her indications from a distance, and moving closer only when careful size-up allows us to do so.

The debris pile here represents years of donated cement from torn-up street department projects. In addition to the jagged concrete, there are lengths of old pipe and an upright series of unearthed water department vaults that once would have contained switching devices. Standing in the center of the pile, the vaults — resting on their sides — look like the world's tiniest apartment high-rise. You can crawl in the ground floor, climb up through a hole in the ceiling to the second floor, then climb up through another hole to the third floor and the "roof," perhaps fifteen feet high. Scent works oddly in this small space, rising or falling and, in strong winds from the east, swifting around inside the little structure like a canned tornado, then pushing out the top to drift down on another part of the pile, yards away. It can be a good place to hide a victim and watch the dogs work out the tough find.

We are fortunate to have access to the pile, a constant challenge with its always changing configuration. Though we are able to work it fairly often, it's not a space to take for granted. One misstep or careless move can easily result in the rescuer also becoming a victim, a risk shared by the dogs. Though none of us have been seriously hurt on training debris or actual disaster sites, the possibility exists. Search dogs have been severely injured doing rubble work, and search dogs have died from it.

Puzzle is on task. She seems to enjoy working rubble. But she has always seemed to me to be aware of her small size and the risks here. I wonder what she makes of debris beneath her paws, with its uneasiness and the vibration of air funneling through its open spaces. Puzzle crosses the pile methodically now, moving over the fractured cement in a series of calculated jumps and scrambles. She has found volunteer victims here before and seems ready to do so again, but a first diagonal pass across it, and then a second in the other direction, have resulted in no locally hot scent. Or so it seems to me, watching her. Though Puzzle is definitely engaged here, she shows me nothing in the low spaces along the edge of the pile. The breeze is variable. I can't be sure how well air is moving across the rubble, so I gesture her around the debris a second time just to make sure. I instantly feel a conscience twitch about the failure to trust my dog the minute I tell her to do it. She circles obediently counterclockwise around the pile but makes no quickening movement there.

Nothing in the debris pile itself, but in three places she has scrambled upward to the highest spot on the upwind side and bobbed her nose appreciatively away from the pile, her little anticipatory gesture I associate with the scatter of faint scent. She doesn't bring her head down toward the rubble, and unhindered by me (this time), she moves away from the debris pile with the easy, dismissive movement of a dog who is certainly willing to find a human but is convinced there is no human here. She was a good girl to circle again when I asked her, but now she switches away from it with a bit of a priss to her step: *The debris pile is clear. Got it?*

We work across the area in wide sweeps, passing railway cars, a partly demolished box truck, a row of wrecked cars. She has no interest in any of them, but on the second sweep, upwind of the debris pile we have cleared, her head pops strongly, and I release her from the sweep to let her run. She dashes across thirty yards of turf to find her first victim, Rob, hidden in a propane gas training tank. Puzzle is ecstatic when he snakes his hand out to pet her; she is all wiggling and crooning, taking her praise as due and her treat as a politeness. She smiles as she takes the jerky, then drops it on the ground. I look back to the debris pile, directly downwind of us, a fair distance away. Was it Rob whose scent she had at the top of the rubble? The wind is blowing the right direction, and because it was funneling through the open tank over him, I think it's likely. Puzzle's proud of her find, but she isn't telling.

We return to the place we had abandoned our sweeps back and forth across the sector, and this time, alongside a railway tanker, Puzzle stiffens, turns her head to the ladder tower and lifts her nose. Again the narrowing of the eyes and the change in her breathing. It is the same gesture I saw earlier on the debris pile: *scent-but-not-scent-here.* I watch her work and note the direction of her nose. She is uninterested in the tanker, rejecting anything nearby, and when we turn to sweep back the other way, she abandons the sweep to head for the base of the ladder tower, where she has to make a choice: go in the enclosed first floor or climb the stairs for the open floors above? Puzzle puts her nose to a crack beneath the door, huffs, and turns away at once for the stairs.

The day has begun to warm, and she's panting heavily. I give her a quick drink from her portable water bowl before she heads upstairs. Puz is a sloppy drinker. Water has settled in the deep pockets of her jowls, and moving more quickly than I, she dribbles on me the whole way up, a 7 percent solution of dog spit and cold water. I get an unexpected charge from this and laugh, trotting upward faster. This is the same ladder tower I rappelled so badly while my twelve-week-old puppy watched. Today it feels a very different place beside her. Puzzle rejects the second floor and the third, not hesitating on the stairs but climbing to the very top, where she finds Teresa crouched in the northeast corner of the roof. We are all excited — Teresa is a perfect second victim. She has honed a lovely high shriek of congratulation that would give any prideful dog a boost, a *good dog!* of such an octave she makes Puzzle facewhip herself with her tail, a puppy behavior I thought she had long left behind.

This is a cert test, so we're not taking Teresa's pulse or offering her water or asking her if she knows what day it is. But we are not totally cavalier, either; we help Teresa to her feet (I lift and Puzzle supervises) — and then we're off again. Back down the stairs. Another drink of water and a return to our strategic sweeps. Puzzle dashes across the next two passes, and I get the sense that she has caught the strategy of this sector and that she would prefer to set the rhythm of it — especially now that I've relaxed a little and have remembered to trust her a lot. Her canter away from me is bright. I get an impression of proud head and flashing blond tail all the way to the brushy fence line, where her passage flushes a dithery bird she does not follow. She meets me coming back the other way.

The next sweep includes a peculiar little structure known as the "maze," for firefighter confined-space training. It looks like a horizontal series of ventilation shafts hooked together or stacked on top of one another. Doors and hatches here and there, a little ladder for access to a door on a second level. Puzzle is interested in the maze. She huffs at one door and rejects it, choosing to trot down the length of the plywood structure to a second door, where she *oofs* and wags and grins in such a way I think it must be one of three family members in there — Matt, or Johnny, or Cindi. And it is. How did I know that? Puzzle belly-crawls into the shaft to give Cindi a wag and a cold nose, and in some first stray flash I recognize that though her alert signals are consistent, Puzzle greets individuals with hellos as specific as a human would greet differently a neighbor, a colleague, and a friend from childhood. Puzzle buries her nose deep in Cindi's outstretched hand, coming up with a smile, gulping slightly, as though she'd just taken a long drink of favorite human and oh, that was nice.

We return to our sweep across the area, which this time includes the burn building. There's been a recent burn here; the interior is black with soot that licks the walls upward, and the building's scent of smoke and ash is strong enough on this warm day that my eyes water. It must be even stronger to the dog, but Puzzle moves through the building without any apparent distress. She sniffs at one pile of sooty, soggy hay before clearing the building of any human scent. Quick work in that dark space, and if Puzzle hadn't had so much experience in the thick air of that building, I might wonder how easy it was for her to distinguish human scent among all the other overpowering smells associated with the earlier fire. Would I smell a single wildflower in a room full of Limburger cheese? But she and the other dogs have literally grown up searching here. With few exceptions, *no* in the burn building means *no*.

Puzzle exits the building wearing stripes across her haunches and a grubby, speckled tail. This may be the first bonus of the day for her. My blond dog loves being dirty. She flashes me a grin as we head next for the multistory high-rise. Puzzle's having a good time. She is undeniably fresh.

I resist the urge to stop, bend over, put my hands to my knees, and take a breather. I'm exhausted without really being tired. I feel strong enough to push a car off a pedestrian, but my neck is tight. As Puzzle bounds into the high-rise, I am really, really glad I skipped the coffee this morning. Caffeine on top of today's nervousness would not have been a good thing. Supercharged with *yi!yi!yi!*, I would have moved like a wind-up chicken on speed, skittering after Puzzle in the dark. Not the best mindset for paying attention.

I flip on my flashlight as Puz takes her bearings in a large warehouse room on the first floor. It is full of ladders, barrels, and red fire mattresses, and it has a couple of closets behind steel doors at the end. Even to me, it is an environment rich with scent. In warm weather, the mattresses smell much like the gymnastics mats of my elementary days, but heavier somehow, and sweatier. Air can move oddly here, a strong current through the middle of the room created by the doors at either end, the stairwell at the north entrance, and windows with heavy metal shutters, while air in the corners can settle motionless behind objects.

Puzzle picks her way confidently to the center of the great

space, stepping over the rungs of ladders lying flat on the floor. She turns her head slowly, her nose lifted. A moment later, she moves to one corner and shrugs out of it, no scent, then trots along a clear space of floor to the back door. There she twitches at the bottom of the door with some interest. It is locked, and before we leave the room, I motion her to check the other corners, the cracks underneath the closet doors. She does so, dismissing them to return to the back door leading out of the building. That return gives me pause. I think of her earlier behavior on the debris pile, scenting Rob in the tank yards and yards away, and in this room we could again be downwind of human scent outside.

We leave the room and circle the building. A few clouds have passed over the sun, and the wind has risen slightly. At the back of the high-rise, Puzzle canters to the flashover bin, and at the moment I'm thinking we may have a victim in the bin, a bent elderly man comes around the corner of it and almost collides with me, Puzzle beside him at his knees. I'm startled. He holds his hands up as though he were being robbed and mumbles something I cannot understand.

Puzzle has found him, but he's not one of our volunteer victims. And he is somehow here but not here. When he speaks to me, his eyes don't connect and his words are unclear. He raises and lowers his hands as if to submit to something or to avoid my dog, but in another way he doesn't seem to recognize she's there. He takes out a card that indicates he is a patient in a care facility and has communication disabilities. He extends the card for me to read.

I am about to direct him to Max when a security guard drives up and with a kind word gently moves the elderly man to her vehicle. Puzzle and I watch her drive him away. He gazes straight forward, anticipation in his posture, as though this change was in his plans. I get the sense he has been picked up in other places and moved to somewhere else before. The last I see of him is the flash of white card as he flips it through his fingers.

"Good dog," I say to Puzzle, who has never seen one of her victims chauffeured away on a golf cart. "Find more!" We return to the cert test and to the high-rise, where there are other rooms to clear.

Don is probably the happiest of our volunteer victims to be found. He's at the farthest end of our sector, and he's been hidden in one of the stuffiest rooms of the high-rise, buried in old uniforms for quite a while, long enough to have sweat a little and spread his scent wide over the tumbled clothing that surrounds him. He is as obvious to Puzzle as a fly vibrating the strands of a spider's web. She snuffles in and finds him; he pushes himself up out of the pile, blinks into the light, and gives Puzzle a pat of congratulations. We watch him walk back to the group waiting at the academy.

Four official victims and one unofficial one; we have another half of the high-rise to clear. Puzzle has dropped her bottom on the cool cement with an air of finality. I give her another drink of water from the collapsible bowl, and when I tell her it's time to go back to work, she rises affably, but I get the sense that she knows the air moving through this building far better than I do, and really, though there's a lot to be interested in — *did you note the scatter graph of pigeon droppings in the farthest room?* — there's nothing to be urgent about; there are no other humans here.

Puzzle wanders through a central room full of lumber. I have always liked this room's fresh wood smell, but its narrow space and strange currents can give dogs trouble. Today, Puzzle pauses intently in one corner and, in a response I have never seen from her, does not alert but begins to paw at something that's caught her attention. She exposes some kind of weighted vest. I bend down to inspect it by flashlight, noting a quarter-size smear of what appears to be dried blood at the back of the neckline, as though the vest had once chafed a raw spot on the person who had worn it. Curious. I can't smell the blood, but I can smell sweat and something like grease. Two scents to the hundreds it must have collected as firefighter after firefighter wore it. Now that Puzzle has inspected the vest and knows that I have seen it, she shows no further interest. *It isn't live,* she seems to suggest, *but it certainly has a lot of human on it.*

We move quickly through the rest of the ground-floor rooms and up the stairs, where Puzzle dashes through the overturned furniture of three apartment rooms and then into the topmost warehouse area. Several plywood structures give it winding air patterns and curious crawlspaces. Puzzle has searched this room occasionally before, and some exciting thing about it always makes her race. She does so here again, her nose low as she gallops its circumference and around again to me, her expression bright. *Great room, terrific space,* she seems to be saying, *and thanks so much, but nada.*

The high-rise is clear. We exit the building, do a quick sweep of the lumber pile and the flashover bin, and with another toss of her head, Puzzle exits the sector. She pauses and turns back to me in a gesture of easy partnership, and something in her ease overrides every nervous urge I have to double- or triple-check the closest spaces we have cleared. I already regret my are-you-sures of the earlier debris pile. Puzzle flops down in the grass and begins to roll. She's happy and absolute, wiggling her hieroglyph across the turf: Trust the dog. Trust the dog. Trust the dog.

Right, I say to myself. *Enough.* We head back to the classroom building, the team, and the three evaluators standing there, ready to make our report.

An hour later, Puzzle's about to have grilled chicken and a kid's cup of ice cream on the patio of a favorite restaurant, and I'm planning on a mimosa — light on the orange juice, double the champagne. We're at a favorite local café that allows dogs. The porch is generous, with heavy cast-iron tables covered by umbrellas; the atmosphere is upbeat. My dog recognizes the scent of the place a block before we get there, and when we turn the corner that leads to the front door, her pace quickens. She's wearing her orange work vest, and those already seated make little comments as she passes, remarking about her size (petite), her coloring (blond), her leash behavior (beautifully improved). Some people remark with open curiosity about her job. They've missed SEARCH AND RESCUE printed on the side of the vest, and I see them bend together a bit as they try to figure her out.

We stand at the door and wait for a table. Puz cranes her head and weaves back and forth a bit as the door opens and closes, either hoping for the beautiful scent of chicken or to catch sight of favorite waitpersons who spoil her. After a long day of search work, there's nothing she likes better than to lounge under a café table and receive a nice grilled chicken breast with rosemary, a to-go carton full of cool water, and the general praise and admiration of young women she's known since puppyhood, young women who smell splendidly of fajitas, melted cheese, and ice cream. This looks to be a very good day.

A young man we don't know seats us at the only available table. I sit, Puzzle quietly lies at my feet, and heads turn to consider her thoughtfully. On the other side of us, a couple is curious. They glance over and put their heads together, then glance over again, as if hesitant to ask something. Their adolescent son, I notice, is pointedly not looking at the dog. It's a strange combination. As Mom and Dad slowly inch their chairs toward Puzzle and occasionally flick an inquisitive glance at me, the boy in perfect counterpoint inches away.

Finally, the father speaks. He says, "We are wondering about your dog. Does it really say 'Search' on her vest?"

When I nod, the son makes another five-inch hitch to the other side of their table.

"What does she look for?" his mother asks.

"Bombs?" asks the father.

"We were thinking criminals, but she doesn't look mean enough."

"I wondered if she might be a drug dog," the father continues. The boy gives another scoot to the left.

When I shake my head and say no, explaining that Puzzle

searches for lost people, the teenager at the table looks up for the first time. I point to the other side of her vest, where the embroidery more clearly reads SEARCH AND RESCUE. The boy relaxes so visibly that I expect his parents to notice, but they are all about the dog at the moment.

"Glad it's not bombs," says the father. "I hate to think of a sweet dog like yours in that kind of danger."

"Drug dogs come to your school, don't they, Cody?" they turn to their son and ask. He shrugs and nods, squinting up at the sun now shining down on him, and he scoots his chair back the way it came, just a little enough to be in the shade.

His mother explains, "They smell the lockers and the cars in the parking lot once a month."

"It's amazing," says the father, "how much dogs pick up on things we humans would otherwise miss."

For a while we eat in silence, then a young man brings his toddler daughter up to ask for a greet and a pet. As the little girl reaches down and says, "Lula, Lula, Lula," her father explains that they lost their Golden a month before to cancer. Lula was an eight-year-old "red dawg," as breed fanciers sometimes call them, a darker field Golden, but the child clearly recognizes the characteristic expression, shape of the head, and plume tail. "Lula," she says. She lifts Puzzle's ear and begins to whisper into it, and Puzzle's occasional wariness with children melts in the presence of this small dark-haired girl, who sits beside her quietly and strokes her shoulder with a forefinger. Her father says little, though he smiles when I compliment his daughter on her gentleness with my dog. He bends down to them both, Puzzle's tail thumps, and I get a sense of the missing dog who would once have completed their circle. When they leave us, the young father's shoulders sag. His daughter may have done the asking, but he apparently needed the contact with Puzzle too.

We go home to lie together on a lounge chair in the backyard. I stroke my newly certified Golden, who wastes no time going belly-up beside me in the deep shade of pecan trees. Any celebration worth doing is, apparently, worth doing upside down, unconscious, teeth bared.

"Mission Ready" is the term we apply to dogs that have trained and passed all initial air-scent tests for living victims — Wilderness, Urban/Disaster, and Clear Building. Puzzle is now ready to deploy on any land search involving potential live finds. The tests have been rigorous, but they have simulated many of the most common search conditions. And like all good tests, they have taught us something as well. Puzzle and I can go forward with a thorough understanding of the hard strategy behind canine search and with a confidence in our working partnership. *What's next?* I wonder, glad to have Puzzle next to me, glad to be ready at last.

But I am thoughtful too. We can take nothing for granted. This decade's unprecedented disasters — the 9/11 attacks, a levee's failure, and the loss of a space shuttle — have already scribbled new rules in the margins of canine search procedure. And the *Columbia* disaster continues to raise debate over what dogs offer this kind of recovery and how they may be changed by it. The shuttle's disintegration at 207,000 feet and at eighteen times the speed of sound still instructs us about fire, compression, exposure, and altitude, about the catastrophic transformation of human scent on the wind.

23

COLUMBIA

A YEAR BEFORE Puzzle was born, the space shuttle *Columbia* fell over Texas on a sunny winter morning already giving way to what seemed like an early spring. I first knew of the disaster when suddenly all my dogs began to bark, jerking me from sleep. The dogs — including deaf Scuppy — erupted as suddenly as though someone had kicked down the door, and seconds later I heard a resonant boom, and then a second one, fainter. I had grown up next to air force bases, and the sound of a sonic boom was familiar to me, though it had been decades since I heard one, supersonic flight being banned over the United States in the late sixties.

Unsure if I had heard a sonic boom or a sequence of explosions, I opened the back door. The dogs rushed out to the yard and there joined all the other barking dogs in the neighborhood. I could identify individual dogs in the uproar: the Wirehaired Terrier across the street, the Border Collie two houses down, the pair of senior German Shepherds a block away. While my dogs raced across the fence line, yapping frantically over something I couldn't perceive, I stood in the sunshine — a beautiful day remarkably similar to September 11, 2001 — and looked up at the sky, wondering if I had heard the first moments of another terrorist attack.

The sounds had seemed to come from the south, the general direction of downtown Dallas, and if something were happening there, the civil defense sirens might go off soon, I thought, or surely police and fire vehicles from all over town would begin their screaming course toward the area. I listened for sirens and heard none. A mystery.

The sounds had been so clear to me. *Boom*. And fainter, *boom*.

I turned on a radio outside and a television inside, where two voices from separate stations quickly broke in on regular programming to release early information. Communication with shuttle *Columbia* lost, the news said — then twenty minutes of deliberation over what that phrase, "communication lost," might mean. On television, there was a tight, curious friction between the official statements and the faces of the people reading them. Though nothing was confirmed, no one on the air seemed doubtful. No one seemed hopeful, either. *Columbia* was gone long before a NASA press release confirmed it. Homeward bound, the aircraft was presumed destroyed across the skies just west, and south, and east of us, the trouble beginning as far away as the Texas Panhandle, they said, and ending in Louisiana.

I looked at my pager, as search team personnel were probably doing across the country, and wondered if we would be called. The immediate question for canine teams would involve not rescue but human recovery, if such was even possible after a high-altitude, high-speed catastrophe of this kind. Unlike the low-altitude loss of the shuttle *Challenger*, where the aircraft itself remained somewhat intact when it fell into the Atlantic Ocean, *Columbia's* breakup and its outcomes were a matter of great question, debated by every aerodynamics expert that newscasters could get on camera as the day progressed.

When the search team met for training later that morning, we still didn't know. Word had it that some pieces of the shuttle were still airborne, some still coming down, and that the lightest debris might be falling for weeks. Hard to imagine, looking up into a blue and seamless sky. We'd learned that federal agencies would join forces to collaborate on the recovery of the aircraft itself, but in those early hours, we had no word about plans for crew recovery and whether dog teams would be needed at all. Guesswork at this point was useless. We set up the day's training scenarios, and the dogs of the team headed out in the field to work.

Late the next afternoon, the pager went off, signaling deployment, followed by a rush of e-mail and faxes. Authorities believed the *Columbia* recovery would be a long one, and our team would deploy in stages, three dogs and human counterparts leaving the first day, another three dog teams to leave five days later as canine units were rotated in and out for rehab periods. The unspoken message suggested this would be a hard search — grueling physically, difficult emotionally, perhaps tough psychologically. Six of us left Dallas the next day in a tandem of cars at midnight, already girding up for a human recovery we could not imagine. We would snake a course through small towns in the five-hour drive southeast to Lufkin, where we would join search teams from across the country convening in the same place.

It was a long drive to begin at midnight after most of us had worked all day. There was a lot of time to think. We made our way out of the Metroplex down a major freeway as far as we could take it, then onto narrow state roads, darkness increasing as civilization gave way to stretches of ranchland and wide plains of undeveloped scruff. Too long a city dweller, I noticed how the night sky changed colors as we drove, shifting gradually from a hazy dark gray to an immense and star-flecked black that stretched from horizon to horizon. I had seen this sky before from my airplane, and beneath it I again felt small, puttering down the two-lane in my red PT Cruiser, insignificant beneath a velvet and diamond drum skin. Normally that anonymity was a comfort, but tonight the size of the sky and the size of the job ahead combined in such a way that I drove with both hands gripped on the wheel.

We drove with our FRS radios on, checking up on one another as the drive wore on and two, then three in the morning approached. A mistake: I'd bought coffee at an all-night gas station on our way out of town — scorched, tarlike coffee that seemed strong enough to melt the thin Styrofoam cup that held it and made my stomach burn as though I were sipping sulfuric acid. The coffee had enough jolt to keep me wide-eyed through Kemp, Mabank, and Eustace, but by Athens I was stiff and achy in the driver's seat, and horribly tired.

Ninety minutes out of Lufkin, I was in trouble. I was so impossibly sleepy that I began to slap myself to stay awake, sharp little pops on the face, the way they do in movies. I thought of Jimmy Stewart in *The Spirit of St. Louis,* playing Lindbergh on his transatlantic flight, dozing off while the plane made a steady descent down to the water, but I couldn't think of it long. This was not a time for thinking about sleepy people in the small hours.

Time to pull over. I was about to key the mike to tell Max I'd have to stop when suddenly something hit the side of my car with the force of a softball, exploding across my half-opened window and, through it, into my face and hair. I jumped, the car swerved, and immediately teammates began calling on the radio. Though they had not seen the object that hit the car, they saw the swerve and feared I'd fallen asleep at the wheel.

No, I had not, and I was certainly awake now. No need to slap further.

Coffee. I could smell coffee, artificial creamer, and the pungent smell of something else. My face was sticky, and the heat of the car and the wind whip from the open window had already begun to dry my hair into crisp, sugary twigs. Someone had thrown a full cup of liquid out of a vehicle going the other way, and whether intentionally or not, they'd broadsided my car — and me — with it. Lufkin was still miles away, but the night was creeping on, and since we were called to an early morning briefing there, this was no real time to stop. I poured a little bottled water into my hand and patted the gunk off my face and eyelashes, figuring I could manage a better wash-up at the Civic Center once we were there.

The road seemed to grow darker before Lufkin's lights pricked the horizon. Now there were occasional objects in the shadows at the edge of my headlights, objects on the side of the road, objects in the grass alongside it. The shapes weren't immediately recognizable as curls of tires or sheared bumpers or the frame of a chair fallen off the back of a truck. One violent twist of metal extended up from the grass like a rabbit on its hind legs, shiny in some places and dull in others. We were moving quickly, and I didn't stop to stare, but I wondered if we were seeing shuttle debris that previous drivers had moved from the road.

Two of the dogs worked me over thoroughly when we arrived and, once out of the car, they got a downwind whiff. Both dogs were busy peeing and shaking off the long sleep, but they weren't too busy to stretch up for the sleeve of my jacket, and when I bent down to them, to examine my face. Intently curious about the odd-smelling Susannah, neither of them attempted to lick the residue off my arm. I wondered about that until Hunter's interest in my splashed jacket was so profound that two of my teammates suspected the coffee-bomber had also taken a pee in the cup. One of them peered at the driver's side of the PT Cruiser and noted the precision of the impact and the wide spray of fluid extending to the back of the car. Huge and goopy, like the bird-splat of a pterodactyl doing a victory roll. Might be good, my teammate said, to find a drive-through car wash sometime soon and get whatever that was off the paint.

The parking lot at the Civic Center was already full. We were early for the briefing, but the area was in motion — a starburst trajectory of uniformed figures walking out and back to vehicles and a number of people moving the other way toward the door. A ring of television trucks circled the action in as close a press to the building as could be managed, bristling with antennae and dishes tilting toward the sky. A passing police officer gestured us in the direction we needed, and we walked into the building caught by a line of cameras marking the new day in the recovery of *Columbia*.

The agencies in charge were still getting established in separate areas of the main auditorium. We gathered to wait at the edge of a corridor, watching food vendors and the Salvation Army arrive to set up emergency support. As we passed, kindly staff offered Happy Meals, hot coffee, doughnuts, and foil-covered plastic cups of orange juice. I had eaten a day's worth of food on the drive, suspecting it might be a long time before I ate again, so I was too full to eat anything. One older woman looked so worried when I declined that I took a cup of orange juice to drink on the ride to wherever.

More movement in and out of the auditorium, then whole groups were ushered out of the main hall and into the corridor. I could hear the tinny whine of a loudspeaker. There was a pointed closing of the doors. We waited there more than an hour, taking turns checking on the dogs in the trucks, who had wisely decided on another nap in the pinkish-gray light of morning. I leaned against a wall and closed my eyes. The corridor was cold and fatigue had stretched my tired nerves to the point that every sensation seemed to leave a bruise.

"You okay?" asked a teammate, who was also a nurse.

"Just figuring out a way to get around the tired," I answered.

She sipped a cup of coffee and said, "I'm trying to tell myself that I've actually *had* a good night's sleep and that what I feel now is just a hard time waking up."

It sounded like a good idea. "How's that working for you?" I asked, cracking an eye open.

"Oh," she laughed, "votes won't be in until noon."

But she looked better than I did, and she'd been up a lot longer. I looked across at the vendors, on standby as they waited for the auditorium briefing to end. They were primed to serve, gazing back at me from behind coffeepots and big bowls full of ice and juice and bottled water. Inspired by self-deception, I returned to the woman who'd fussed over me as tenderly as a grandmother and tried my colleague's line: "I'm having a hard time waking up." She poured me a cup of coffee the way, she said, her husband the trucker drank it: five plastic thimbles of cream and three sugars. I thought of my earlier car bomb, and I felt my teeth curl, but I had to admit this hot coffee milkshake smelled delicious. The lady pressed me to take an iced-chocolate doughnut, and I did not re-fuse her, returning to the group charged with enough sugar and caffeine to make an elephant tap dance.

The auditorium doors opened. An intense young woman ar-rived to brief us, or rather, to brief Max while we stood in earshot. She identified the chain of command—who we should report to and who, in turn, would report our information upward. She de-scribed the small town we would stage from, told us to make cer-tain we took no cameras into the field, and confirmed the place we would return to sleep. We should leave immediately, she said, and expect to be in search sectors by 10:00 A.M. We were to watch out for the media, to refuse to respond to reporters, and to refer them to the designated NASA and FBI spokespersons. As she moved away, she stopped and turned back briefly to look at the group of us. "And," she said, her expression somber as she nodded to the row of media vans outside, "no jokes. No jokes about *anything* at all." It was a comment out of nowhere, relayed downward perhaps from incident management and designed to forestall gallows hu-mor, that desperate levity that sometimes shows up on searches.

Easy to comply. We weren't laughing and didn't have a joke be-tween us, but we left Lufkin duly cautioned. Dawn had given way to another mild day in late winter, and we drove to the place of de-ployment on a gray ribbon of road beneath a dome of blue sky.

Shadow's ticked coat threw sparks in the sunlight as she moved confidently, person to person, introducing herself and petition-ing for treats. We were standing outside a small-town meeting hall with our dogs and our gear amid a number of other canine teams. From a distance, the crowd of people, backpacks, and dogs on this bright day might have suggested a happier gathering. It would have seemed a good day for a group hike or a geocache expedi-tion. But here where we stood, the dogs alone were lively among us. They had all had naps. They were experienced enough to rec-ognize their handlers' gear and their own. Perhaps they smelled the surge of human scent each time the door to the meeting hall opened and someone pushed definitively through, as though an announcement were about to be made.

Search management personnel braided their way through the crowd, accounting for us as resources and prioritizing locations on the map where we should be sent. Something about the process seemed a little slippery. We'd been on standby for hours. We'd given our team IDs, our names, our dogs' names to a sequence of persons who have come out with clipboards to crosscheck how many of us were able to deploy. So far, we'd seen no canine teams move from the command post into sectors, but long standbys can be the rule on major searches. One police officer from a Houston suburb said that he and his dog sat here in the grass all day the day before, on standby to work but never sent out. *At least,* he said, *I'm getting paid for this.* I couldn't tell if he was grinning or gritting his teeth. He looked at two brothers who had taken vacation days from work to assist the search. *How much vacation you got?* he drawled.

The officer's story circulated, causing the occasional mild exclamation and a number of squared shoulders, drooping heads.

Many of us removed our packs and arranged them in lumps that doubled as pillows; some of us stretched out on the rolling slope of pale grass to make up for lost sleep. The rest stood and watched the dogs as they idly wound back and forth at the ends of long leads. One young man seemed particularly nervous about the TV cameras trained on the group from a distance. He repeatedly shifted to the middle of the group, borrowed a dark jacket to cover his bright shirt, and turned his back to the parking area across the street. He had called in sick to work from three states away and was worried his boss might see him on national television. One of his teammates suggested a temporary hair dye, pointing to a supermarket just across the street. She was only half-joking; she said their team rarely had the luxury of employer support. The camera-shy young man would have a hard time avoiding attention. He was tall and his lovely German Shepherd bitch was a stunner, a showy girl with dark eyes and an intelligent expression. Ready to go and sensitive to every change, she occasionally barked with excitement, causing her handler to speak sternly to her in a low voice, afraid her exuberance would turn cameras their way.

"A Husky," said one woman to Jerry. She had a Border Collie at her feet, a bright boy so keen to get on with it he seemed to crackle where he stood. She looked down at Shadow, who amiably returned the gaze. "I would have thought they are too much a one-person dog for search work."

Jerry shook his head. "Well," he said, "she only works for one person, me, but there's no question she wants to do it."

Shadow grinned upward and mumbled something in Husky that could have been *You betcha.* Shadow, the dog of many consonants and vowels.

Jerry's leadership and Shadow's commitment had made them a strong team in the field. I had watched their accord a long while. Though I had not seen Shadow evolve from puppyhood, I'd seen the working outcome. Theirs was a unique partnership managed differently from the Lab or German Shepherd pairs. Definitive, unforced, amicable. Jerry knew how to tell her what he needed from her, and he knew how to reward her for doing so. The woman appeared unconvinced, but she admitted she'd never seen a dog like Shadow work. Jerry was equally undisturbed. There are all kinds of breed biases in canine search-and-rescue. He gets the Husky comment a lot.

A helicopter descended into a clearing half a football field away. Its rotor continued to *woop-woop-woop* at a low RPM after it landed, suggesting this was just a short stop. But it sounded to all of us like progress, and the rotor-wash excited the dogs too as it stirred the border of low brush at the periphery of the clearing and scattered scent every which way. They raised their noses and wuffled. Some huffed and some bobbed their heads; some knitted their nostrils rapidly together and apart. One older Retriever seemed to just close his eyes and savor, like an aging vintner of scent, his mouth slightly open and his jaw working as though the smells were rich enough to chew. I could imagine the dogs happily sorting today's squirrel and yesterday's rabbits and the passage of a coyote ten days before — and all our human scents — greasy, tired, car uphol-stery-and-fried-chicken us. A row of dog ears perked. Two men with notebooks and dark jackets ducked out of the helicopter and dashed purposefully across the grass to the command post, disap-pearing inside.

Afternoon had raised a breeze, and the clear blue sky above had begun to give way to mare's tail cirrus. The pilots among us looked up. Our good weather was about to change; tomorrow would not be fair. Someone inside the command post with access to a fore-cast must have heard the same, because minutes later, two men were rigging an antenna, and five others were raising a tent. The command post itself suddenly seemed to stir. We could hear the clatter of chairs and the occasional bump against a wall.

"Is this it?" asked the young man with his back to the cameras. "Do you think we're about to go?"

"Believe it when your feet hit the sector," said a woman as she shredded the top of a hamburger bun into neat chunks and dropped them in a clean poop bag. She was obviously experienced at this, and we watched her with a sort of fascination as she shred-ded each piece almost identically to the one before and after, neat little cumulus puffs of hamburger bun, as though she were about to make bread pudding and was worried about the presentation. Dog treats? A field snack, maybe? Pigeons back at the motel? We watched without asking why. At this point, we were easily — and groggily — engaged by anything at all.

Later that day in the tent put up against forecast bad weather, I continued to wait to be deployed, sitting by a man called JD from a sheriff's department several states away. He'd arrived the day be-fore and was already a little grumpy with frustration. Between us, we counted seven roll sheets we'd signed in an eight-hour day of standby, all brought by different people saying, "Don't leave. Don't go anywhere, but be ready to deploy. And sign this so we know who's here."

"Obsessive-compulsiveness?" mused JD about the seven roll sheets. "Or incompetence?"

"Evolving situation, change of leadership maybe," I said. I was as eager to go to work as any of us, but I wondered how someone plans a large-scale search even as they recognize they don't really know what's out there. And how do you know what's really out there when things are still falling? This was catastrophe beyond known poses. I could imagine all the issues of combustion, trajectory, physics, and mundane things like personnel safety and jurisdiction. Man, I was impatient to get out there and search too, but I felt a certain sympathy for search management, many of whom were red-eyed and gray with fatigue.

"Did you search yesterday?" I asked JD.

"Nope," he said. He and the earlier police officer compared notes. JD's weary Coonhound had melted into the grass, now consoled himself this second day by worrying a hotspot on his forepaw and farting.

"It was like this, then?"

"A-yup."

Not long after that exchange, we were fitfully, finally deployed — with warnings about the media, the locals, and our own behavior ("no jokes, no press . . . no goddamn cameras in the field"). We loaded up our packs into cars and trucks and headed out, ten vehicles of dogs and searchers, and twenty minutes later, as we reached the edge of the sector we were about to search, we met the lead vehicle coming the other way.

"Back to base!" the driver called. "We've been called back." The cords of the driver's neck were tight. He mouthed something else and spat, screeching away with a chain of us behind him. JD was quiet in the seat next to me. His face darkened to a purplish red. *Believe it,* the woman among us had said, *when your feet hit the sector.*

While her handler and I watched, a search dog inspected human effects found in an area of dense, unpopulated wood. "Will she find more of this?" the NASA representative asked her handler as the dog worked her nose across several items he had offered. Her handler nodded, and after a brief discussion about direction, we were off. The dog's head was up. A gray and shining creature, she moved on long, muscular legs toward the deepest part of the wood.

"The question is," I heard one man say to another, "will she find it fast?"

She seemed to. We moved quickly — handler, assistant, and two agency representatives — behind the dog as she penetrated the wood, and after a series of passes across the sector, stiffened and paused in a clutch of young trees.

"There's interest," said her handler quietly, watching.

A light breeze threaded fitfully through the wood, and the dark gray dog began moving more rapidly across the small area, perhaps fifteen by twenty feet. She worked methodically at the periphery, her nose to the air, the trees, and the ground — clearly trying to isolate where scent began and where it ended and to find a cone to follow to the scent's source.

"What is this?" asked an agency representative quietly. He was a dark-haired, youngish man with his hands thrust deep into the pockets of his jacket, intently watching the dog move. She was all concentration, her body taut with focus.

"She's got something," said her handler, "and she's trying to narrow it down so she can give me a location."

The dog's circling became more rapid, and as the wind rose a little, I heard her mutter with frustration. She pawed at the turf, passed her nose along the brush, as though the source of the scent was elusive.

I looked up into a young tree next to where I stood and thought I saw a bright red and blue fleck of something in its topmost branches. Putting my hands to its supple trunk, I shook the tree once, then harder. The flitch of fabric fell and with it, apparently, fell a riot of scent. The dog grew frantic, circling haphazardly, stumbling now and colliding with trees, her mouth open as she huffed and ferreted for a source.

"Jesus," said the other man with us, who had been silent all the way from the command post.

After a dizzying few minutes the dog returned to her handler, dropped down to sit beside him, and moaned. It was an exhausted, anxious sound, as if to say she'd tried to show him something, but the scent was too much everywhere here.

"What she's got?" asked the second man.

"She's got a whole lot of scent, but it's not — coming from one place," said her handler. He spoke with confidence in his interpretation. "I don't know if there's anything here large enough to recover."

We stood a moment, then without a word crouched carefully where we'd been standing. I rolled cautiously onto my knees, spidered my fingers apart, and leaned forward on them, scanning the turf. The dog did not move but lay among us, panting rapidly as we studied the ground by inches, looking for anything we might be able to identify. The breeze now was both friend and adversary. The gentler gusts turned over the smallest leaves, revealing areas we were reluctant to touch, but the moving air seemed to worry the search dog. She didn't rise again but lay where she had dropped, her head between her paws, her expression tight.

"Nothing," said the dark-haired man.

The dog's handler shook his head also. He couldn't see anything either.

"Just this," said the second man, and he pointed to the ragged scrap of red and blue fabric the size of a tarot card that had fallen onto a patch of raw ground. They studied it together. One took out a recovery bag as his colleague unfurled a length of crime-scene tape. From my knees, I marked the spot with the GPS, jotted the coordinates in my notebook as backup, then pushed up awkwardly to stand.

The handler moved and his dog rose to follow. Waiting for a signal that I too could step free of where I stood, I watched the pair leave the area. I could hear her handler's praise, but the young dog's head and tail were down. Was there too much scent for her?

Did she think she had somehow failed? Her confident demeanor was gone. She seemed to have withdrawn even from her partner, moving stiffly away from us as though she were old.

Columbia fell over towns, farms, and forests. The developing search began to reveal just how great an area was affected. In the days we worked there, we heard the circulated stories of miraculous misses and amazing recoveries. Hot chunks of metal that had barely missed school buildings or wedding parties, heat tiles flung across a pasture like cards from a bad hand of poker. The debris field was generous.

At the command post, someone wondered if we would recover more than the shuttle in the deep woods we were searching. This area had its meth labs and its body dumps, we'd been told. There could be anything — or anyone — out there. We were to report all human finds, but it could well be that some of them would be entirely unrelated to the loss of *Columbia*. Someone else commented that there were probably some mighty anxious criminals straining forward on their barstools, watching the evening news in a state of wince, unprepared for the presence of thousands of search personnel across the woods of East Texas and Louisiana.

Perhaps due to the careful choices made by search management, perhaps because shuttle fragments were so widespread, every sector I searched beside canine units recovered something of *Columbia*. Though the dogs were charged with crew recovery, human colleagues also took GPS readings and noted the fall of the shuttle's physical debris for written reports when we returned to base. Some pieces were recognizable — straps, switch panels, or fragments of studded circuit board the size of a stamp. One great upended object resting against a tree in deep wood was, we were told, a toilet. Dogs had apparently shown great interest there the previous day, tugged their handlers a fair distance to arrive at the spot. Their handlers debated whether it was the ammonia in its cleaning solution or the associated human scent that had caused the dogs to respond so strongly.

Though I can't speak for everyone associated with the recovery of *Columbia*, the teams I worked with — my own and others from across the country — approached the work soberly. We made no jokes, took no cameras into the field. Sometimes a NASA representative, often an astronaut, accompanied us into sectors. We flagged mechanical debris with strips of brightly colored construction tape. When the dogs indicated human scent, our response to the finds was respectful: we alerted search management and remained beside the find until an official and a NASA representative could complete the recovery. Unlike the knots of pink, green, and orange construction tape that marked shuttle debris, areas with finds of the crew or personal effects were marked with yellow crime-scene tape. As the search extended over days, it became possible to read the recovery on the long roads leading through forest to new sectors, the tails of colored tape revealing the end result of *Columbia's* fall.

That first day in the shadows of late afternoon, the sunlight filtering through the trees to land on charred or shining debris seemed a kind of blessing. "God light," said one of the searchers a little wryly. He was a student cinematographer from Georgia, less faithful than visual perhaps. But I was glad of the sun; we needed light sometimes in the private spaces where debris had landed.

This was a region of hardship. On some farms, we sidestepped thin, hungry livestock. We slip-slid past empty chicken coops, into slaughtering pits with our notebooks and our GPS units, wading through old blood and skin and feathers to mark a single shard of motherboard thrusting upward from the sludge. We found corkscrews of metal and tiny actuators from the shuttle deep in the woods, scattered across makeshift tent cities suggesting profound human poverty.

On one farm where debris had peppered the top of an aged mobile home, we were met at the end of a long dirt drive by a little boy in a suit and bow tie, scrubbed pink to the hairline. Skittish of the search dog, he appeared close to tears, uneasy and babbling. He was reluctant to lead us back to the house. At first he confused us, until we pieced together his conversation and realized he knew nothing about the space shuttle. But someone in his family must have learned that federal government representatives were in the area, without knowing why. This boy was the youngest son of a family of a dozen children. His mother had sent him down the twisting drive to assure federal agents that all the boys and girls got food on the farm. They did their school at home. They had clothes and shoes, and there was no real need to take her children away.

Another homeowner met three of us in her driveway. She was dressed for work, a coat folded over her arm, fidgeting with her car keys as she explained she had to leave and her small farm was ours to search. She had been out already, had seen some new damage on her roof. She'd found a few computer parts, she said, and something she thought looked like upholstery. She knew for a fact that the things she had seen hadn't been there long. She'd be glad if we'd move all of it as soon as possible. She said it was like living in the middle of a train wreck — all these strangers and all this stuff everywhere. The knowledge that it was even there made her uncomfortable on her own land, and very sad. She balanced her purse on her shoulder to gesture how far her farm reached, pointing down a graduated slope that led to a creek that was sometimes there and sometimes not.

And then she turned back, remembering to warn us about her dogs: five dogs out on chains, where they lived at the corners of her land and nearest the pens for the animals. They were lean dogs and half-wild, and they were there to keep the wild hogs and coyotes away from her stock. She said the chains were secure enough, but not to get too close. These dogs weren't hunt partners. These dogs weren't pets. They weren't dog-friendly. They weren't human-friendly, not even to her, except for feeding time. They didn't really have names.

"How long are the chains?" asked the handler, a colleague from another team, his pretty Border Collie sitting at his side.

The woman thought a minute. She couldn't be sure. The chains had been there since her grandfather's day, forty years or more. *So go*, she said. *But don't take your dog off that leash. And good luck.* Her voice was tired.

When she left, the handler said grimly, "This will be interesting." With his dog in a tight heel, we entered the land through a gate not far from the house. The farm was not a large one, but the land was difficult to see to the fence line, choked with standing farm equipment and old cars, dipping down as it did toward the creek bed. We could see two pens of goats and beside them a pair of dogs chained not far away, instantly aggressive, barking angrily — a female and a young male, much alike in their postures and voices, straining to get to us. I saw the Border Collie stiffen beside her handler. With a quiet word, her partner said to let it go.

Two dogs known and three unseen. The handler gave his girl her command, and as we headed for the most downwind point of the sector, out of nowhere another dog leaped out of the brush as though conjured, a roaring, rust red creature that seemed to be on us before he was checked by his chain. He missed the Border Collie by only feet. She froze, ears down and tail tucked, trembled as her handler pulled her in.

"Let it go," he repeated, his voice shaking with the nearness of this. While the chained dog raged, it took a moment for us to assess his tie-down, mentally calculating arc and just how possible it would be for us to get to the farthest point of the sector. We stood still, and the rust red dog also quieted — growling low, watching us with cold eyes. I had no doubt that if he broke free, it would be short work for him to maul two humans and kill the search dog.

A long, considered moment. A breeze rose as we stood there, and something in it made both dogs turn the same direction. The Border Collie woofed a shy single note, and her handler looked to her, then at me. The red dog's gaze turned back our direction.

"All right," said the handler. "We'd better get in there. And we'd better hope that chain holds."

He gave a command to his partner and she stepped forward, still trembling slightly, her head up and eyes forward despite the

angry drone of the other dog. Moving down the slope, I walked behind them with an eye to that chain. It's a fine line, working past
aggressive dogs in the field, whether fenced, chained, or held in .
check by a human: don't engage, don't provoke, get on with the
work, but don't underestimate the situation either. We were still
uneasy when we moved down the rise out of sightline. The back of
my neck prickled. Red dog's absence was somehow scarier than his
presence.

We sidestepped what appeared to be slaughtering ground with
an acrid stench of its own — dried blood, remnants of skin, and
bristly hair. Rounding a truck and battered trailer, on the other
side of the creek bed, we could see chunks of raw metal and
scorched circuitry in the thick brush ahead, a swatch of fabric, en-
twined strands of wire caught on a roll of old fencing. The search
dog sprang forward with intention: from some artifact or another,
human scent, whether *Columbia*'s or not.

"Ah," said her handler, looking at the brush, the wide scatter of
debris. "God." And then he said quietly, "We're going to be here
awhile."

Fine weather in the early days of the search gave way to rain, then
freezing rain and sleet by Wednesday of the first week, changing
the complexion of the recovery. Now I was assigned to a different
group of searchers — a collection of personnel from three separate
teams. We were covering areas already searched by others, perhaps hundreds of others, and yet there were still finds, all of them
small. Tomorrow there would likely be more. One official said it
might take months for any sector to be clean, that every gust of
wind brought more of *Columbia* down.

We'd been out in the freezing rain since early morning, and in
some cases individual searchers stood over human remains for an
hour or more, waiting for the process of official recovery to occur.
An astronaut and a handful of dogs worked among us, as well as a
gridline of young men from a military school who walked the uneven terrain at arm's length from one another, their eyes on the

ground. Two of them passed near me as I stood waiting for the recovery team. "Ma'am," they said politely, without looking up. They parted slightly around the tree where I stood, then came together again, their heads bowed, taking careful steps.

I now stood over a fragment of vertebra, tilted upward among the stones and leaves. Knobbed edges and an internal fretwork gave it a tiny, bony alien face. I had nearly missed it earlier. We had entered the sector in ice pellets and sleet, and though the ground was still too warm for much accumulation, parts of the ground rapidly crusted with ice. Rocks had grown slick. Somehow in the press forward, negotiating the terrain with my head bent against the sting, scanning, scanning, I had walked past it. I don't know what provoked me to turn around, but in the different light behind me the bone stood in sharp relief against the dull brown of old leaves. I called out the find.

"Yes," said the officer running the sector, bending down to look at it. "Call it in. And stay here."

I made the required phone call used for human finds and stood there a long while, slapping my gloved hands together and occasionally wiping a glaze of ice from my glasses. Though there were perhaps sixty of us working across that wood — some moving, some standing as I was, waiting for recovery teams — tucked deep into our coats we seemed isolated from one another, so quiet amid the *tic-tic-tic* of falling ice that I could hear both the ragged crunch of the cadets as they moved down slope and the individual snuffles of the dogs as they passed yards away.

The dogs' heads worked low today. Perhaps time, sleet, and cold, heavy air had pressed scent down. I could see their noses crossing back and forth, lifting occasionally a few inches from the turf. One sniffed thoughtfully at the boots of a nearby cadet, then lifted his head to his handler and barked. There was little energy in it. To keep the dogs encouraged, last night we'd arranged live finds for many of them by stepping out of our hotel rooms and hiding volunteers there. This dog had been in that group, but now he showed none of last night's exuberance.

"*Barrow*," I heard a Bloodhound cry about another find some-where else in the wood. "*Barrow*."

I crouched in place, arms wrapped around my knees. The offi-cer running the sector returned to verify that I'd called in the find. He said, "*You* look a little green."

"Just cold," I answered, and that was the truth of it, after days of disturbing human finds.

"There's counseling back at the command post when you need it."

Did I need it? I couldn't be sure if the numb I felt was cold or some kind of event saturation that made me feel little at all. No more horror, no longer deep, abiding grief. I had seen enough of *Columbia* that the vertebra before me provoked only a weary sense of inevitability. I watched the dogs and handlers make their small, tight sweeps, the dark dogs subdued, their backs frosted with ice. The ground around us was rapidly going white. Kneeling there, I cupped my hands above the little bone as though I could warm it. I felt the freezing rain stitch both of us down tight to the earth.

Days later, outbound along the same road we'd come in on, I led several other cars full of personnel who were also cycling off the search as new responders were due to arrive. We would drive in train until our paths diverged. Two cars would head west. One, northeast. I would drive back to Dallas. The other drivers put me in the lead, saying my red car was the easiest to see in bad weather. As we drove, I occasionally glanced back and could see dog heads in silhouette, sticking up from the back seats of the cars behind me. After a time, I could see only drivers. The dogs were no longer there. They were all tired, surrendering to the long drive and the rhythm of the cars. This had been a hard week.

Some dog teams had left the day before. There were circulating stories that this dog or that one had been overcome by the work. Not one of them physically injured, but several of them affected by the search. "Too many days of too much scent, none of it good," ex-plained one handler, speaking of his dog now curled in his crate, a normally outgoing German Shepherd, an experienced recovery dog that had stopped eating the day before and had withdrawn from play and affection. Was this illness, stress, field exhaustion, or a canine form of compassion fatigue? The handler shrugged. He said that when a dog gives signals like these, you pay attention. His German Shepherd had had enough.

The true nature of canine grief — if this was grief — was a mystery to me. I had listened to experienced handlers at this search, and opinions were strongly divided. Some said dogs didn't share grief in human terms, but that critical incident stress was as real for them as it was for their human partners. It could overwhelm a dog in the field, or it might take a while to surface. They said that handlers and dogs would need to proceed cautiously across the coming weeks. Easy, motivating practice searches for the dogs. Lots of play. Upbeat rewards. Pushing too hard could create an aversion to the work and shut a dog down from search for good. Perhaps some humans too — though none of us talked about that before we packed the cars to go.

We left East Texas in heavy rain that gradually tapered to drizzle, then ceased altogether beneath fringed clouds giving way to blue sky. The road lightened. The woods on either side of us were quiet, the hundreds of searchers who had penetrated them now gone. For a while we could see the twitch of colored tape among the trees: pink, green, orange, and the occasional curl of crime-scene yellow. Less and less of it as we drove free of the area, none at all for a long stretch — then suddenly two trees wreathed in pink, something of the shuttle far apart from everything else. We all slowed. At the base of the trees, a hand-painted sign read GOD-SPEED, COLUMBIA. Someone in our group keyed his radio, then thought better of it and left the call unsaid.

24

NO BAD NEWS

I 'LL LET YOU get dressed," the nurse says as she leaves the small examining room where I've lain for an hour or so, staring alternately at a diagram of the eye and a video on cholesterol. The door clicks shut, but for a moment I am unable to move. The room is meticulously impersonal, like a public bathroom, its furniture all hard, slick sides made for wiping down the more embarrassing truths about being human. Though there's probably good news now and again, they are prepared for tears here. There's a box of tissues on the counter and another on a small cabinet near the examining table. It is the kind of room that hears the kind of news that warrants seatbelts on the single chair for family members and a roller coaster's pull-down, lock-tight bar over the space where patients wait for the sudden drop.

I haven't cried. Having lost a good friend to cancer nine months ago, I easily see that my own prognosis, while not wonderful, doesn't throw the long shadow that Erin's did. But as I step into jeans that once fit and turn my T-shirt inside-in, my fingertips are curiously numb. The clothes slide on easily, but I feel no connect with them, as though I'm dressing a mannequin using robotic arms while looking the wrong way through a telescope. Buttons are tough. Zippers hard to grasp. I am still finding buttonholes to account for the mismatched alignment of my blouse when the doctor returns.

He is a tall man with wiry brown hair that doesn't settle neatly around his ears. Glasses worsen the problem, so that sometimes he has sticky-uppy tufts protruding over the earpieces. He is young enough to have been my son if I'd been particularly enterprising, or maybe my much younger brother, and some remaining vulnerability in him makes me want to smooth down those tufts, pat the front of his lab coat, and say, "There." His expression is kind, but it is clear he gives this kind of information often enough that the lines of his face quickly settle into a kind of bad-news barrier, and that he speaks from behind that necessary distance. He is there, but not there, with his frequent glances to my medical record. He is compassionate in the way one might be at the sight of a car accident a block away. And he is brisk with his list of recommendations and protocols, clear about what the future might hold in a year. He says, "There will probably be days when you're going to feel very bad."

He's right. That's already happened. Some days, it's hard to make my feet move. Other days, I feel too weak to stand. And then an unexpected reprieve: I'll go for a few months feeling completely normal, with all the energy I had in my twenties.

I've had a while to prepare for this. The condition has been a known possibility since I was a toddler — a birth defect combined with factors of heredity have made it a question mark during my adolescence and young married life, which had seen a number of related infections. In short, I have lousy kidneys. I'd grown up with kidney infections that occurred so frequently I could sense the earliest symptoms when they were coming on, but in adulthood I'd decided I would strong-arm the condition and ignore it to the best of my ability. Eat the right things, yes. Avoid the wrong things, absolutely. See a doctor regularly. But other than that, I refused to think about two organs that could become old-lady kidneys even while I was relatively young.

For the most part, such optimistic thinking has worked. I responded well to medical intervention and found it easy to follow the suggested diet. I continued to fly, worked a few weeks as a deckhand on a tall ship a couple of summers in a row. But a bad episode at age forty seemed to be significant. Was the condition stepping up? My treatment reconfigured and I adapted to it, and when I joined the search team in 2001, I did so firmly believing that I could work despite the illness, planning to stand myself down from searches during the bad periods and deploy during the good ones. I must have done something right. I chugged liters of water and followed the medical protocol. I never failed to show for a search due to illness. Puzzle's chaotic arrival in 2004 seems now to have been such a bright point of distraction that, looking back, I can remember few bad days during her puppyhood.

Now I leave the office with a sheaf of papers in hand, heading out of the tinted-window gloom of the building into a summer day that has relented, this one time, and traded heat for heavy cumulus clouds and a breeze with the sound of thunder at its back. Any cool in a Texas summer feels like a gift. I don't want to outdrive the coming rain, so I get in the car and wait. I watch drops slide down the windshield and quiver one upon another above the wipers, stacked like circus acrobats waiting for a fall.

The dogs have known something was wrong for some time. Just weeks after Puzzle's certification tests, Jack and Puzzle were the first to behave differently in my presence, the first to begin to hover when I moved through the house. On bad days, I come home too exhausted to turn on the lights for evening. I throw my jacket over a chair and fall into bed fully clothed, shoes thumping to the floor. Jack has taken to pulling the jacket off the chair and curling up on it next to the bed. Puzzle leaps up on the bed to lie beside me, pressing her forehead to my cheek. Whether the scent of my changed chemistry or the altered homecoming have provoked this, I don't know, but this is the first time I have seen Jack and Puzzle consistently act in common accord. They follow me every evening to my bedroom, and there they stay until I get up again. In recent weeks,

Sprits'l too has joined the entourage, following the others as they trail me through the house. Sprits mutters and circles worriedly on the floor when I lie down.

For several evenings after work, I retreat to the semigloom of my bedroom, drinking ginger tea and considering the future. The dogs like this. Their natural response at the end of hot days is to lie still. They join me in everything but the tea, the Golden lying long across the bed and the Poms stretched wide, bellies to the breeze of the fan. My thoughts are as much on them as they are on illness. The most immediate concern is strength, which I'm told will come and go. It's mostly gone these days, and it isn't difficult to realize that right here, right now, managing the house and the dogs will be difficult. And right now I'm certainly not strong enough to work Puzzle in the field. As my doctor wrangles treatment protocol, this might improve in coming months. Or not.

Lying beside me on the bed, belly-up, the Golden is oblivious to my private debate. Extended strategically beneath the air-conditioning vent, she has her forepaws bent like a praying mantis and her back legs inelegantly splayed. Her ears extend outward like wings, and her mouth is open; the seed-pearl bottom teeth show. Some of her snores must tickle, because as they come out she gives them a final, unconscious chew with those bottom teeth, which makes a little dipthong of the snore. Or perhaps the chew means she is dreaming of doughnuts, which she nibbles in much the same way. Even in the heat of these late summer evenings, Puzzle presses close. She's my dog now, by choice, and we both know it.

A firefighter friend and I used to talk about the "tap on the shoulder"—the moment when emergency responders make a choice to put themselves at risk on behalf of another. There are taps and there are *taps*, he said to me once. The first tap tells a person she wants to become a firefighter, or a police officer, or—and he elbowed me—run after some dog in the dark. Another tap tells him to go into a burning structure when every natural impulse says no. At its most extreme, the "Courage Meets Oh Geez" moment, he called it and laughed, not wanting to claim that he is some kind of saint.

Now it occurs to me that in this working partnership with Puzzle, I might be the one to fail, and that the tap on the shoulder might instead be saying step aside. *Oh geez,* I say aloud the way my friend does through his nose, but there's little courage in it. The dogs twitch awake at the sound of me, stretching and grinning with an optimistic eye to the kitchen. *Treats?* they seem to ask. *Did you just say "Treats"?*

I can lie in the dark with a teacup only so long. I remember Erin, who ten weeks before she died was at Home Depot buying mulch. In the heat of the "meanest summer ever," as she put it (and 2005 was a right scorcher), she put in new flower beds full of moss roses and vinca. Fierce gardening for anyone in that vindictive heat, and though I thought it was Erin's sort of karmic make-peace with fate and an unkind universe, she shook her head. No, she said, she liked the bright colors, but her mind was on her aging mother, who would have to sell the house after she died. Theirs was a neighborhood full of foreclosures; Erin wanted her house competitive. She would dig for hours in the garden, then be too weak to stand for several days.

After she died, her two little Poms came to live with me. They remind me of her often this year after we lost her, and for some contrary reason on a day I'm feeling pretty good, I go to Home Depot to wander the garden department. I tweak a vinca or two and pat several bags of mulch in honor of my friend, before wandering takes me outside to a row of prefab storage sheds in architectural postures. There are red barns and log-cabin look-alikes, and one with a wrought-iron star on it has a distinctly Texas prairie feel. Why am I looking here? I don't need a storage shed, but I walk the row of them, anyway, stopping at the final example. It's not a storage shed at all, but a child's cottage playhouse, complete with porch, shutters, dormers on the roof, and window boxes. Unfinished on the inside, the exterior is already primed taupe and crimson. A sign promises that the primer will take any paint color, and that the whole thing can be delivered and built in a half-day or less.

SURPRISE YOUR CHILD, a sign on the cottage reads.

Inside, the scent of raw plywood smells like possibility. I ignore the adult-size side door and choose, instead, to walk through the little Dutch-door entrance. It's not a tiny playhouse. Six adults could stand up and have cocktails in here, if they were feeling friendly. I bend down to look out the four-over-four cottage windows. When another woman opens the door to come inside, I feel a little silly kneeling there. But she enters with a grin and bends to peer out the other window.

"I always wanted a playhouse," she says.

Me too. At forty-six and childless and on the trailing edge of bad news, there's no reason for me to want one now, but I do. I pull loose a free-take-one flyer and make a crazy-lady circle of it next to my head. My companion laughs and asks, "Are you gonna do it?" When I walk out of the little house and across the parking lot for a cashier, I can still see her in there. She's shifted to the other window and gives me a little wave, one elbow on the sill as she looks out at the world.

I convince myself that I'm building a *dog* house — a luxe little space to share with my crew and any doggy visitors. Friends are not convinced. "Uh huh," says one of them. "And where are you gonna put the dolls?"

The cottage arrives on a flatbed truck two weeks later. Two young men spread its sections out across the backyard in a sequence they understand, but which to me looks as though the little house has been felled by a particularly organized tornado. While inside the house the Poms are going nuts against every available window, the two men assemble the house with almost no conversation between them. Cinderblock foundation, floor, walls, roof, dormers, porch, doors, window boxes. They pause only when I come out with canned soft drinks and cups of ice. One shows me a manufacturer's metal tag that's supposed to be screwed onto the roofline of the cottage. He doesn't speak much English, but he holds the sign up where it should go, looks at me, and shakes his head.

"Ugly," he says.

"Ugly," I agree.

He points to the cottage's serial number for warranty's sake, then slides the little sign under the right edge of the front porch. He taps his forehead and then mine, as if to say *remember.* I lift a soda can in tribute.

The dogs rush out of the house when the cottage is finished. They stream to the fence to bark away the last remaining scent of the two men that still hovers across the yard, and without breaking a stride, they rush to the cottage to examine it. Though the adult- and child-size doors are open, they first dash around it in a circle, examining it on the fly. It's their old game of chase with a new objective. Puzzle is in the joyful lead, Sprits'l is already acting a little territorial, and I get the sense that Puz is much less interested in the cottage than she is in its current ability to provoke a chase from the Poms. She wheels around and play bows to Sprits'l, who takes the gesture as a challenge and an insult and begins to chase her around the cottage in earnest — *stay-away-from-this-thing-that's-now-mine* — her canter leading his furious hop-chop-chop of a gallop. The other little dogs pick up on the energy and follow, yapping and nattering at her heels.

Around and around the cottage they go, never once dashing inside until Sprits'l ducks through the adult door after Puzzle blazes around a corner ahead of him. Smart boy. She doesn't realize he isn't back there still chasing her; the other Poms are slathering behind her and haven't missed their ringleader, either. When Puz circles around the cottage again, Sprits'l leaps out from the door with a yap that sounds very like *hiiii-ya!* They collide, spin briefly together like Elmer Fudd and the Tasmanian Devil, then fall apart panting, a cue for the other dogs to collapse on the grass and look dazedly at the cottage and one another. One by one, they recover themselves and totter into the little house to claim it.

Friends insist that the cottage needs to have a name. In the days before its delivery, I have considered a few pretty, artful titles, but nothing seems to fit until the dogs' chase makes the house their own. Charlotte, a Canadian, suggests *La Folie des Chiots* — the madness of the pups — which seems completely right. The house is my folly, in the English architectural sense, a structure built for no reason other than pleasure, but it is also — yes — a place to share with the dogs. There is much to do to complete the cottage and integrate it into the garden. It needs a complete paint job over the primer, its window boxes planted, and walls, a floor, perhaps furniture on the inside. I imagine a faux-tin ceiling and a small electric heater that mimics a wood-burning fireplace. There can be no question that I'm about to play house for a while. What I don't understand is why the project seems necessary and why, from the moment I buy the first cans of paint to bring home, the future seems a little brighter, if not entirely clear.

Field assistant Ellen has never wanted to work a search dog, and she doesn't want to work one now. Not even Puzzle, though she has long collaborated on her training. It's a hard moment when I ask if she'd be willing to learn to run my dog in the event I can no longer do so. And it takes a while for her to respond. For her, it's not a matter of disliking dogs. She has dogs of her own. For Ellen, it's the question of vulnerability. She has seen a dozen dog-and-handler relationships and she's seen the environments where they work. She has never wanted to become a handler, because the risk of loving and losing a dog is too great, and she doesn't know that she'd be able to bear that loss. And, she says, knowing she would be working *my* dog makes all those concerns even greater.

Trouble is, all the team handlers have dogs of their own, many of them in their prime and far from retirement. If Ellen doesn't want to handle Puzzle, and if I get too sick to partner my dog, I'll need to decide what's better for her: leaving to work with another handler on another team, or living quietly with me as a pet. Either option makes my stomach twist. Puzzle seems to love her job, and she seems to love me. I cannot retire her before she's been on a single search. On good days, I refuse to think I'm going to have to make a choice. On bad days, I make a note to call her breeder to discuss this. Somehow word spreads to other handlers in other states and to strangers. I get an e-mail from Mike in Vermont titled *I will take your dog.*

Kindly meant, I'm sure. But I think, *The hell you will.*

That e-mail is a snap-to message. There are alternatives I can make peace with, and alternatives I cannot.

I ask Ellen again. It's a little easier when I tell her that learning to run with my dog is a backup plan, a what-if safety net. I don't want to think that the past two years of hard training and testing have been for nothing. And I also want to be fair to Puzzle. When she isn't working, she seems to watch and wait for some sign from me that we're heading out — the pager, the gathering of the search gear, the words, "Are you ready to go to work?" She's a good girl, young and motivated. I don't think she'd be happy as a housedog yet. And there are larger issues here: quite apart from our history together is the truth that she's a dog able to make a contribution. The job is still there to be done, with or without me in the search field beside her.

These are all arguments that make sense to Ellen. One day after training, she gives Puzzle's ear a tug and says she'll give it a shot.

Puzzle seems to know where she is the minute she hops out of the Jeep, bounding across the parking lot to the greenbelt beside the road, happily nosing through the brush. This is the same hiking area where she certified for wilderness search months ago. It is warmer today, humid and airless. Nevertheless, the winding trails, hilly terrain, and thick brush seem to excite her in ways that urban landscapes do not, reminding me that Goldens have a love of the field in their genes and that the crashing and bounding required here must feel very right to Puzzle. She has her head up now, and her tail waves a wide, happy flag as she greets dog friends and human colleagues alike. Johnny and Cindi with Labs Buster and Belle, Rob and Belgian Malinois Valkyrei. Deryl and Max with German Shepherds Sadie and Mercy. Birgit and Pit Bull Ali. Terry and Border Collie Hoss. Jerry and elegant Husky Shadow.

On a good day with three sectors working here, every dog on the team can get in four to five searches during a three-hour training session. We will take turns as victims or as FAS team if necessary, rotating the dogs in and out across the area so that all canine units get a chance to work and everyone also gets a chance for water and rehab on this hot day. While the dogs stretch their legs and socialize, revving up for the work, each of us organizes the backs of our vehicles for ready access to training records, water, scent articles for the dogs working scent discrimination, and medical supplies both for dogs and humans. I toy with gear in the back of the Jeep longer than I really have to, tidying and re-tidying my first-aid kit and breaking up training treats for Puzzle.

I look up to see Ellen standing beside the Jeep. She's been there a while, watching. When I have no more excuses to keep rearranging my pack, I close the back door to the Jeep and tug Puzzle's long lead, calling her to me. She trots over easily, her smile deep and her tongue already out sideways. I take up her backpack of gear and move to a stretch of grass where we will wait together.

"Puzzle's number four to go out," Ellen says. "I'm going to go hide for Val, and then I'll come back and get . . ." She can't say it. She gestures to Puzzle. We both know what she means. While we settle in the grass, Ellen heads out to hide in a sector. We watch her disappear up the winding curve that marks the entrance to the second trail. Puzzle's head is up. She tilts it a little and moans when Ellen disappears from sight, looking at me in the way she does when one of her supposed pack leaves the group and goes off solo. Puz has seen the process for a couple of years now, but she shoots me a look every time, as though I were pretty sloppy about pack maintenance and in just a few bounding steps she could fix that.

We watch Deryl and Sadie head out for a sector off the first trail, while Johnny and Buster take their places, waiting for word to search, at the head of trail number three. Rob and Val are also ready to go. As soon as Ellen is hidden deep in the sector, they will be off. And running. Belgian Malinois Val never takes things at a lope that would be much more fun at a gallop.

Puzzle lies beside me, but her posture is alert, and each time she hears a handler give the "Find!" command, she starts a little where she lies, the product of hundreds of searches bound in muscle memory. As the third handler disappears, she sighs but does not relax. Though she cannot see the dogs and handlers work each search, she seems to be able to follow their progress through scent and sound. We are down slope and downwind from two of the sectors, and as I watch her, I wonder how much she makes of all of this that totally escapes me. I see her head turn as though she were watching, but the bob of her nose and the delicate working of her nostrils suggest that even here where we sit together she has a good idea where dogs, handlers, and victims already are.

Johnny and Buster return quickly, two victims in tow. Val makes short work of finding Ellen. They also return in less than ten minutes. Rob is laughing and Val's bright dash around him suggests hers was a tight, efficient search. Ellen and Rob confer a minute at the edge of the wood; he glances over to the place where I sit in the grass with Puzzle. Then he puts Val in her crate, and after a word to two other teammates, Rob disappears up the third trail.

As Ellen approaches, I push awkwardly up to stand, and when I stand, Puzzle also rises, shaking herself and giving a little whimpering strain at the lead as if to say she's ready to run. Without comment, Ellen takes the treat bag from my hand and clips it on to her belt. I hand her Puzzle's lead. In a low voice, she asks Puzzle if she'd like a drink. Puzzle puts her nose to the bowl and takes a casual lap, but she isn't thirsty and she's eager to head out, and she isn't confused about the change of leadership until Ellen gives her lead a tug and asks if she's ready to go to work. The phrase is a familiar one, and at the sound of it Puzzle responds with a shiver of anticipation, but as they step away from me, she turns and looks at me with a bewildered expression on her face. I can't be sure what I'm seeing from her, and I wonder if what I do see is merely a reflection of my own feelings: confusion, hurt, and a hint of betrayal.

Ellen gives another command and urges Puzzle away. I watch the dog's reluctance shift to subdued obedience, the tension of her walk away from me giving way to a loose-lead trot. As they move to the edge of the sector and wait for word to begin, Puzzle stands quietly beside Ellen, her focus already deep in the woods. This is the first time I've seen Puzzle begin a search from a distance, and I'm struck by how my girl has grown up, and how rapidly. She is a different dog just in the five months since her certification, as though the tests had given her a sense of purpose that training had only hinted at.

Ellen seems anxious. I watch her gather and ungather the long lead in her hands, bunching it against her stomach and then dropping it free. She checks her watch and pushes the hair back from her face. She encourages Puzzle, the usual rev-up words. Puzzle flicks an ear and stands, as though she knows something about the sector before Ellen has had word of it. When Max, who has hidden Rob as victim, comes down the trail and gives Ellen the word, they are ready to search. Ellen glances at me once, then quickly away. She clicks Puzzle off-lead. When she shouts "Find!" to Puzzle, the dog springs forward to meet the woods. For a moment, I can see her flash through the green. She bounds quickly up the trail. She does not look back.

There are good days and there are bad days. On the good days, I train with Puzzle as I always have — a little slower, perhaps, and bathed in sweat and nausea, while she bounds ahead of me, alight. On the bad days, I stay out of sight while Puzzle runs with Ellen. Sometimes I wait in cars parked outside the buildings where we train, watching for the flick of my blond Golden Retriever running past a window, Ellen and FAS team assistant in trail. Sometimes I see her. Once, from a parking lot and through the glass of two windows, I witness the moment when Puzzle orients from faint scent to the location of her hidden victim. I watch her pivot on that upturned nose, a 90-degree change of direction so sudden that her back end spins out a little, the way it did in her puppy days, before she scrambles out of sight and into the room she has chosen.

"How's it going?" I ask Ellen of their work together, and she says, "Fine," but adds after a pause that Puzzle is different — she's doing the job, but completes the training searches without her usual joy. Refusing treats for the most part, shrugging away from praise.

"Not even *weenies*?" I ask, thinking this dog can surely be bought.

"Not even weenies," Ellen answers.

Returning from one training scenario, Puzzle spots me sitting half a football field away. She abandons Ellen and ignores nearby teammates and dashes across the turf, exuberant with success, colliding with me, wiggling the way she did as a puppy. *I-was-wonderful-you-are-wonderful-I-was-wonderful.*

"She'll do it for me," says Ellen, who has caught up with her, breathless, "but she wants to search with you."

Birgit is always acute about dog-human relationships. She says, "Susannah, you better get strong."

During the months while my strength boxes the compass, Puz and I train at every opportunity, large or small. Friends and teammates are generous. Some hide for us in the park a couple of blocks away; a few come over and hide in the house, the yard, the garage, or in cars for Puzzle: currency training that doesn't require as much stamina from me. On Labor Day weekend, one neighbor brings his own son and two little nieces, giving Puzzle the opportunity to find three giggling children wedged in small spaces. One friend gives me four pairs of old shoes for scent discrimination training, so that I can scent Puzzle on a single shoe and ask her to find its match amid the other ones. Having the Golden fetish for shoes in general, this is a game Puzzle enjoys. She puts her nose deep in the chosen shoe and huffs her bliss, then scrambles around the yard to find its mate.

"Oh," I cry out when she makes an accurate find, shrieking in a nasty, guttural voice that Puzzle has always loved, "she's FABU-LOUS." Puzzle tosses her head at that and begins to race through the yard, galloping a figure-eight around the cottage and the fire pit that I've come to call her "Folie 500." "FABULOUS," I shout again, throwing up my hands, and she races a little faster. Around and around again, until she stops, flopping down on the slate path and bobbing her head up to me with the *yo-babe!* expression I've come to associate with her own pride. "Good job. You're fabulous," I say, but softer, stroking her ears while she grins up like *I so am*.

On a particularly awful pair of bad days, I lie on the couch and fiddle with paint swatches and decide to paint *La Folie* candy-box colors — a bright green called "Picnic," and for the trim a butter yellow, a periwinkle blue, and a pearly white called "Marshmallow." Gerand once said that the right colors together inspire energy, and maybe I've stumbled onto a clutch of good ones, because one late-summer morning, I feel strong enough to lug the paint cans out into the yard, prizing them open and stirring the paint with fat sticks. That's my goal for the day: just to open the cans and stir the paint with fat sticks. But the paint smells fresh and good, and the row of bright cans is cheerful. And I think there are brushes in the garage, and what would it hurt to get a little of the base coat up?

This is a day I should feel lousy. Certainly my neighbors do, creeping like suspects from their cars into the artificial cool of their houses, where the central air has droned since June. I don't blame them. Even beneath the deep shade of pecan trees, the heat is palpable, roaring up from the street beside the house. There's a row of grackles on the lowest power lines, their mouths open wide in an attempt to cool.

Against all better wisdom, I let the dogs out in the yard, where they circle and yap the grackles and are immediately curious about the paint, putting their noses to the open cans and coming away with their dark whiskers tipped green and yellow. While I get pans and brushes and drop cloths, the Poms assume supervisory poses on the slate sidewalk, frog-legged to press their bellies against cool stone. Puzzle prefers to saunter into the garage and out of it beside me.

The day progresses, the heat rises, and by midafternoon, two-thirds of the cottage is green and all of the comfort-loving Poms are back inside the house, worshipping the central air, draped like roadkill across the tile beneath the ceiling fan. Puzzle alone has remained with me. She lies inside the cottage and watches me paint through the open doorway, panting lightly, her smile wide in easy camaraderie. When I head for the garage, she follows. When I take a break from the painting, she shares my water, then offers me a ball to toss or simply lies against my feet. We study the humming-birds as they hover along the Turk's Cap, sometimes inches away from both of us.

At the end of the day, we both seem pleased. It's 102 degrees, and Puzzle and I look a little goofy as we stand admiring *La Folie* with our mouths open against the heat. I'm liberally smeared with green. Puzzle has somehow avoided the green, but in the process of inspecting the paint for the doors, she's acquired a spot of periwin-kle on her muzzle, another smudge on her haunch, and the waving feathers of her tail are so liberally streaked blue on one side that when she wags, she appears to be waving a Go Team pennant.

"Whoa," says trainer Susan about the cottage later that after-noon. "You got a lot painted for a sick girl. Actually . . ." she amends, "you got a lot painted for a *well* girl." She looks down at my peri-winkle-smeared Golden. "Puzzle in her blue period?"

She is. And across the coming weeks, she's in her yellow period. Her white period. And, at last, her green period, when I give a few sections of the cottage a second coat. Whatever the weather of the day and whatever my own strength directs, Puzzle seems deeply content beside me. Indoors or out. I look down at her and find it hard to remember the puppy that, two years ago, turned away from me with a shrug.

But it is not hard to remember the search dog. One afternoon the pager pips, and green-speckled Puzzle springs up to stand eagerly at the door while I scramble for the cell phone. It is a call to search, but it's a drowning call, an advanced water search that Puzzle has not yet certified to work. I am able to deploy. For a few anticipatory minutes, she seems sure she's heading out too, and it is as though the world is back in the greased grooves she remembers, but when I head for the door without her vest and long lead, her face falls. I am heading out to work, she is ready to go to work, *and I'm not taking her.* She huffs to the back of the couch muttering, clearly aware there's something very wrong with this system.

This summer was initially quiet with regard to search call-outs, and then in late July we began to get a series of drowning calls leading into August. Summer 2006 is a season of hard drought. The lakes are low, and our area is critically short of water, but for recreational enthusiasts it is also dangerous. Since only one Texas lake is natural and the rest are reservoirs, boats are now sitting just over the remnants of trees or other rubble that make up parts of manmade lake beds. When swimmers jump from the boats, they come to grief in the trees that once would have been fifteen to twenty feet below the surface.

This September call is a search for a middle-aged missing man who'd gone boating with his mother on a late Friday evening in the moonlight. At one point, he stood up in his boat and turned to speak to her, took a misstep, and pitched over the side of the boat and into the water. She threw him a life preserver, but she said he never reached for it. Down he went in a sort of tangle, a thrash and down out of sight, and he never came up again.

Fifteen hours later, we are out on the boats with the dogs. We've been briefed on the accident's history by the local sheriff's department, and the story of a drowning off a boat with two life preservers in it makes me grit my teeth a little with frustration. Every drowning we've had in the last three years has been someone off a boat with a life preserver in it, but no life preserver on the victim. You want to headbang a little after weeks of lost daughters, fathers, fiancés, and best friends.

At one point, after I've been out on a boat assisting another handler and his dog, I am walking back to the command post and stop to wipe my face next to a woman eating half a sub sandwich and gazing out to the water. I initially think she is one of the Red Cross volunteers, but she introduces herself and is, rather, the mother of the man who had drowned.

She says, "I'm so sorry you've had to give up a Saturday." She says she's always loved boats and water, and that this outing the evening before had been inspired by good intention: an evening with her boy after she'd had a serious illness. Neither could swim.

She speaks of a double mastectomy and a chemotherapy follow-up in May, and says her son had taken her out the night before because it was the first time she was well enough to go. The pressure of the life preserver was too painful for her to wear on her chest, so she did not, and because she couldn't, he chose not to wear his also. She is slight and pale beneath a large hat, her eyes shadowed with fatigue. But she is out in the heat, will stay out here until he's found. Her tired voice is laced with tenderness and respect as she speaks of her son — he was just trying to do something nice for her at the end of a very bad time. He said, "You need to have a little summer," and he took her out on the boat. It was a beautiful evening. The water was calm. The way he fell over the side, she says, makes her think he'd had a heart attack or something acute and unexpected. She wonders what he'd been about to say before he fell.

We stand for a time together, watching the other search boats go out, back and forth across the area, the dogs' noses up, then down to the water. From where we stand, a hundred yards away, their alerts are absolutely clear, and I wonder what it is like to be her, watching us debride that wound. She says that when she was diagnosed with cancer earlier in the year, a friend told her, *There is no bad news, only information.* She says she grew up with a dad who raised Labs. Now, when a dog on the boat tenses over the edge, his bark ringing across the water, she doesn't ask me what it means. She offers me half her turkey sandwich, and though I am a vegetarian, I take it. We sit in the grass and make our separate sense of what will happen next.

Summer's sullen heat gives way to the cooler temperatures of late autumn. By October, *La Folie* is painted and its window boxes planted, and most days its doors are thrown open wide for the dogs to enter and exit at will, while I sit inside reading *Cadaver Dog Handbook*. There are dog beds and a water bowl inside it, a white tin of dog biscuits on a little table just inside the front door. The tin has a lid that snaps tight over its contents for freshness, but one day I walk past one of *La Folie*'s open windows and see Puzzle sitting before the table, staring earnestly upward at the tin while Fo'c'sle Jack stands on his back legs and fantasizes about height and opposable thumbs. When I call the two dogs, they come out of the cottage, Puzzle immediately and Jack more sluggishly. He glances back and forth to the tin as though weighing the hazards of disobedience or the advantages of begging. He's a good boy, but only just, and I grin watching Jack's internal debate: "You . . . the treats . . . you . . . the treats . . . (sigh) . . . well, all right . . . you." With the Golden, there's no longer any doubt.

I feel stronger in the cool air — more up than down — able to work more training sessions with Puzzle, who at two and a half is physically changing also. I'm seeing the early shape of the mature dog. She is taller and sturdier. Her winter coat has begun to come in, a thatch of waves across her chest, her haunches deeply feathered and tail feathers thickened. On wilderness workdays, we're getting close to the 2:1 ratio Fleta used to joke about: for every hour searching, the handler of a long-coated dog spends two hours combing out the search.

Apart from training, we walk together daily. I try to be careful. Short walks some days. Longer on others. I have a tendency to push myself hard, and it rarely works out well. We add blocks and increase speed incrementally. On bad days, which sometimes still happen, we back everything down several notches. Puzzle, who two years before was determined to set the pace of every walk (*faster! faster!*) from a lead taut as a ski rope, now looks to me to set the standard. She's still showy and prideful. She is pleased to be out and about. But if I need to stop, we stop. If I want to jog a little, we jog. A little. As the holidays approach, I put on her red and white velvet jingle-bell collar, and Puzzle walks beside or ahead of me, depending on the command, the steady *jing-jing-jing* of her lope causing the neighbors to wave and lean over the fence to admire her. They shake their heads and smile, remembering the puppy that bucked and snorted and shot me the paw.

On a cool, foggy morning just after Thanksgiving, I decide to try the pace test required of all team members for Senior certification with the team: a circuit around the training academy campus that must be done with a forty-five-pound pack in fifteen minutes or under. I did the circuit successfully in January 2004 and again in summer 2005, but have not attempted it this year, and certainly not since I've been sick, when stamina newly emerged as an issue.

Puzzle stands next to me as I lean into the Jeep and rebalance the pack's contents. Something is up, and she knows it. I'm going to take her with me on the circuit, interested in what kind of time we'll make together. The sight of the pack excites her, and I briefly wonder if she'll be too wound up to keep pace beside me. It'll be a test for us both — and maybe an affirmation that things are looking up.

I give a nod to the timekeeper, say "With me" to Puzzle, and we head onto the track. We begin the circuit with a walk that slowly escalates to a jog and from there, halfway through it, to a run for a fifth of the distance. I haven't felt like running, haven't run at all in six months, and my feet seem awkward thumping over the track in thick-soled boots. The pack is heavy too, and maybe one strap's not quite right — there's a slight *galumph-galumph* against my left shoulder with every step. But the balance is good.

And this feels good and strong. For a little while.

Puzzle canters off-lead beside me, and I'm so intent on not falling and not failing at this that for a long period I'm aware only of the muffled sound of her tags jingling in the fog. But the track widens a little, and I catch better sight of her beside me, this former Dog Who Would Not Heel, her light coat curly in the thick air, up-down-up-down ears punctuating every step. A neighboring dog rushes the fence as we pass. From another direction, a car door slams and two voices raise from some disembodied distance. I hear the clink of metal and the word "alternator," but Puzzle ignores it all.

As the path curves down to a low point, I huff and wobble, nursing a stitch. The fog thickens, and the air through my open mouth feels thick enough to chew. We are passing a row of fire trucks now, and ambulances, and I'm thinking wryly of collapsing behind one of them when we make a last corner to the home stretch. Puzzle looks up at me, all snort and dance and challenge. She's still fresh, and I'm somewhere in the nether between dazed and brain-dead, but we are going on just this little last way.

The sun is moving high over us, and here in the thickest part of the fog, Puzzle is spectral in the filtered light. She is my dog but filtered somehow and unfamiliar, rendered in aquatint. We push for the end of the circuit and, at the end of it, flop down together. Now she is real again. I can smell her damp coat and her warm dog breath, and as the timekeeper calls "13:08," I hear the *thump-thump-thump* of Puzzle scratching a sweet spot behind her ear.

"13:08," I say to Puzzle, who I'm sure has no clue why that's a good thing. But she rolls over onto her back and wiggles across the damp grass and exposes her belly, and from where we lie, she tilts her head to my shoulder and looks at me, grinning. It's not the hardest push we've ever done, but it's a hint of what we were.

Good job, she seems to say of us. *Fabulous.*

25

JIMMY

I N T H E H A R D G L A R E of headlights from a police car two houses away, Puzzle puts her nose to a single sock in a plastic bag on the ground, working thoughtfully over it a moment, then looking up for her release command.

"Ohhhh —" says a bystander from across the street. "Look at that."

All the dogs glow when they are backlit, and blond Puzzle shines silver in the light. Huffing frostily in the cold air, she looks like the dog angel one sees on condolence cards that come from the vet, but she's flexing her right paw a little, a characteristic gesture associated with scent and unease. Puzzle likes her space. She's a little uncertain about the ring of officers that leaned forward as she put her nose to the bag, watching her with fixed intensity. This is her *let's-go-let's-go* signal to me. She will flex that paw until I send her out to search. When a nearby officer drops a cup and coffee explodes across the cement, she quivers and shoots me a *can-we-get-on-with-it* look, and I do.

"Find *that*," I say to her. *That* is the scent she has taken from the article in the bag. Without hesitation (and with some suggestion of relief), she makes her immediate choice of direction: east not west. She lopes, then canters easily down the residential street away from the police cars and the crowd. I follow behind her; a young officer and Jerry working FAS team walk behind me. Puzzle is easy to see in the darkness. She moves confidently, her plume tail flicking across the beam of our flashlights.

This is her first official search, and she's running with me. Her job is clear: *find him if he's in this sector or communicate absolutely that he's not — and because this search is scent-specific, ignore any other human scent you find.* My job is to make sense of all she communicates.

We have seen photographs of the missing man. We can perhaps overtake and identify him if Puzzle and the other dogs isolate the direction he's walked tonight. Jimmy is a senior citizen of diminished capabilities, who hears well but cannot speak. He is described as friendly, outgoing, and childlike in his attraction to bright lights and sweets. The photo we have of him seems to verify the description. He has a long, narrow face and a thinning swath of hair combed neatly back over the top of his head. His face is ducked slightly as he looks into the camera, as though he isn't sure whether to trust the camera, the photographer, or both. In sync with his posture is a fixed, wide smile that reminds me of the grin of a shy dog about to roll over in submission.

Caregiver interviews describe a man who has had difficulties negotiating the everyday world from childhood, and his expression in the photograph suggests a long history of misunderstanding, coupled with a desperate, inextinguishable hope. He's a tractable man with those who know him, but he's got gumption too — an adventurous fellow with an eye to the main chance. Last night in warmer weather, he slipped out of his assisted-living residence and walked northwest a few hours before he was found by police officers, who took him to McDonald's for a milk shake before driving him home. Tonight he has walked away again after spying the unlocked front door to his house, perhaps bent on repeating the adventure of the night before.

Tonight, however, he has walked out in striped pajama bottoms and nothing else, and though the weather was warm earlier in the evening, a cold front has pushed through the area, dropping temperatures by thirty degrees with the promise of subfreezing temperatures by morning. His caregivers and local police searched for hours after he disappeared, and when Jimmy did not turn up at his previous haunts, the dog team was called.

The three of us move quickly behind Puzzle. We are bundled in winter jackets and hats against a bitter wind from the north. A few clouds scud across stars in the night sky, but rain is not in the forecast — a positive note. Jimmy is already at risk for hypothermia in his half-clothed state; falling precipitation would increase his risk, and quickly too. He has been out four and a half hours, and unless he's found shelter, he's been in the cold for two of those.

There are other potential harms. An approachable man like Jimmy is an easy target. Though his neighborhood is a quiet one, gang activity has been reported at its fringes. I saw the painted tags on Dumpsters and telephone poles driving in. Tonight much of Jimmy's safety depends on the direction of his travel and whether those whose paths he crossed were kind.

Still heading east, Puzzle elects to enter the driveway of an apartment complex. She sniffs thoughtfully at the curb, then lopes into the complex parking lot and turns left along the long row of cars beneath carports. Though it is late, there are a half-dozen residents in the lot — some getting into and out of cars, two talking with their heads bowed and their arms crossed, as though their subject is mutually uncomfortable. We pass a woman wearing scrubs and a sweater tied around her waist, carrying a sleepy child toward the door of an apartment. She has her boy on one arm and her purse slung over the other. She pauses at the sight of the search dog and the officer, but she doesn't stop to ask questions. Puzzle ignores her as she sweeps past and ignores every other person in the lot. *Good girl*, I think. *She's working a specific find, not a general one.*

At the fifth apartment, Puzzle turns back the way she came. Though something provoked her interest here, she's dismissed the area now, trotting out the driveway and eastward again. At the intersection of the street we are on and a busy road bordering our sector, we turn south. There's a moment's pause. Puzzle pulls briefly eastward again, perhaps interested in crossing the major road that forms the edge of our sector. It is a light tug from her rather than a hard, urgent pull, as though she has a little scent she'd like to eliminate, but the busy road separates one city from another here. The officer with us confirms it: to cross the road would be to pass out of the local jurisdiction and into a separate city requiring permission for us to search. After the slight tug of interest, Puzzle heads south again, then obediently turns west at the next intersection as we continue to sweep the streets for some indication that Jimmy has passed this way or that Jimmy is here.

A hundred places to hide in any one block of this street, and none of them warm. It could take a team of humans hours to visually search the same night sector a dog can clear in an hour. Puzzle works calmly, either unaware of her great responsibility or unafraid of it.

The houses are mostly dark. Here and there, a lamp for a walkway, but not too many of those. These are long, flat neo-Colonials or ranch houses built in the eighties, it appears — brick and siding, vinyl-clad windows and painted shutters that were never meant to shut. Mature trees throw long shadows across doorways; the streetlight that filters through their branches turns the pale winter grass a silvery blue.

There are vehicles parked on both sides of the street, I zigzag Puzzle back and forth as we pass along them. A single unlocked car or truck might be enough to shelter Jimmy, and from his caregivers' description, I think he might be enterprising enough to climb into an unfamiliar vehicle. I wonder also about him huddling in the darkened doorways of houses, but Jimmy's scent would be quickly apparent to Puzzle even if we couldn't see him.

Puzzle has no interest in any of the cars. She puts her nose to the edges of doors and beneath each one itself, but it's a trained check, not one provoked by the scent she remembers from Jimmy's sock twenty minutes ago. Behind us, the police officer flicks his flashlight into each car as we approach it, briefly revealing their interiors white-bright in sequence, as though each were caught by the flash of an intruder's camera. We see knobby seatback massagers, cardboard pine trees hanging from rearview mirrors, a stack of textbooks, and a mound of fast-food bags in a passenger seat. In one car, an adult magazine lies on the dashboard. Trotting ahead as the officer works behind us, Puzzle has already cleared the cars, and the officer also dismisses every vehicle on this street in turn.

We move briefly south at a cross street, then turn into an alley to work our way back east. Here are private spaces and a great deal more light than we found on the street. Whether fearing break-ins or not yet down for the night, the residents on either side of the alley have their garage lights on. We walk more slowly here as Puzzle threads her way behind each house. Some have motion-sensitive security lights; our passage causes a *click-click-click* and a sudden blaze to warn us away.

The cold front has thoroughly arrived; the wind is fitful and irregular around the fences and the boats, campers, and spare vehicles parked on driveways. No uninterrupted scent cones here. I try to frame this environment as Puzzle experiences it: I imagine human scent swifting between houses, slamming into the sides of campers, and parting there to wind around each side or slip underneath. I watch Puzzle raise her nose and circle slightly, maneuvering the odd spaces as she ferrets this human scent and that one — new, older, and oldest — dismissing all of them as irrelevant.

"What's she got?" asks the officer, watching the movement of her nose. He has never seen a dog work before.

"Looks like a lot of human scent. All of it old at this point. And none of it Jimmy."

Though the area is more brightly lit, the houses here seem more vulnerable from the alley. Not just vulnerable to theft, naked in the display of owners' private lives: the rusted car up on blocks over dark spots of old grease beside the speedboat carefully cocooned in its tarp. An open garage door reveals an aging Honda motorcycle next to an empty playpen and a set of four upside-down wooden chairs in various stages of sand and stain. Would any of these spaces appeal to Jimmy? Puzzle poises, nods in the direction of them all, but turns away. Behind one house, she bobs her head but also turns away from an elderly man in a bathrobe who sits in the lit doorway of a pop-up trailer, smoking a cigarette. His legs and feet are bare. He sits easily, as though he cannot feel the cold.

"Evening," he says to the officer.

"Sir," the officer responds. "Any chance you've seen a man about this tall" — he gestures — "wearing blue and white pajama pants?"

The man shakes his head and thumbs the filter of his cigarette. Ash falls, sparks bright on the cement, and slides away in the breeze.

We move on. Puzzle sets the pace, a quick trot in some places and a thoughtful walk in others, but I do not see the canter or the low stir of wuff-wuffling excitement I've come to recognize from her when desired scent is close on the wind. She is not difficult to follow on this urban search, and her light color makes her easy to read in the shadows. Jimmy isn't in this alley, and from what I can make of Puzzle's signals, he hasn't been here tonight.

From some dark place against a house, a pair of dogs rush a fence she passes, barking furiously, startling us all. Puzzle shudders and is about to spring away when she recognizes there's a barrier between them. She stands still, her tail waving faintly and her ears pushed forward, ready to pass them, but wary. Two mixed-breeds, both bigger than she is, one white, the other blotchy with liver-colored spots and a mouth so wide it would have a great grin if the dog weren't so busy savaging Puzzle through the fence three feet away.

Whether they are pissed at her for her proximity or pissed at her because she's with three unfamiliar humans in the night, I have no idea, but they are glad to make noise about it. The spotted dog is the shorter one, and he leaps up at the fence in a sort of competitive besting of the other, landing on the bigger dog's back a couple of times before the white dog shudders him free, no offense taken. We can hear the *ting-ting* of their nails catching on chain link.

This looks like a ritual. There's a raw spot in the dirt where they've done it before. The dogs are territorial and maybe a little jealous of her freedom of the alley. Certain now about the fence that separates them from her, Puzzle turns away pointedly, like a snub.

We pass out of the alley at the easternmost point, turning southward again. Puzzle seems more interested in this side of the sector, something I noticed before and, on the next sweep, will notice again. It is no more than slight interest, though, a small, subtle intensifying of body and quickening of step, but that's it. The more westward we move, the less interested she is in the sector. She has remained true to the designated scent. When a man gets out of a car upwind of us on a fourth street, Puzzle lifts her head in acknowledgment but doesn't quicken her pace. His is human scent, sure, but it is not the scent we want.

At the southernmost end of the sector, we find a bridge over a small creek bordered by a ravine and an elementary school. The school is surrounded by a wide, fenced yard with a playground, bare of trees, the turf immaculate. There is a long curl of black hose lying at the edge of a student garden. Puzzle steps over it without a hitch in her step.

Jimmy, like most victims, does not fall neatly into a lost-person classification, which means he also does not precisely fit one of the many lost-person behavior categories suggested by research. He does not have Alzheimer's or another diagnosed dementia. He is a senior citizen, but on the hardy end of that spectrum. He can hear, but he cannot speak. He isn't manic; he isn't depressed. He's not despondent or aggressive or angry. One of his caregivers suggests he is like a curious five-year-old with a toddler's emotional maturity in the body of a sixty-eight-year-old man.

Lost-person theory suggests that a majority of people, when wandering without a specific goal in mind, will turn right when they first set out to walk. Right-turnedness is linked to right-handedness, and right-handed Jimmy had, in fact, turned right when he headed out the night before. When he disappeared tonight, caregivers and officers searched the area he'd explored on Saturday, but he was not in those locations, nor had he been seen there again. The dogs confirmed this. Every dog scenting Jimmy's sock headed left — east — not right and westerly tonight.

Where Alzheimer's patients will follow travel aids like sidewalks or paths until they run out, or "go until they get stuck," Jimmy is less likely to have done so. His feet are bare, and he may well have chosen what surface to walk simply by what was most comfortable underfoot, but his processing capabilities are sound enough that when a sidewalk ran out, he could have easily crossed a street to find another.

Some walk aways, whether influenced by Alzheimer's or other dementias, will walk with a memory-driven goal in mind. They walk to pick up now-grown children from school; they head for a bus that would have taken them to work in another city forty years before. Jimmy is likely more aware of chronology than this. If he has a goal in mind, it may be similar to the goal a child would have — a high-value attraction frequently passed by car — a playground, creek, restaurant, video arcade, or store. Or something else he has seen and stored and wants badly to connect with that searchers might not recognize: a piñata hanging from the limb of a tree. A friendly cat with a bell sitting on a porch stoop. Because he does not speak, caregivers have not heard repeated themes from him: *Want this. Go there.* If Jimmy has given nonverbal clues about his interests, they have not passed them on to us.

As I pause to give Puzzle a drink, I look at Jimmy's photo again, aware that we work across two terrains here: the physical one and the unknowable territory of Jimmy's impulses. Where in the Venn diagram of his wandering would those two conditions intersect? I wonder how his priorities have shifted, if at all, in the almost five hours he's been gone. Would staying warm replace Jimmy's urge for a candy bar? Would he know not to approach unfriendly strangers for money or would he overlook risk in the pursuit of bubblegum?

Potential hypothermia adds another layer of question. Irrational behavior often occurs with severe hypothermias, including a condition called paradoxical undressing, where the victim receives false signals from the hypothalamus, believes he is warm, and sheds his clothes. *Keep your clothes on, Jimmy,* I think. *Get out of the wind.*

Puzzle finishes her water and I shake out the collapsible bowl, then fold and tuck it into a pocket. We are off again, across the bridge and into the ravine. The creek below is a shallow one, sparkling occasionally from a corner streetlight. Water is always relevant on missing persons searches: a perpetual fascination, a potential hotspot for children — even in the cold — and though Jimmy might also be attracted, Puzzle is into the creek bed and out of it in less than a minute. She loves water too, but she is clear about it. Nothing there.

We head into the schoolyard to begin sweeps across it. The school itself is perpendicular to the wind here, and because I can't know how scent might be distorted around its edges and deep side-door pockets, our sweeps are closer together than they need to be, perhaps. It's Puzzle's first formal search, and this new environment has made me cautious. We work across the schoolyard as the officer flashes light into its empty doorways.

When we move to the side of the school, Jerry suggests that I circle Puzzle around a Dumpster as we pass. She has little interest in the area, and when we circle the Dumpster, no interest at all, but there is precedent for Jerry's suggestion: Dumpsters are often the sad endpoint of searches, and scent there can be muddled through their heavy lids and slide-hatches or muffled when a victim has been wrapped in garbage bags. Puzzle moves away from the Dumpster as the officer verifies by peeking in, and I feel a little twitch of relief that Jimmy hasn't been discarded there. Whether he'd climb in one to keep warm is anyone's guess, but clearly he hasn't made that choice, either.

The schoolyard marks the end of our assigned area, and we return to the command post along the easternmost side of the sector. Puzzle has indicated interest, mild interest, only on the eastern side. I want to return the same way to see if that interest intensifies or goes away altogether. We move quickly north along the street we had previously used to head south, and twice Puzzle twitches eastward. Again, it's only a twitch, not the body shiver I've felt from her when desired scent was hot and close, nor the gathering to run that I associate with a very near alert. Jerry has reported this repeated interest to the search manager, and we move quietly back to the command post in the early hours of the morning.

We arrive to find the search manager bent over a map and in conference with the police officer coordinating the search. Fleta has tallied all indications from the responding dogs, and when asked what the next sectors might be, indicates that the wisest move would be new sectors to the east. Several dogs had interest that direction. She begins to mark the map while the officer in charge discusses the situation with police in the neighboring town.

Handlers full of hot coffee and the dogs now warm from a rehab period in cars, we are ready to go out again, waiting for authorization to head east. We've now been on-scene for a couple of hours. Jimmy has been missing for almost seven. Most of us have added a layer or two of clothing as night has deepened and the temperature has continued to drop. Even so, it doesn't take much exposure to the wind to feel cold again. An officer raises the question we all carry: would Jimmy be aware enough to seek shelter and come in from the cold, or would he regress as hypothermia advanced, losing the ability to walk, in time unable to stay awake as his brain and body began to shut down? If Jimmy made all the wrong choices three hours ago, he could have died soon after the front had passed.

I look down the line of teammates already in packs and ready to head out again. They stand queued and ready to receive second sectors, gloved hands in pockets, shoulders up and heads retracted into the collars of jackets. Quiet. Conserving energy. Most of them are due at work in a few hours. Those who can stay will stay until Jimmy is found, then go on to work second or third shift. This is not the first time any of us will have searched most of the night and gone straight to work afterward, a little punchy and disembodied. I can see the puffs of exhale that mark each of my colleagues — the slow, steady thought bubbles above those who have learned to rest standing, waiting; the erratic steam-engine puffs above those whose conversations I cannot hear.

Puzzle's little exhales are also visible as she stands knitting scent. I have draped one of my down vests over her back as we wait. She doesn't whine or bark or strain at the lead, but I can see the steam of deep breaths and small ones, the occasional round huff of her mouth as some new Not Jimmy person steps onto the scene. When I touch the back of her neck, I can feel the tension of her readiness for *Next*, whatever it is, whenever it comes.

We hear a burst of static and unintelligible words over a distant radio, and suddenly there is a rush of feet and a huddle of officers, and Fleta is eclipsed within a ring of taller men. The dogs pick up the changed energy and transmit it, dog to dog and rapidly, their ears perked and tails in new motion. We humans lean forward where we stand. We strain for a single clarifying word. "Found" would be a good one. "Alive" would be even better.

The word I think I hear is "chips," and I'm trying to make sense of that when information crackles down the line that Jimmy has been found, alive, and just a few blocks east of the road that separated his neighborhood from the next town. "East" a few murmur and look down at their dogs. Alerted to the search, police officers in the adjoining town quickly began to sweep nearby streets and had located Jimmy in an all-night fast-food restaurant.

For the second time in two nights, Jimmy returns in a police cruiser with lights blazing. His forehead presses against the window, and his eyes widen at the sight of the luminous, frosty dogs pacing beneath the street lamps. Jimmy is cold. He is small and huddled when he gets out of the car, barefoot still. His feet curl and he hops a little when he steps onto the chilly sidewalk. He is staccato there in the flash of emergency lights, *pop-pop-pop*, looking gleeful and impossibly young. He points to the dogs and smiles wide.

There have been some good Samaritans and possibly some scavenging in tonight's history. Jimmy wears a worn blanket like a shawl and struggles to hold it closed across his chest while managing his armful of prizes: a martial arts videotape, a half-empty bag of corn chips, a Twinkie, and what's left of a soda in a supersize cup. He seems a little chastened by tonight's experience, but as a huddle of people move him to the front door, he appears genuinely delighted over the light show, the gathered crowd, and the atmosphere of victory over his return.

Though Lassie and Rin Tin Tin have schooled the world to Hollywood dogs and Hollywood victories, Puzzle and I celebrate a much quieter one. Jimmy is alive. Puzzle did her job thoroughly. She did it well — no distractions, no abandonment, no false alerts. We ran pace for pace on this first official search of our partnership. She never once stopped, and I never once had to.

We return home wide awake, hungry, and renewed. Oatmeal and Milk Bones at three in the morning, e-mail at four, and at five I'm still up playing Tug-o-war with the Golden, who by now would gladly wind down if I would. The Poms have grumbled themselves off into deeper rooms of the house, their sleep disturbed by our late, late entrance that will not resolve. But Puzzle, who is also tired, is generous. She has shared a bit of the oatmeal, which she doesn't like much, and put her head on my boots while I read e-mail, and now she will tug as often as I drop the Booda rope before her, though I notice more and more often that she's tugging recumbent — giving me a little deadweight game while she hints that it might be time to let go of the search.

Which is one of her many gifts, this moving forward, this letting go.

I bend down to Puzzle and kiss her street-worn paws. These are early days in our career together, and there will be more stumbling places ahead, few easy lessons. "Good girl," I say without a referent, a generic thank you for the partnership and the history, for the anarchy, the instruction, and the solace of her. We go to bed at first light, and we leave the pager on.

EPILOGUE

Despite the amazing capabilities of new technology in the search
field — the pinpoint GPS units, sidescan sonar, tiny cameras, and
hypersensitive microphones — canine search-and-rescue continues. Law enforcement agencies recognize that for some search scenarios, there is no substitute for a well-trained dog with a gift of
nose and a handler who can translate even the most subtle cues.
Canine SAR teams exist worldwide, partnering other rescue resources, serving communities ravaged by natural or manmade
disaster, and deploying with the same commitment to search for
a single person gone lost. Many dogs and handlers give the best
years of their lives to this service, retiring only when injury demands it, or when age and strength begin to fail. It is a quiet message in the long dialogue between partners: *enough*.

The dogs of MARK-9 remain beside us even after they retire, much-loved family members after their partnership days in
the search sector are done. German Shepherd Hunter, a second-
chance dog rescued himself just days before scheduled euthanasia,
worked a long and distinguished career. Hunter retired in 2004
and died at home in 2007, his handler, Max, beside him. Roughcoat Collie Saber, another of MARK-9's foundation dogs and an
AKC ACE Award recipient in 2004, took on the gentler job of
bringing in the mail after retiring from the search field. Saber died

at home just three weeks short of his sixteenth birthday in 2008. An off-duty injury forced brilliant Shadow into retirement from SAR, though she participated in the occasional training search and helped instruct the team's youngest dogs for as long as she was able. Shadow's heart surrendered in 2008. She was the last of the team's foundation dogs, whose ashes are jointly scattered across their favorite training spot.

At the time of this writing, Buster, Belle, and Hoss continue in the field, still driven, focused, successful — and opinionated. High-energy Valkyrei remains full of dash and go beside Rob. Max and Fleta continue to work beside their talented second partners, Mercy and Misty. Puzzle is no longer the puppy upstart: Jerry's second partner, the clever Aussie Shepherd Gypsy, certified in 2008. And youngsters have joined the team: Border Collie Pete recently certified with his partner, Sara, and Border Collie Scout is training hard with new handler Michele now.

Puzzle and I are still partners in the field. Puz is happy to be a part of any search, period, but wildly happy to bust brush in the wilderness. With her dog and human colleagues, Puzzle has participated in urban, wilderness, and weather-related disaster searches, once surprising a reporter hidden deep in a search sector with an unexpected *wroo!* In 2006, Puzzle and many of her canine teammates trained for and successfully challenged the certification test for Texas Task Force 2, a state disaster-response unit.

At home, Scuppy, Sophie, and Whisky died in successive years, rescues themselves who learned love and shared joy. The cats thrive. Fo'c'sle Jack and Mr. Sprits'l are very much alive and happy to tell you about it. And tell you about it. And tell you about it. The puppy discord when Puzzle first arrived is gone. Her affinity for fragile senior dogs continues. I'm aware how much we owe all the little dogs that came through the house in those early years, who taught and challenged Puzzle, from whom she learned the ways of canine compassion. She also learned how to *insist*. In 2007, Puzzle met an abandoned calico kitten she was determined to bring home. Enter: Thistle. Cat and Golden are inseparable playmates.

In the prime of her strength and drive, Puzzle is a joyful dog, a daily instruction. I like to think I have brought her something too, and that we achieve things together neither of us could have ever done alone. And I'm aware how thoroughly she is one of her own kind. At the end of a recent search for a child found unharmed, I watched Puzzle bob her nose with the other dogs as the boy stepped beneath a street lamp and his mother rushed to meet him. The tired, street-greasy search dogs came alive, nostrils working and tails in motion. "Yes," they seemed to huff happily in the second scent of him, "you're the one we're here for."

July 2009

ACKNOWLEDGMENTS

Behind lucky writers, there are good souls throwing sparks. I could not be more grateful to my agent, Jim Hornfischer, and editor, Susan Canavan, for their faith in this project and rigorous encouragement throughout.

A special thank-you to seven authors — Tony Broadbent, Lee Child, Cornelia Read, and Hallie Ephron for urging me to do this thing in the first place, and early readers Robin Hemley and Irene Prokop for showing me how to do it better. And to Michael Perry, that decent soul in Wisconsin whose work always resonates, and who was kind at a critical point — more kind than he probably knew. Thanks also to Mitch Land, George Getschow, and Ron Chrisman of the Mayborn Literary Nonfiction Conference, where this project received important critique and quite the jump-start!

To Devon Thomas Treadwell of Pollywog Naming and Branding, Minneapolis — thanks for so many things, including intuitive Googling and long-distance assistance on multiple searches, and for a working title here that made the cut! And to Marina Cing Hsieh, a fine woman of candor and unconditional love.

Thanks to Kim Cain, of Mystic Goldens, who brought Puzzle into the world, and to Susan Blatz, obedience instructor, who helped me teach my smart dog how to love a "Sit!" Special thanks to Manny Yzaguirre, DVM. Puz is in such good hands.

At Houghton Mifflin Harcourt, no writer could ask for better support than I have received from Carla Gray, Taryn Roeder, Meagan Stacey, Martha Kennedy, Bridget Marmion, Laurie Brown, Melissa Lotfy, Lisa Glover, Shuchi Saraswat, Mary Kate Maco, and Lori Glazer. Thanks also to copy editor Beth Burleigh Fuller and to photographers Debbie Bryant and Chris Moseley. Woot! and Yowza! I am so fortunate.

Thanks to the staff at Legal Grounds, Dallas, for a quiet place to write. (I recommend the grilled mozzarella sandwich.) And to Tom and Karen Watson at the Tartan Thistle Bed and Breakfast, McKinney, Texas, for weeks of safe haven and really good shortbread. More than half this book was written there. I am grateful, grateful to Elaine Harris, of PomRescue.com, who brought four-pound Pomeranian rescue Tupper into my life. From first draft to final edits, Tup was beside me every time I sat to write — a loving presence, my unfailing muse. Thank you to Megan Glunt of Borders, Lovers Lane, Dallas, who did a rescue of her own, helping me retrieve a third of this edited manuscript when it was caught by a thunderstorm and blown yards away. All kinds of gratitude to Chef Duff Goldman, Mary Alice Fallon Yeskey, Anna Ellison, and the staff of Charm City Cakes, Baltimore, for keeping a secret and making one *amazing* cake.

To my colleagues at MARK-9 Search and Rescue: bless you, thank you. Dog and human — you had me from the very first "Find!"

And in the largest sense, thank you to every officer, EMT, paramedic, and firefighter, to every dog and volunteer who goes out in the middle of the night on behalf of another.

BIBLIOGRAPHY

Ackerman, Diane. *A Natural History of the Senses*. New York: Vintage, 1995.

Bidner, Jen. *Dog Heroes: Saving Lives and Protecting America*. Guildford, CT: The Lyons Press, 2002.

Brown, Ali. *Scaredy Dog! Understanding and Rehabilitating Your Reactive Dog*. Allentown, PA: Tanacacia Press, 2004.

Coren, Stanley. *How Dogs Think: Understanding the Canine Mind*. New York: Free Press, 2004.

Ellman, Vikki. *Guide to Owning a Pomeranian*. Neptune City, NJ: TFH Publications, 1996.

Fischer, Cindy. *Our Pets Have a Story to Tell*. North Chelmsford, MA: BGB Publications, 1998.

Fleming, June. *Staying Found: The Complete Map and Compass Handbook*. 3rd ed. Seattle: The Mountaineers Press, 2001.

Kalnajs, Sarah. *The Language of Dogs*. DVD. Blue Dog Training and Behavior, 2007.

McConnell, Patricia. *The Other End of the Leash*. New York: Ballantine Books, 2002.

Rebmann, Andrew, Edward David, and Marcella H. Sorg. *Cadaver Dog Handbook: Forensic Training and Tactics for the Recovery of Human Remains*. Boca Raton: CRC Press, 2000.

Shojai, Amy D. *Complete Care for Your Aging Dog*. New York: New American Library, 2003.

Volhard, Jack, and Wendy Volhard. *The Canine Good Citizen: Every Dog Can Be One*. New York: Howell Book House, 1994.

Wood, Deborah. *Help for Your Shy Dog: Turning Your Terrified Dog into a Terrific Pet*. New York: Howell Book House, 1999.